TEACHING DANIEL

From text to message

BOB FYALL & ROBIN SYDSERFF

SERIES EDITORS: DAVID JACKMAN & ADRIAN REYNOLDS

TEACHING DANIEL

From text to message

BOB FYALL & ROBIN SYDSERFF

SERIES EDITORS: DAVID JACKMAN & ADRIAN REYNOLDS

PT RESOURCES

CHRISTIAN
FOCUS

Copyright © Proclamation Trust Media 2016

ISBN: 978-1-84550-457-1

10 9 8 7 6 5 4 3 2 1

Published in 2016
by
Christian Focus Publications Ltd.,
Geanies House, Fearn, Ross-shire,
IV20 1TW, Scotland, Great Britain
with
Proclamation Trust Resources,
Willcox House, 140-148 Borough High Street,
London, SE1 1LB, England, Great Britain.
www.proctrust.org.uk

www.christianfocus.com

Cover design by Moose77.com

Printed and bound by Nørhaven, Denmark

Contents

Authors' Preface

Robin Sydserff writes:

This book has been a long time in coming and that is largely my doing! In that regard, I want to record my special appreciation to Bob Fyall, Adrian Reynolds and David Jackman. Bob is a friend and scholar. As a scholar, he knows the Old Testament Scriptures inside out and I have thoroughly benefited from his penetrating insight and depth of knowledge. As a Christian friend he has the patience of a saint! My thanks also to Adrian Reynolds and David Jackman as Series Editors, for their encouragement along the way to get the job done.

I have taught Daniel in various contexts and want to record my thanks for the many comments, questions and conversations that have sharpened the material over the years. My thanks to delegates at the Proclamation Trust Bible Training Weekend, NIMA Preaching Conference, Free Church of Scotland Spring Conference, Cornhill Servants of the Word and Faith Mission Edinburgh Convention; church weekends with St Luke's Wimbledon and Holy Trinity Lyonsdown; and student weekends with Carrubbers Christian Fellowship, Plymouth and Strathclyde Christian Unions.

My thanks to students on the Cornhill Training Course, both in London and Edinburgh and the Faith Mission Bible College, where I had the opportunity to teach Daniel. And a special thanks to the participants on the Free Church of Scotland Saturday Course who really helped knock the material into shape over a number of months.

A very personal thanks to my wife Sally and parents George and Anne Sydserff for constant prayer, encouragement and their godly example. And to our children, Lucy, David and William – may you live like the young Daniel.

It has been my privilege to pastor *Chalmers Church* in Edinburgh now for seven years. They have heard Daniel preached right through twice as well as various one-off talks. A local church living in the text of a Daniel for a few months is the best preparation for writing a book on Daniel. I would like to dedicate this book to the elders and congregation of *Chalmers Church* who have shown what it means to live distinctively in light of God's rule.

Bob Fyall writes:

It is good to be at this stage after long delays and we hope those who read this book will judge the wait to have been worth it. Robin Sydserff is to be thanked for his collaboration in the writing. Robin is one of a generation of younger leaders who have emerged in recent years and the book has greatly benefited from his clear and imaginative thinking and his gift of application. I thank him and hope we see more written material from him in years to come.

Thanks also to Adrian Reynolds and David Jackman whose patience has been exemplary as successive deadlines passed.

I have taught Daniel with increasing pleasure over many years and thank all who have listened to the sermons and lectures. In my ministry in Claypath Church (now Christchurch) in Durham I began my preaching there with the book and returned to it near the end. It was also the subject of talks at Preachers' Conference in Melbourne as well as at other weekends and conferences. It also featured in my teaching in Cranmer Hall, St John's College, Durham.

I am particularly glad to have had the privilege of teaching this book (along with Revelation) at the Scottish Cornhill Training Course over the last nine years. It was stimulating to share insights with successive generations of students and see at least some of them overcome their fear of Apocalyptic literature. It has also occasionally featured in my preaching ministry at the Tron Church in Glasgow. I would like to thank the staff both of Cornhill and the Tron for the seriousness with which they take the responsibility to teach and model living in the kingdom of this world while witnessing to the kingdom of God.

In 1998 my earlier commentary on Daniel appeared as part of the *Focus on the Bible* series. There is some overlap but I consciously set out to write my part of this one without too much reference to the earlier book.

In that commentary I thanked my wife Thelma for all her loving support which continues to be the bulwark for my life and ministry. I dedicated the book to my then teenage children, Carmen and Drummond with the prayer that they would grow up to be 'people who know

their God'. They are now married, and Naomi, the first
of the new generation is fast growing. My prayer for my
family is still that prayer of eighteen years ago and indeed
that all who read this book will be strengthened in their
pilgrimage.

ROBIN SYDSERFF
AND BOB FYALL
Edinburgh
March 2016

SERIES PREFACE

Daniel is a Bible book like almost no other. At the same time it contains some of the best known stories in the Bible (the lions' den, for example) and some of the least. It is used and misused to prove all kinds of points, moral lessons and detailed eschatological timetables. Moreover, for preachers and teachers, there is a significant mismatch between the time given to the first half of the book (often preached) and the second (seldom preached).

Our conviction is that God has breathed out by His Spirit the entirety of Scripture, including the book of Daniel. What is more, He has wisely and sovereignly bound up the 'easier' parts of Daniel with the 'harder' parts. We shall see that these are, to some extent, false distinctions. Nevertheless, Daniel comes to us as an entire book – all twelve chapters – and we must read and teach it as such.

Teaching Daniel is therefore an essential contribution to our growing series. We need direction to get the familiar parts right and guidance to help us tackle those sections we assume to be trickier. Bob and Robin have spent a long time getting this help right and this volume brings the book together in a way which should thrill every man or woman in evangelical word ministry.

The volumes in this series are purposely practical, seeking to offer real help for those involved in teaching the Bible to others. The preacher or teacher, the sermon or talk, and the listener are the key 'drivers' in this series. The Introductory Section contains basic 'navigation' material to get you into the text of Daniel, covering aspects like structure and planning a preaching series. The 'meat' of the book then works systematically through the major sections of Daniel, suggesting preaching or teaching units, including sermon outlines and questions for Bible studies. These are not there to take the hard work out of preparation, but as a starting point to get you thinking about how to preach the material or prepare a Bible study.

Teaching Daniel brings the number of published volumes in the series to [16]. We are encouraged at how the series is developing and the positive comments from the people that really matter – those at the chalk face of Christian ministry, working hard at the Word, week in week out, to proclaim the unsearchable riches of Christ.

Our thanks must go to Celia Reynolds for help with proof reading and checking references. As ever, our warm gratitude goes to the team at Christian Focus for their committed partnership in this project.

David Jackman &
Adrian Reynolds
Series Editors
London 2016

How to use this Book

This book aims to help the preacher or teacher understand the central object and purpose of the text, in order to preach or teach it to others. Unlike a commentary, therefore, it does not go into great exegetical detail. Instead, it helps us to engage with the themes of Daniel, to keep the big picture in mind, and to think about how to present it to our hearers.

'Introductory Material' examines the book's themes and structure as well as seeing why it is considered a difficult book to preach. This material is crucial to our understanding of the whole book, which will shape the way we preach each section to our congregations. There are two short helpful appendices on preaching narrative and preaching apocalyptic literature.

The remainder of the volume contains separate chapters on each preaching unit considered in the Introductory Material. The structure of each chapter is the same: it begins with a brief introduction to the unit covering context and how the section fits within the overall book ('Setting in context'). This is then followed by a section headed 'Working on the text.' This section outlines the structure and context of the unit and takes the reader through a section by section analysis of the text. All good biblical preaching begins with careful, detailed listening to the text and this is true for Daniel as much as any other book.

Each chapter then continues with a section called 'From text to message.' This suggests a main theme for each preaching unit, some ways to engage hearers, lines of application and then some possible sermon outlines. These suggestions are nothing more than that – suggestions designed to help the preacher think about his own division of the text and the structure of the sermon. We are great believers in every preacher constructing his own outlines, because they need to flow from our personal encounter with God in the text. Downloading other people's sermons or trying to breathe life into someone else's outlines are strategies doomed to failure. They may produce a reasonable talk, but in the long term, they are disastrous to the preacher himself since he needs to live in the Word and the Word to live in him, if he is to speak from the heart of God to the hearts of his congregation. However, these sections provide a few very basic ideas about how an outline on some of these passages might shape up.

Each chapter concludes with some suggested questions for a group Bible study split into two main types: questions to help study the passage and questions to help apply the passage. Not all the questions would be needed for a study, but they give some ideas for those who are planning a study series.

The aim of good questions is always to drive the group into the text, to explore and understand its meaning more fully. This keeps the focus on Scripture and reduces speculation and the mere exchange of opinions. Remember the key issues are always, 'What does the text say?' and then 'What does it mean?' Avoid the 'What does it mean to you?' type of question. It is much better to discuss the application more generally and personally after everyone understands the intended meaning, so that the Bible really is in the driving-seat of the study, not the participants' opinions, prejudices or experiences! These studies will be especially useful in those churches where Bible study groups are able to study the book at the same time as it is preached, a practice we warmly commend. This allows small groups to drive home understanding, and especially application, in the week after the sermon has been preached, ensuring it is applied to the daily lives of the congregation.

Introductory Material

Getting Our Bearings in Daniel

What kind of book is Daniel?

(1) Familiar, yet unfamiliar

Daniel contains some of the best known material in the Bible. Hananiah, Mishael and Azariah (we'll call them by their Hebrew names) in the fiery furnace, Belshazzar and the writing on the wall and Daniel in the lions' den all feature prominently in children's story Bibles. Yet these are not children's stories. A danger of the familiar, particularly stories like Daniel in the lions' den, is that our understanding is superficial.

Moreover, while parts of the book are familiar, other parts are unfamiliar, particularly the prophetic material. Most series on Daniel stop at chapter 6, or if you are particularly brave, chapter 7. Yet, this leaves out so much of what the book has to offer. As teachers of Daniel ourselves, one of our hopes in writing this book is to encourage you to teach right through the book, unlocking some of its unfamiliar treasures, as well as revisiting familiar ground.

(2) *Diverse and exciting*

The book of Daniel is diverse and exciting. Its diversity is seen in the different types of literature – mainly narrative and prophecy expressed in apocalyptic language, but also poetry, and in chapter 9 one of the great prayers of the Bible. Such diversity, while presenting challenges to the Bible teacher, is a real asset in sustaining an effective and engaging teaching series. When you teach Daniel, you are not just conveying the content of the book, but the richness of the Bible's literature. The stories are exciting and dramatic to teach, the spiritual warfare and cosmic conflict revealed through the prophetic chapters, equally dramatic. And in the prophecies that point to the coming of the Lord Jesus and God's everlasting Kingdom, there is great encouragement, both in the content of the prophecies and when they were given. For example, at the heart of the book, the description of one like a son of man crowned as King of God's everlasting Kingdom (Dan. 7:13-14), written hundreds of years before Jesus, gives us confidence not only in God's sovereignty but in the inspiration of His Word.

(3) *Striking contemporary relevance*

While the entire Bible is relevant all of the time, there are times and circumstances when particular Bible books have an added edge. Daniel is a book for our time. Whether as Christians living in the secular West, feeling increasingly marginalised as exiles, or as Christians living in the East at the frontline of spiritual progress, Daniel has much to teach us. The fact that God rules is a vital message of encouragement. And the challenge to God's people to live distinctively in light of His rule, is a message the Church, particularly in the West, needs to hear and obey.

Authorship and Date

(1) *Authorship*
Although there is some debate as to authorship, the most likely author is the prophet Daniel, who lived in Babylon during the Exile. There are a number of references in the text to 'I, Daniel' which support his authorship (e.g. 8:1, 15; 9:2; 10:2). And the fact that Jesus attributes authorship to the prophet Daniel (Matt. 24:15) is conclusive.

(2) *Date*
Scholars argue over an earlier or later date. The earlier date is shortly after the end of the Exile. The Exile was from 605 B.C. to 539 B.C. Daniel 10:1 records the date Daniel received his final vision as 'the third year of Cyrus king of Persia' (536 B.C.). It is reasonable to assume Daniel would have written his book around then.

Other scholars argue for a much later second century date. Various reasons are suggested.

- The detailed nature of the prophecies in chapters 8 and 11 focusing on the persecution under Antiochus IV Epiphanes in the second century (Antiochus reigned from 175 B.C. to 164 B.C.) suggests that the material could only have been written after the events described.

- Apparent historical anomalies (e.g. over the identity of Belshazzar, Darius and Cyrus) suggest a date much later than the period these people lived, thus explaining the anomalies.

- The fact that the book is written in two languages
  – Hebrew (1:1-2:3; 8:1-12:13) and Chaldean (early
  Aramaic) (2:4-7:28) – differentiates Daniel from
  the rest of the Old Testament Scriptures and
  suggests a much later date.

For the most part, those who argue for a later date are
liberal scholars who will not accept the divine inspiration of
the prophetic material. None of their arguments, however,
is sufficiently compelling to justify a later date, and a date
around 536 B.C. is most likely. That is the position we take
in this book.

Account of the Exile
At one level, the book of Daniel is an account of the Exile.
The Exile began in 605 B.C. when Nebuchadnezzar king
of Babylon besieged Jerusalem, defeated Jehoiakim king
of Judah and took Daniel and his friends to Babylon as
part of the first 'phase' of exile (Dan. 1:1-2; 2 Kings 24:1-2;
2 Chron. 36:5-7). The second 'phase' was in 597 B.C.
(2 Kings 24:10-14), with the final phase in 586 B.C., when
Jerusalem and the temple were destroyed (2 Kings 25:1-24).
The Exile ended in 539 B.C. when the Babylonian dynasty
fell to the Medo-Persian kingdom under Darius the Mede
and Cyrus the Persian (Dan. 1:21; 5:30-31; 6:28).
Cyrus decreed that the Exile should come to an end
(2 Chron. 36:22-23; Ezra 1:1-4; Isa. 45:1). The identity
of Darius and Cyrus is a matter of debate. Are they two
different people at the head of the Medo-Persian kingdom?
Or is it the same person with two names / titles? We can't
be dogmatic either way, and it doesn't much matter. For
the purposes of this book we'll assume Darius / Cyrus is
the same person.

Most of the events recorded in the book and the prophetic visions Daniel received are precisely dated. Where there is no precise date we can make reasonable approximations. Fig. 1 summarises.

Fig. 1 Dating events and prophetic visions in the Exile

Exile begins 605 B.C.

Events during the Exile

Ch. 1	Daniel in Babylon	605 B.C. *(1:1)*
Ch. 2	Daniel interprets Nebuchadnezzar's dream	603 B.C. *(2:1)*
Ch. 3	Hananiah, Mishael and Azariah in the furnace	Approx. 580 B.C.
Ch. 4	Nebuchadnezzar's humbling, conversion and restoration	In period 580–570 B.C.
Ch. 5	Belshazzar and the writing on the wall	539 B.C. *(5.30-31)*
Ch. 6	Daniel and the lions' den	539 B.C. *(6:1)*

Prophetic visions received during the Exile

Ch. 7	Vision 1	552 B.C. *(7:1)*
Ch. 8	Vision 2	550 B.C. *(8:1)*
Ch. 9	Vision 3	539 B.C. *(9:1)*

Exile ends   **539 B.C.**

Ch. 10–12	Vision 4	536 B.C. *(10:1)*

Message of Daniel

The message of Daniel can be summarised as follows:

> **God rules, is building an everlasting Kingdom, and calls people to live in light of that fact.**

It is helpful to unpack this a little, and then draw a distinction between the message of the book for *God's people* and the message of the book for *all people*.

(1) God rules and is building an everlasting Kingdom
This is the main theme of the book, the dominant note
sounded in every chapter.

Right at the start, in the introductory verses, it is clear that
God rules. It is the Lord who delivers Jehoiakim into Nebuchadnezzar's hand along with some of the articles from the
temple (1:2). History might record a weak Judah and Jehoiakim
overpowered by the mighty Babylon and Nebuchadnezzar,
but God's Word reveals where true power lies.

Chapter 1 describes Nebuchadnezzar's strategy to put
God out of the lives of Daniel and his friends. Behind the
scenes, however, God orchestrates events, influences state
officials and gifts His people to put them into the heart of
public life in Babylon with a clear faith. Nebuchadnezzar
is a powerful ruler with a strategic plan but God is more
powerful and confounds his plan. God has the upper hand.

The interpretation of Nebuchadnezzar's dream in chapter 2 is that God rules. While human kingdoms rise and fall
(including Nebuchadnezzar's Babylonian kingdom) God
will build an everlasting Kingdom that will fill the whole
earth. Moreover, the fact that God alone can interpret the
dream through His servant Daniel means that God is not
only sovereign in *rule* but sovereign in *revelation*.

God's rule is seen in chapter 3 as Hananiah, Mishael
and Azariah defy king Nebuchadnezzar by appealing to a
greater authority and power. God demonstrates His rule
by delivering Hananiah, Mishael and Azariah unharmed
from Nebuchadnezzar's furnace. This is an astonishing
miracle as the Kingdom of God breaks into the world.
Moreover, God made sure Nebuchadnezzar saw it.

Chapter 4 describes Nebuchadnezzar's humbling and
conversion. His conversion demonstrates God's sovereignty

in salvation. In spite of what Nebuchadnezzar did to oppose God and His people, God consistently revealed the truth to Nebuchadnezzar in order to bring him to faith. That is astounding grace. In order to save him, God took all Nebuchadnezzar's power from him. He also took his dignity and sanity. When Nebuchadnezzar acknowledged God's rule and was converted, God gave everything back to him. God takes and gives at will.

While God's sovereignty in salvation in seen in Nebuchadnezzar's conversion (Ch. 4), it is seen in a very different way in His judgement of Belshazzar in chapter 5. Over many years God brought Nebuchadnezzar to repentance and faith (Ch. 4). In one night, God judged Belshazzar (Ch. 5), God took his life and that same night his Babylonian kingdom fell to the Medo-Persian dynasty.

In chapter 6, faced with the king's decree, Daniel will not stop worshipping his God. His allegiance is to the rule of God. God demonstrates His rule by delivering Daniel unharmed from the lions' den, events that play a significant part in bringing the Exile to an end. Another astonishing miracle as the Kingdom of God breaks into this world. Chapter 7 is a prophetic vision that conveys God's universal rule. There are strong parallels with Nebuchadnezzar's dream in chapter 2. Human kingdoms and kings rise and fall but God will build an everlasting Kingdom that will never be destroyed. In the vision we see God as the Ancient of Days on His throne and one like a son of man crowned as God's all-powerful King of His everlasting Kingdom.

Chapter 8 is a prophetic vision that conveys God's rule in a particular period of history when God's people experience intense persecution. God rules not only on the big canvas of human history but in the detail.

In chapter 9, Daniel prays that for God's own glory He will bring the Exile to an end. The prophetic vision that follows (an answer to the prayer) confirms that the Exile will come to an end with Jerusalem restored. But the vision looks forward down the centuries to a day when the Anointed One will be sacrificed for the sake of God's people. This event will secure their ultimate victory.

Chapters 10–12 record a single prophetic vision. First, we are taken behind the scenes of human history to witness the cosmic spiritual warfare between good and evil (Ch. 10). Evil is powerful but God's power is greater and will prevail. Next the vision focuses on the detailed events already described in chapter 8. God's people may face intense persecution but will never be destroyed (Ch. 11). They will endure and rise again. And God will destroy those who oppose Him and His people. Finally, the vision broadens out to the big canvas. There will be tough times ahead for God's people, particularly the End Times, but the saints will endure and inherit God's everlasting Kingdom (Ch. 12).

(2) God calls His people to live distinctively in light of that fact

God rules and is building an everlasting Kingdom. This is the main theme of the book running through every chapter.

In light of that fact, God calls His people to live distinctively, testifying to His rule. The distinctiveness of God's people is an important way God reveals His presence in the godless world of Babylon and advances His Kingdom. God also reveals His presence in other ways, for example, through His control of events, miraculous intervention and in His prophetic revelation. God's presence in the world is inescapable, providing a constant challenge to other beliefs and worldviews.

Living distinctively in light of God's rule is a key focus of chapters 1, 3 and 6. Often referred to as conflict chapters, in each situation God's people face conflict and oppression. Will their faith stand up under pressure? What will they do? Where does their true allegiance lie? While there are similarities between the three chapters, the situations described and the responses of God's people are different. These differences are intended, part of the richness of the book that needs to be brought out when we teach it. In chapter 1, a young Daniel resolves not to defile himself with the royal food and wine. That was his way of living distinctively and pledging his allegiance to God. In chapter 3 the situation is quite different as Hananiah, Mishael and Azariah face a direct and hostile challenge to their faith, necessitating a bold and courageous stand as they speak in open defiance to the king. Similarly, in chapter 6, Daniel faces a direct and hostile challenge with great courage. The events of chapter 6 also reveal Daniel's consistency – a faith that pervades every part of his life, lived out over many years. In all these situations, the decision of God's people to live distinctively is used by God to advance His cause.

The conflict / oppression God's people face is a direct consequence of living distinctively in the world. Oppression ranges from pressure to conform to worldly thinking and behaviour, through to direct hostility and persecution.

But God's people can also experience oppression as a direct result of their sin and disobedience. God's covenant with His people promises blessing for obedience but punishment for disobedience (e.g. Deut. 28). The Exile is a direct consequence of such disobedience and sinful behaviour, warned of repeatedly in the Prophets (e.g. Isa. 3, 5). Yet even as God judges His people there is purpose. God put His people into exile as a consequence of their loss of distinctiveness in order to make them distinctive again. God's covenant means He is totally committed to His people. His purposes for them are always good, however remote that may seem at any given point. Ultimately God's covenant loyalty to His people is seen in their inheritance of the blessings of His everlasting Kingdom. The text of Daniel's prayer in chapter 9 is a powerful appeal based on God's covenant with His people. Daniel prays corporately, on behalf of God's people, confessing their sin. He acknowledges the justice of God's punishment in putting them into exile. He then appeals to God's mercy and promise of future blessing if His people are faithful. This is covenant praying.

(3) *God calls all people to submit to His rule*
While Daniel has a clear message for God's people, it is relevant for *all people*, in particular the section from 2:4 to 7:28 which is written in Chaldean (early Aramaic). Aramaic was the court language of Babylon and the lingua-franca of the ancient world. The use of Aramaic suggests the content of these chapters is of universal significance, a message for *all people* as well as God's people. The Hebrew chapters, in particular 8-12, deal with matters concerned with the future of God's people.

The Aramaic section also has a clear structure (referred to as a chiastic structure) suggesting thematic coherence.

Fig. 2 Aramaic section

Two languages – Hebrew and Aramaic

Ch. 1:1–2:3   Hebrew
Ch. 2:4–7:28   Aramaic
Ch. 8:1–12:13   Hebrew

Chiastic structure of Aramaic section

a Ch. 2   Prophetic vision of four-part statue, rock and mountain

   b Ch. 3   God delivers His people from the furnace

      c Ch. 4   God saves Nebuchadnezzar

      c Ch. 5   God judges Belshazzar

   b Ch. 6   God delivers Daniel from the lions' den

a Ch. 7   Prophetic vision of four beasts, Ancient of Days and son of man

The parallel prophetic visions in chapters 2 and 7 convey God's universal rule. God reveals that He alone rules. Chapters 3 and 6 (in parallel) indicate that God is all-powerful and will deliver His people. God's presence is seen in the distinctive witness of His people and through His miraculous intervention. The central chapters four and five express God's sovereignty in matters of salvation.

The relevance of this section of the book for all people is also evidenced by the conversion of King Nebuchadnezzar (Ch. 4) and the response of Darius (which may also be conversion) on seeing Daniel delivered from the lions' den (6:25-27). From the lips of these pagan kings we get a psalm of praise testifying to God's rule and everlasting dominion (4:34-35; 6:25-27). Darius decrees that all people must fear and reverence the God of Daniel whose Kingdom will last for ever.

Message of Daniel then and today

(1) Message of Daniel then

If, as we believe, Daniel was written shortly after the Exile, its relevance to the people of God then is obvious. Daniel wanted God's people to learn the lessons of the Exile, not only why God put them into exile, but God's sovereign control through the Exile, His bringing the Exile to an end and His promise to restore His glory.

The book would have provided much needed encouragement in the years that followed, with the frustrations and delays in rebuilding the temple and city of Jerusalem. The historical books of Ezra, Nehemiah and Esther record the difficult period that followed the Exile. From Cyrus' decree in 539 B.C. through to the repopulation of Jerusalem after the temple and walls have been rebuilt (around 444 B.C.) was close on a hundred years, a period full of frustration, discouragement and opposition. The message of a book like Daniel, along with prophets like Haggai and Zechariah who ministered in this period, would have encouraged the people of God to press on through adversity, living distinctively, trusting in their God.

When the temple and the city were finally rebuilt in the fifth century, it seemed a pale shadow of the glory days of the great kings, David and Solomon. In that light, one wonders what effect the prophecies in Daniel about God's everlasting Kingdom and all-powerful King would have had on God's people back then? The prophecies do refer to the rebuilding of Jerusalem on the near horizon (9:25) but their dominant focus is on the far horizon. Like a mountain range with peaks stretching into the distance, the prophecies point forward down through the long centuries. And more emphatically of all, they point to a time much later when God's people would face intense persecution. And most of all, they point to a time when God would establish His everlasting Kingdom under the rule of His all-powerful King.

And one can imagine that during that awful period in the second century B.C. when Antiochus nearly wiped out

God's people, the encouragement they would have taken from reading Daniel. What was happening to them had been prophesied in detail. And they would know that Antiochus would not have the last word. God rules.

(2) *Message of Daniel today*

What is the relevance of the message of Daniel for today? Much of what is prophesied in Daniel has happened. We look back in history and see the restoration after the Exile, the rebuilding of the temple and Jerusalem. We look back in history and see the persecution under Antiochus. And most of all, we look back to Jesus who has come in fulfilment of prophecy to inaugurate the everlasting Kingdom of God. We look back to Jesus, God's Anointed One, cut off as a sacrifice to save God's people (His death on the cross). We look back to Jesus' coronation as God's all-powerful King over His everlasting Kingdom. All of that, prophesied in Daniel, has been fulfilled. With Jesus the Kingdom of God has broken into this world and Jesus reigns as God's all-powerful King. But there is stuff prophesied in Daniel that is still to happen. For example, the Kingdom of God has not yet come in all its fullness. That will happen when Jesus returns. Only then will the people of God come into their inheritance spoken of in chapter 7. Only then will they reign with Jesus. The last verse of the book points Daniel, and all God's people through history, forward to the day when all that is prophesied is finally and fully fulfilled: 'As for you, go your way till the end. You will rest, and then at the end of the days you will rise to receive your allotted inheritance' (12:13).

What is our experience living as God's people today? The New Testament picks up the language of Daniel to describe what it's like for God's people to live in the world today. Peter's first letter is a good example of this. Peter writes to a group of churches scattered throughout Asia Minor who are experiencing persecution for their faith. He ends the letter with a statement explaining his reason for writing: 'I have written to you briefly, encouraging you and testifying that this is the true grace of God. Stand fast in it' (1 Pet. 5:12). This is followed by: 'She who is in Babylon, chosen together with you, sends you her greetings' (1 Pet. 5:13). Peter is referring to the Church ('She') in Rome ('Babylon'). Rome / Babylon represents the world. The message of 1 Peter is that God's people live as exiles (aliens and strangers) in the world (1 Pet. 1.1). They are God's 'chosen people' (1 Pet. 2:9) with a guaranteed glorious inheritance to look forward to (1 Pet. 1:3-5), but in this world their experience will be suffering for the sake of the gospel (1 Pet. 1:6-9; 4:12-19; 5:8-11). God calls His people to live distinctively in the world, thus revealing His presence. A key text is 1 Peter 2:11-12 – 'Dear friends, I urge you as aliens and strangers in the world, to abstain from sinful desires, which war against your soul. Live such good lives among the pagans that, though they accuse you of doing wrong, they may see your good deeds and glorify God on the day he visits us.' These themes are picked up throughout the New Testament. The final outcome of the battle is seen in Revelation 17 and 18 when Babylon is destroyed, followed by the coming down of the holy city, the New Jerusalem, in Revelation 21 and 22.

A final point in terms of the message of Daniel for today. Although different from the covenant between God and His people in the Old Testament, the Church is in a covenant relationship with God. God expects His people, the Church, to live distinctively in the world. He promises blessing if they do and warns of judgement if they don't. This is clear, for example, from the letters to the seven churches in Revelation (Rev. 1-3). God is not indifferent to how we live as His people, whether in the sixth century B.C. or the twenty-first century A.D.

(3) Realism of the message of Daniel

A danger in studying Daniel is that we bring our pre-conceived ideas to the text. In Christian culture Daniel is portrayed as a hero of the faith. Hymns like *Dare to be a Daniel* are great but can give the wrong impression. Daniel is not the hero of the story. God is the hero. The book of Daniel is primarily about God. Daniel and his friends were courageous, but their decisions were logical. They knew that God rules. Moreover, as we will see, they didn't fight every battle. They were shrewd, wise and at times tactical in how they operated. Most of all, they were steady and consistent. The book records significant events that happened during the Exile – Daniel's training in Babylon (Ch. 1), Hananiah, Mishael and Azariah in the furnace (Ch. 3), Daniel in the lions' den (Ch. 6) – but such incidents are rare. In between are many years of faithful, consistent witness. Likewise, the big tests may come for us, but the long years of faithful, consistent, distinctive witness in between are just as important.

Reading Daniel from our vantage point in salvation history, we can see how the decisions Daniel and his friends made to live distinctively were caught up in the outworking of God's purposes to build His Kingdom. But on the ground, in the day to day of life, they would not have seen that. The book of Daniel is an encouragement to consistent, faithful, distinctive living, knowing that

God rules and is building His Kingdom. We know the big picture, but in the day to day of the Christian life it is difficult for us to see what God is doing, how the different pieces of the jigsaw fit together.

Structure of Daniel

In terms of structure, the book can be divided in a number of ways.

(1) Two parts – events and prophetic visions

Typically Daniel is divided into two parts – chapters 1–6 and 7–12. Chapters 1–6 record events that took place during the Exile. Chapters 7–12 record the prophetic visions Daniel received at different points in the Exile. Fig. 3 summarises:

Fig. 3 Two parts – events and prophetic visions

Part 1 – Events during the Exile	Dating
Ch. 1 Daniel in Babylon	605 B.C.
Ch. 2 Daniel interprets Nebuchadnezzar's dream	603 B.C.
Ch. 3 Hananiah, Mishael and Azariah in the furnace	Approx. 580 B.C.
Ch. 4 Nebuchadnezzar's humbling, conversion and restoration	In period 580–570 B.C.
Ch. 5 Belshazzar and the writing on the wall	539 B.C.
Ch. 6 Daniel and the lions' den	539 B.C.

Part 2 – Prophetic visions Daniel received during the Exile	
Ch. 7 Vision 1 – four beasts, horns, little horn, Ancient of Days, son of man	552 B.C.
Ch. 8 Vision 2 – ram, goat, four horns, little horn	550 B.C.
Ch. 9 Vision 3 – Daniel's prayer and vision of seventy weeks	539 B.C.

Chs. 10–12	Vision 4 – spiritual warfare, kings of south and north, king who exalts himself, End Times	536 B.C. (after Exile ends)

Within this broad division there are a number of more detailed parallels and contrasts, for example, the conflict chapters 1, 3 and 6 and chapters 4 and 5 where God's saving Nebuchadnezzar is contrasted with His judgement on Belshazzar. And in the prophetic material there are numerous parallels (see section below).

(2) Two types of literature – narrative and prophecy

The division of the book into two parts – chapters 1–6 and 7-12 – broadly reflects the different literature types in the book. These literature types (or genres) are narrative history and prophecy expressed in apocalyptic language. We prefer the term prophecy expressed in apocalyptic language to simply apocalyptic. The material is essentially prophecy, pointing forward to future events. It is written, however, in apocalyptic language with the stylistic feature typical of that genre, e.g. beasts, horns and numbers.

The simple division between chapters 1–6 and chapters 7–12, obscures the fact that there is a good deal of prophetic material in the first half. Nebuchadnezzar's dream of the four-part statue in chapter 2 parallels the vision of the four beasts in chapter 7. Chapters 4 and 5 which deal with Nebuchadnezzar's salvation and Belshazzar's judgement contain prophetic material = the dream of the tree (Ch. 4) and the writing on the wall (Ch. 5).

In addition to the literary genres of narrative and prophecy, the book also includes one of the great prayers of the Bible (Ch. 9) and a number of examples of poetry, e.g. the description of the Ancient of Days (7:9-10) and the testimonies of Nebuchadnezzar (4:34-35) and Darius (6:26-27). Their recorded testimonies read very much like Psalms.

(3) *Two languages – Hebrew and Aramaic*
Another feature of the book (as we have already observed) is that it is written in two languages – Hebrew and Chaldean (early Aramaic). And within the Aramaic section there is a clear structure (see Fig. 2 above).

(4) *One coherent revelation*
These are some of the structural divisions and patterns within the book. Which of them is the key that unlocks the structure of the book as a whole? The answer is that they are all structures within the book but none *the* legitimate way of structuring the book as a whole. The numerous parallels and contrasts lead us to see the book as one coherent revelation from beginning to end. As we preach or teach systematically, chapter by chapter, drawing out the different parallels and contrasts as we go, then we will communicate the message of the book in the way the author intended.

Understanding the prophetic material
Some introductory comments on the prophetic material will be helpful for orientation. More detail on the individual prophecies and the correspondence between them can be found in the individual chapters. Also, at the end of this chapter an Appendix is included which explains how to understand apocalyptic language.

(1) *Extent of prophetic material*
Fig. 4 shows the extent of prophetic material in the book.

Fig. 4 Prophetic material in Daniel

Ch. 2   Dream of four-part statue, rock and mountain

Ch. 4   Dream of tree

Ch. 5   Writing on wall

Ch. 7   Vision 1 – four beasts, horns, little horn, Ancient of Days, son of man

Ch. 8   Vision 2 – ram, goat, four horns, little horn

Ch. 9   Vision 3 – Daniel's prayer and vision of seventy weeks

Chs. 10–12   Vision 4 – spiritual warfare, kings of south and north, king who exalts himself, End Times

All the prophetic material conveys the main theme of the book – God rules and is building an everlasting Kingdom. Within this broad framework, however, some prophecies take a big-picture, wide-angled view of the future, while others focus on the detail with more of a zoom-lens approach.

(2) Big-picture prophecies

The big-picture prophecies are in chapters 2, 7, 9 and 12. Chapter 2 is Nebuchadnezzar's dream of a four-part statue and a rock not cut by human hands that smashes the statue and becomes a great mountain. Each part of the statue represents successive human kingdoms in world history – Babylon, Medo-Persia, Greece and Rome. The rock which smashes the base of the statue (in the time of Rome) is Jesus Christ. The fact that the rock is not cut by human hands reveals His divine origin. This rock becomes a great mountain which is the everlasting Kingdom of God inaugurated with Christ's coming. The reference to the mountain filling the whole earth points forward to the end of time when Jesus will return and the Kingdom of God will come in its full and final form in the New Creation.

Chapter 7, at the centre of the book, gives us the widest-angle frame on the future. The vision is of four beasts, ten horns, a little horn, the Ancient of Days and one like a son of man. Like the four-part statue, the four beasts represent the kingdoms of Babylon, Medo-Persia, Greece and Rome. The fourth beast, which has features of all the other beasts, also bears a general interpretation to all human kingdoms. Out of the fourth beast come a number of horns and a sinister little horn. This little horn represents the Antichrist at the end of history (Paul speaks about 'a man of lawlessness' in 2 Thessalonians 2:1-10). The Ancient of Days establishes His everlasting Kingdom and crowns the son of man as King. The one like a son of man is Jesus (e.g. Matt. 24:30; Mark 10:45). The beasts and the horns are destroyed and the saints of the Most High (the people of God) inherit the Kingdom of God. This vision, therefore, looks forward not only to the inauguration of the everlasting Kingdom of God, but to its final consummation where the people of God will reign with Jesus for ever.

The vision of the seventy sevens (9:20-27) looks forward to the rebuilding of Jerusalem and the temple after the Exile and then down through the long years of history to the coming of the Messiah. The vision focuses in detail on the death of Jesus and then beyond to the destruction of the temple in A.D. 70.

Chapter 12, the final chapter in the book (the last part of the single vision that runs from chapters 10–12), focuses on the End Times, and specifically the time of the End. God will protect His people and nothing will prevent this final consummation of His everlasting Kingdom.

Taking stock for a moment, and remembering these prophecies are sixth century B.C., their scope and significance is astonishing. What confidence this gives in the inspiration of God's Word and His sovereignty over history. From our particular vantage in salvation history, in possession of the full revelation of God's Word, we look back to Christ's coming and the establishing of God's everlasting Kingdom. And we look forward to Christ's return and the consummation of that Kingdom where we will live and reign for ever.

(3) Detailed prophecies

While chapters 2 and 7 give a panoramic survey of history, the prophecies in chapters 8 and 11 focus in detail on a particular period, the fall of the Medo-Persian kingdom to Greece under Alexander the Great and, following his death, the division of his kingdom under four generals. Two of these generals, Ptolemy in Egypt and Seleucus in Syria, dominated, their successors referred to as the Ptolemies in Egypt ('the king of the South') and the Seleucids in Syria ('the king of the North'). Chapters 8 and 11 describe the Seleucid kingdom in Syria and the attack on Jerusalem and desecration of the temple under Antiochus IV Epiphanes, who reigned from 175–164 B.C. From the perspective of world history, Antiochus was not a particularly significant figure compared, for example, to someone like Alexander the Great, but in the history of the people of God, the persecution under Antiochus was of great significance.

The vision in chapter 8 is of a ram and a goat. The goat represents the Medo-Persian kingdom which falls to Greece under Alexander the Great (the goat with a prominent horn). Following Alexander's death the horn is broken off and replaced by four horns, representing the four generals. The vision then quickly focuses on another horn, one of their descendants, Antiochus IV Epiphanes.

Chapter 11 is the most detailed of the prophecies. The text deals quickly with the fall of the Medo-Persian kingdom to Greece under Alexander. A great deal of detail is devoted to the battle for power between the king of the South and the king of the North and the eventual emergence of Antiochus IV Epiphanes.

(4) Relationship between the big-picture and detailed prophecies

The big-picture prophecies embrace the detail and the detailed prophecies point to the bigger picture. For example, chapter 7 which concerns God's universal rule in history embraces the detail of chapter 8 with its focus on a particular period in history. Similarly *the* Antichrist in chapter 7 embraces all antichrists through history, including Antiochus in the detailed vision in chapter 8. And it works the other way round. The experience of God's people in a particular period of history illustrates their experience throughout all history. And the outworking of God's rule in a particular period of history is a picture of His rule over all of history.

The relationship between the big picture and detailed prophecies is also expressed in common apocalyptic language. For example, the big-picture prophecy in chapter 7 and the detailed prophecy in chapter 8 use very similar language / imagery.

(5) Specific prophecies concerning Nebuchadnezzar and Belshazzar

The prophecies concerning Nebuchadnezzar and Belshazzar are specific to the individuals and cover a short period.

Figure 5 summarises the nature and scope of the prophetic material.

Fig. 5 Nature and scope of prophetic material

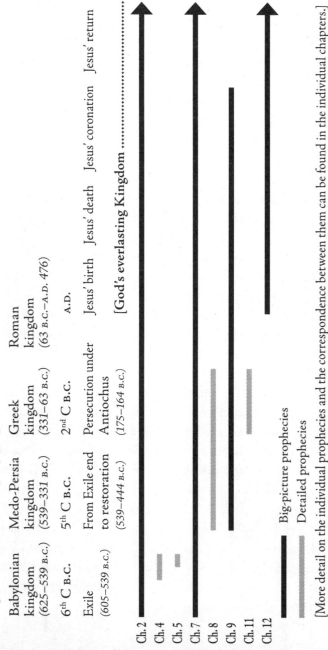

[More detail on the individual prophecies and the correspondence between them can be found in the individual chapters.]

Other matters

Christ in Daniel

The focus on Christ in Daniel is seen primarily in the prophecies that point forward to the establishing of God's everlasting Kingdom under the rule of Jesus, God's all-powerful King. The coming, death, coronation, reign and return of Jesus are all prophesied in Daniel. He is the major focus of the prophecies. The title Son of Man which Jesus uses extensively in the Gospels to refer to himself (e.g. Matt. 24.30; Mark 10.45; Luke 21:36; John 6:27, 53) is taken from Daniel 7:13-14.

In the narrative chapters we do not regard Daniel as a 'type' of Christ in the way that, for example, Joseph, Moses and David are. While there are parts of the book where Daniel's life foreshadows Christ (e.g. the events in Ch. 6, Daniel in the lions' den), Daniel is primarily God's Prophet and a model believer who shows what it means to live distinctively in the world. He does not deliver or rescue God's people from Exile (as a 'type' of Christ). Nor is he a ruler of God's people (as a 'type' of Christ). Rather, he lives *distinctively* in exile. That's his function in biblical revelation. And so we are to follow Daniel's example, drawing applications from his life and witness to ours. This is the line we take and the way we teach the narrative chapters, in particular the conflict chapters 1, 3 and 6. It is very important, however, that we don't preach or teach moralism (in other words 'Be like Daniel to gain favour with God' or 'Be like Daniel in your own strength'). We live distinctively because we are Christians (people who live in light of God's rule) and in the power of the Holy Spirit. As indicated above, drawing parallels with a New Testament letter like 1 Peter will guard against moralism.

(1) Miracles in Daniel

The miracles in Daniel happened as described. The accounts are written as eye-witness testimony and that is how we should take them. The miracles described in chapters 3 and 6 are astonishing. Walking out of a fiery furnace or a lions' den is not of this world. That is the point. They show us the Kingdom of God breaking into this world. They reveal God's absolute rule and omnipotence.

(2) Nature of revelation

Dreams and visions abound in Daniel. Should we regard this as a normal mode of God's revelation or exceptional to these times? While it would be quite wrong to say that God no longer speaks through dreams and visions, we live at a point in salvation history where we have God's full and final revelation in Scripture. That is how God primarily speaks to us.

Walking through the book

Daniel is not a simple Bible book and getting our bearings is important. Figure 6 summarises.

Fig. 6 Walking through Daniel

Text ref.	Description	Theme
Ch. 1:1-2	Introduction to book	God rules
Ch. 1	Daniel in Babylon First conflict chapter	Living distinctively in light of God's rule
Ch. 2	Nebuchadnezzar's dream of four-part statue, rock and mountain Daniel interprets Nebuchadnezzar's dream [Big-picture prophecy]	God reveals that He rules

Text ref.	Description	Theme
Ch. 3	Hananiah, Mishael and Azariah in the furnace Second conflict chapter	Living courageously in light of God's rule
Ch. 4	Dream of tree Daniel interprets Nebuchadnezzar's dream Nebuchadnezzar's humbling, conversion and restoration	God rules in salvation: Nebuchadnezzar's conversion
Ch. 5	Belshazzar and the writing on the wall Daniel interprets the writing Belshazzar's life is taken and the Babylonian kingdom falls	God rules in salvation: Belshazzar's judgement
Ch. 6	Daniel in the lions' den Third conflict chapter	Living consistently in light of God's rule
Ch. 7	Prophetic vision of four beasts, horns, little horn, Ancient of Days and son of man [Big-picture prophecy]	God's universal rule
Ch. 8	Prophetic vision of ram, goat, four horns, little horn [Detailed prophecy]	God's rule in stressful times
Ch. 9	Daniel's prayer and prophetic vision of seventy weeks [Big-picture prophecy]	Praying in light of God's rule
Ch. 10*	Prophetic vision of spiritual warfare	Prayer and spiritual warfare

Text ref.	Description	Theme
Ch. 11*	Prophetic vision of kings of south and north, king who exalts himself [Detailed prophecy]	God's rule through history
Ch. 12*	Prophetic vision of End Times [Big-picture prophecy]	God's rule in the end

* Chapters 10–12 are all one prophetic vision. Following the chapter headings we will treat it in three parts for ease of study.

Planning a Teaching Series on Daniel

Comprehensive series

The book of Daniel is a coherent, inspired revelation, intended to be read as a whole. In planning a teaching series on Daniel, tackling the whole book should be our starting point. The following series of thirteen sermons / Bible studies is suggested. This series will constitute the structure for the rest of the book, with a separate chapter devoted to each sermon / study.

Title of series: **Living in light of God's rule**

Talk/study	Text ref.	Title
1	Ch. 1:1-2	Introduction to Daniel: God rules
2	Ch. 1	Living distinctively in light of God's rule
3	Ch. 2	God reveals that He rules
4	Ch. 3	Living courageously in light of God's rule
5	Ch. 4	God rules in salvation: Nebuchadnezzar's conversion

Talk/study	Text ref.	Title
6	Ch. 5	God rules in salvation: Belshazzar's judgement
7	Ch. 6	Living consistently in light of God's rule
8	Ch. 7	God's universal rule
9	Ch. 8	Trusting God in stressful times
10	Ch. 9	Praying in light of God's rule
11	Ch. 10	Prayer and spiritual warfare
12	Ch. 11	God's rule through history
13	Ch. 12	God's rule in the end

Thirteen weeks is a manageable length for a series. Aside from the introductory sermon / study, taking a chapter at a time will maintain a consistent pace. Some of the chapters are quite long (e.g. Chs. 2, 4, 11), but they are self-contained narratives and need to be taken as a whole.

The series could be split in two (indicated by the shading above). This might be necessary, for example, if you are studying Daniel in a small group Bible study say over two terms. Or it might be helpful to preach it in two blocks to fit in with your preaching schedule.

Because of the perceived complexity of the prophetic material in the second half, series on Daniel often stop at chapters 6 or 7. One of our aims in writing this book is to help dispel fears about teaching the prophetic material.

Shorter comprehensive series
If you're looking for a shorter series (to fit, for example, a term of studies) that nonetheless takes you right through the book, there is scope for taking larger sections. For

example, the introductory sermon / study could be included as introduction to an exposition of chapter 1. Chapters 4 and 5 could be taken together with the title: 'God rules in salvation'. The writer intends a clear contrast between these chapters – the remarkable conversion of Nebuchadnezzar (Ch. 4) and his swift and sudden judgement of Belshazzar (Ch. 5). The downside is the amount of material to cover, but with the right discipline and careful selection of which passages to read (and excellent readers!) it can be done. Chapters 7 and 8 could be taken together with the majority of the sermon / study on chapter 7, with brief reference to chapter 8 as an illustration of the main teaching point of chapter 7 (i.e. in stressful times remember God's universal rule). Chapters 9 and 10 can be taken together. Although chapters 10–12 are a coherent unit in describing Daniel's fourth vision, there are strong thematic parallels between chapters 9 and 10. Chapter 10 is a powerful description of the spiritual conflict we engage in as we pray; a helpful perspective to Daniel's prayer in chapter 9. In that light chapters 9 and 10 could be taken together. Finally, chapters 11 and 12 could be taken together with the title: 'God's rule through history' with the sermon / study covering God's rule through history (Ch. 11) and of the end of history (Ch. 12).

This would give a series of eight as follows.

Title of series: **Living in light of God's rule**

Talk/study	Text ref.	Title
1	Ch. 1	Living distinctively in light of God's rule
2	Ch. 2	God reveals that He rules
3	Ch. 3	Living courageously in light of God's rule

Talk/study	Text ref.	Title
4	Chs. 4 and 5	God rules in salvation
5	Ch. 6	Living consistently in light of God's rule
6	Chs. 7 and 8	God's universal sovereignty
7	Chs. 9 and 10	Praying in light of God's rule
8	Chs. 11 and 12	God's rule through history

Although the chapters that follow are based on the comprehensive series of thirteen studies, suggested sermon outlines and Bible studies are also included for this series of eight.

Another approach to shortening the series, while at the same time covering the book as a whole, would be to leave some chapters out. For example, the strong parallels between chapters 2 and 7, between the conflict chapters 1, 3 and 6 and between chapters 8 and 11, suggest some flexibility. The problem with this, however, is that people feel short-changed if you miss out the 'classic' chapters! More importantly, recognising that the whole book is a coherent, inspired revelation, it is better to take chapters together than omit them.

Mini-series
Mini-series on Daniel can also be helpful, for example, for church weekends, student house parties, youth weekends, etc. Here are some suggestions.

Series 1
This series focuses on the conflict chapters 1, 3 and 6, together with chapter 7 as the central chapter. The purpose of the series would be to encourage Christians to live distinctively in light of the fact that God rules. Comparing

and contrasting chapters 1, 3 and 6 allows careful reflection on the different circumstances and pressures Christians face living in the world and the different responses God looks for. Concluding with chapter 7 allows the series to finish on the key note of God's universal rule. That's important, because our motivation as Christians to live distinctively in the world is not primarily through the example and inspiration of people like Daniel (inspiring as they are); but rather the fact that God rules.

Title of series: **Living in light of God's rule**

Talk/study	Text ref.	Title
1	Ch. 1	Living distinctively in light of God's rule
2	Ch. 3	Living courageously in light of God's rule
3	Ch. 6	Living consistently in light of God's rule
4	Ch. 7	God's universal rule

Series 2
Similar to series one, but focusing on some of the key chapters on God's sovereign rule rather than the conflict chapters. The overall title would be the same.

Title of series: **Living in light of God's rule**

Talk/study	Text ref.	Title
1	Ch. 1	Living distinctively in light of God's rule
2	Ch. 2	God reveals that He rules
3	Chs. 4 and 5	God rules in salvation
4	Ch. 7	God's universal rule

Series 3 and 4

These series give a fair flavour of the major themes in the book as well as the different types of literature.

Title of series: **Living in light of God's rule**

Talk/study	Text ref.	Title
1	Ch. 1	Living distinctively in light of God's rule
2	Chs. 4 and 5	God rules in salvation
3	Ch. 6	Living consistently in light of God's rule
4	Ch. 7	God's universal rule
5	Chs. 9 and 10	Praying in light of God's rule

Talk/study	Text ref.	Title
1	Ch. 1	Living distinctively in light of God's rule
2	Ch. 7	God's universal rule
3	Chs. 9 and 10	Praying in light of God's rule

One-off sermons / studies

While any chapter of God's word is profitable for study, if you are preaching a one-off sermon or leading a one-off Bible study, we would suggest one of the following chapters: 1, 3, 6, 7 or 9. These chapters are manageable as stand alone studies.

Reading Scripture effectively

The reading of Scripture must never be done casually. It is God's inspired word and merits care and attention. The chapters in Daniel (both the narrative and apocalyptic material) make exciting reading, and if read well, really add to the study. If you are not reading the passage yourself, it might be helpful to brief the person reading, alerting them to the narrative structure. For example, it makes a difference if the reader is aware of the movement of scenes and the key turning point in the narrative chapters. The chapters should be read in full, although for the longer chapters (or when two chapters are taken together) the readings can be split. It's good to be creative and work hard to keep people's attention.

If you are looking for New Testament readings to parallel Daniel, 1 Peter and Revelation are the most obvious.

Structure of chapters which follow

The chapters that constitute the major section of this book are based on the comprehensive series of thirteen studies. A separate chapter is devoted to each talk / study. Although this is our starting point, as indicated above, we also include suggested sermon outlines and Bible study material for the shorter series of eight.

Each chapter follows a similar format, specifically geared to help the Bible teacher get to grips with the text in order to teach it. Some brief comments here by way of explanation will be helpful.

Setting in context

It is important to set the particular passage in context. We do this in three ways.

(1) Dating

Many of the chapters in Daniel are dated precisely, both the narrative chapters describing incidents that took place during the Exile and also the visions Daniel received. This is an important aspect of the structure and sequence of the book. For example, the three conflict chapters, 1, 3 and 6, record incidents over the entire period of the Exile, many years apart. Daniel is a teenager in chapter 1, Hananiah, Mishael and Azariah in their late thirties or early forties in chapter 3, and Daniel an old man in his eighties in chapter 6. Being aware of this has a bearing on the way you teach the passage. The vision in chapter eight is dated as 'the third year of King Belshazzar's reign' (8:1). The toughest time for God's people in the Exile was during Belshazzar's reign, which ties in with the content of the vision about God's commitment to His people in times of particular stress and opposition. Or the events of chapter 6 (Daniel and the lions' den), the timing of Cyrus' decree to end the Exile (Ezra 1:1) and Daniel's prayer recorded in chapter 9, are all dated as 539 B.C., the end of the Exile.

(2) Context – *structure of book*
Setting the passage in the context of the whole book is also important. As indicated in the introductory chapter '*Getting our Bearings*' there are numerous parallels and links between chapters. Again, this reflects the writer's intention. For example, an awareness of the relationship and progression across the three conflict chapters is important; the intended contrast between chapters 4 and 5; the striking parallels between chapters 2 and 7; the relationship between the big-picture vision of chapter 7 and the detailed visions in chapters 8 and 11 (which are similar) and the connection between chapters 9 and 10.

(3) Context – *message of book*
As well as being aware of the place of a particular passage or chapter within the context of the book's structure, it is equally important to approach the chapter in light of the

message of the book as a whole. Every Bible book has a key message and when dealing with individual passages and chapters, it's important to keep that main message in view. This should not be seen as a constraint leading to a sameness in each study. The richness of each individual passage or chapter should be brought out to the full, but in the context of the message of the book as a whole. This reflects the writer's intention and will give a coherence and sharpness to your talk or study. In 'Getting our Bearings in Daniel' we suggested the following as the message of the book: *God rules, is building an everlasting Kingdom, and calls people to live in light of that fact.* This determines how we teach, for example, the conflict chapters. The way Daniel, Hananiah, Mishael and Azariah lived was courageous and inspirational, but also logical. Their decision to live distinctively while in exile in Babylon was motivated by the fact that God rules; that great as the power of Nebuchadnezzar was, they knew there was a greater power and a greater King.

Moreover, an awareness of the big picture of God's rule and the fact that He is building His Kingdom, is an important reference when you're preaching on the detailed prophecies in chapters 8 and 11. These chapters are about times of particular difficulty or stress for the people of God. In applying this today – perhaps referring to the increasing secularisation of Western culture and consequent pressure on the Church to conform to that culture – keeping this big picture in view is important when it neither looks like, nor feels like, God rules.

Another good example of understanding the point of a chapter in light of the message of the book as a whole is Daniel's prayer in chapter 9. The title of the study, 'Praying

in light of God's rule', not only reflects the key message of
Daniel, but builds a bridge to Jesus' teaching in the New
Testament about the pattern and priorities in our praying
(e.g. Matt. 6:9-13).

Working on the text

This is the main section in each chapter. Hard work on
the text is indispensable to good teaching. We begin by
identifying the structure of the chapter and then work
through each section in turn. Hard work on the text,
however, is not an analytical or forensic activity. We need
always to keep in mind that the outcome of the process
is not a passage to explain, but a message to proclaim. In
his book, *Working the Angles*, Eugene Peterson helpfully
reminds us that we approach the inspired Word of God,
not as cool analysts, but as passionate hearers. The former
approach will have us taking a tool kit to the text; the latter
(and right approach) will first find us prayerfully meditating
on the text and then, appropriately and sensitively, picking
up our analytical tools.

As we work on the text these are the kind of questions
we should be asking:

- What is the writer saying?
- What bearing does the context have on what he
  says?
- Why does he say it like this?
- What did it mean for the first readers?
- What does it mean now?
- What should I do about it?
- What pictures is the writer using?

Having engaged with the text in this way, it would then be appropriate to consult the detailed commentaries (we suggest a number at the end of the book – 'Further reading').

From text to message

By this stage we should have got to grips with the essentials of the passage. As we sit at our desk, we have a 'text to explain'. If that's the end point, however, our preaching on / study of the passage will be dry. An effective and engaging talk or study needs to move beyond having a 'text to explain' to a 'message to proclaim'. A number of steps can be identified in this movement from text to teaching. These are not prescriptive, but simply a guide as to the kind of logical process we should be working through.

(1) Get the message clear

Our concern is to identify the big idea of the passage. The big idea is the central theme or key message of the passage. A helpful analogy is to think of a Bible passage as containing a boulder as well as rocks and pebbles. The boulder is the main point or the big idea of the passage, the central teaching point. The rocks and the pebbles are the details that contribute to the big idea. And so when you preach / study the passage, by all means look under the rocks and the pebbles, but don't neglect the boulder, the big idea of the passage.

(i) Big idea

In identifying the big idea, helpful questions to ask are: 'What does the passage say?' and 'What's the point of the passage in terms of the message of the book as a whole?' It's helpful if you can state the big idea in one or two sentences. This discipline helps ensure you are focusing on the main point. As you prepare your sermon or Bible study always keep this big idea at the forefront of your mind. For example, the big idea in Daniel 7 is:

God rules and is building an everlasting Kingdom.

That's the 'take-home' point of the talk or study, the point from which the key applications are developed.

(ii) Key questions

Having settled on the big idea, it's helpful to conceptualise it in a series of questions. These are the questions your talk or Bible study will answer and frame the key applications. Raising these at the beginning of the talk or study shows the relevance of the passage. For example, these are the questions you would be looking to answer in a study of Daniel 7.

- What is human power like?
- In contrast to human power, what is God's power like?
- What is God's everlasting Kingdom?
- Has God's everlasting Kingdom come?
- What does the future hold for God's people?
- What will happen to those who oppose God and His people?
- How should humanity respond to the fact of God's rule?

In determining the relevant questions, each one should be tested against the text in order to determine whether it is being answered by the passage. If a question is posed that is not answered by the passage it will lead to confusion.

(2) *Engage the hearer*

Two issues are of relevance here: what we term 'point of contact' and 'dominant pictures / illustrations'.

(i) *Point of contact*

By point of contact (sometimes called 'hook') we mean something that grips the listener at the start of the talk or study. This can be helpful in getting people's attention and orienting them for the talk or study that follows. A good introduction and conclusion add to a talk. It's important, however, that the way you begin and end reflects the heart of the passage. A brilliant introduction that has little bearing on the substance of the passage is worse than an average introduction that gets to the heart. For Daniel 7, a point of contact we suggest is the coronation of a monarch or the inauguration of a president. This is chosen because it takes us to the heart of the passage and the coronation of the son of man as King of God's everlasting Kingdom. A good principle in determining the appropriateness of a point of contact is to consider whether it connects with the big idea.

(ii) *Dominant pictures / illustrations*

Illustrations in talks or Bible studies are helpful, again provided they are good illustrations! The same principle applies as point of contact – an illustration is only helpful as far as it reflects the point of the passage. A good way to work on illustration is first to determine the dominant picture(s) in a passage and then work on illustration by filling out that picture. For example, the first two verses of chapter 1 (which we take as the text for an introductory study to the book as a whole), draw a sharp distinction between appearance and reality. While it looks like Nebuchadnezzar is the dominant player, in reality God is in control, orchestrating events. Illustrations along these lines would be appropriate.

(3) Work on application

Aware of the importance of thoughtful application of the Word of God, we suggest a number of pointers to application. This is not an exhaustive list; rather we try to identify what might be considered the main lines of application arising from the passage.

(i) Primary application

The primary application takes us to the heart of the passage. This is how the passage applies to everyone all of the time and might be considered the authoritative application. For example, in the conflict chapters 1, 3 and 6, the authoritative application to all God's people is that God expects us to live distinctive lives in the world as His witnesses. In the chapters concerning God's sovereignty in salvation – God's grace to Nebuchadnezzar (Ch. 4) and His judgement of Belshazzar (Ch. 5) – the authoritative application for all people is that we need to repent and seek God's forgiveness. There are no exceptions.

(ii) Secondary applications

Secondary applications relate to how the passage might apply personally to different groups or individuals. Again, using the conflict chapters as illustration, what might it look like for different people to take a stand for God?

Outline for a sermon or talk

We offer a suggested outline for a sermon or talk on the chapter. Again, this is not meant to be prescriptive in any way. It's simply intended to provide a helpful starting point. This outline would also be useful if you're giving a short introductory talk followed by a Bible study.

Leading a Bible study

Finally, each chapter ends with a Bible study. The Bible study is divided into four sections: *(i) Introduce the issues, (ii) Study the passage, (iii) Apply the passage, and (iv) Pray it through*. It may be that in your Bible study group everyone has a copy of *Teaching Daniel*, with each person reading the text and the relevant section in the book by way of preparation. Or, you might feel that the material in the book is too detailed or difficult, in which case you, as the study leader, would do the preparation, using the book and then distribute the questions to the larger group for the study. As indicated above, you might begin the study with a short talk on the passage.

While you will know what is best for your group, we have tried to write this book in a way that makes the material accessible. And so we would encourage the approach where everyone has a copy of the book and reads through the relevant chapter. The benefit is that it teaches people how to read and understand the Bible by giving them practical tools to that end. It also encourages them that they can read the Bible for themselves.

Appendix 1
Teaching Old Testament narrative

We offer some brief reflections here on teaching Old Testament narrative. More detail on interpretation and application is included in the individual chapters.

(1) Understanding how stories work

Stories have structure and plot lines, beginnings and endings. Moreover the author will describe the events in an engaging and dramatic way. It is important to reflect these principles in the way we teach narrative. Our teaching should be as engaging, after all the events described are dramatic and gripping. Daniel 3 and 6 are good examples. These chapters have a clear, logical structure and we should reflect that in the way we teach them. Moreover, the author builds tension throughout the narrative before Shadrach, Meshach and Abednego are thrown into the fiery furnace (Ch. 3) and Daniel into the lions' den (Ch. 6). That heightened tension takes a further turn as God miraculously delivers them. We need to teach these stories conveying the tension and drama of real life events. This stuff happened.

(2) *Teach the turning point*

The key to teaching narrative is to identify the turning point. The turning point is the main teaching point / application point. In Daniel 1, the turning point is verse 8, when Daniel resolves not to take the royal food and wine. In Daniel 3, the turning point is Shadrach, Meshach and Abednego's defiant statement of faith (3:16-18). The turning point in chapter 6 is Daniel's reaction to the king's decree (6:10). In light of the message of the book all of these turning points illustrate God's people living distinctively in light of God's rule.

(3) *Keep to the main points*

It is important to keep to the main points. The details are important but are there to illustrate the main points. And the key applications should be built around the main points rather than the details. Daniel 1 is a good example. The beginning of the chapter looks at the pressure these young people faced to conform to the culture of Babylon. There are fascinating details like changing their Hebrew names to Babylonian names but you need to be careful not to get bogged down in the detail and miss the key point which is the timeless pressure to conform (and the applications that arise from it).

(4) Teaching Christ from Old Testament narrative
There is a discussion of this in the section entitled 'Christ in Daniel' in the Introductory Material ('*Getting our Bearings in Daniel*').

Appendix 2
Teaching apocalyptic literature

(1) Apocalyptic literature makes things clear
The first thing to say (and one of the most important) is that the purpose of apocalyptic literature is to make things clear, to reveal what is hidden. As a literary genre it is often considered difficult and obscure but that is precisely at odds with the reason this literature is in the Bible. In this regard, a helpful way to think of apocalyptic literature is that it is different rather than difficult. Once you get your head around the way it works, it is not that difficult to understand and great to teach.

(2) A significant literary genre
Apocalyptic literature is a significant literary genre in Scripture. While Ezekiel, Daniel, Zechariah and Revelation would be the main examples, apocalyptic writing is also found in the Gospels, for example, Jesus' words on the Mount of Olives (the so-called 'Olivet Discourse', sometimes called the 'little apocalypse') spoken just before the events of the Passion and Resurrection (Matt. 24, Mark 13 and Luke 21). There are also elements of apocalyptic writing in the New Testament letters – the end of 1 Thessalonians, 2 Thessalonians chapter 2, and 2 Peter, especially chapter 3.

(3) What is apocalyptic literature?
In the Introductory Material ('*Getting our Bearings in Daniel*'), we suggested the term 'prophecy expressed in apocalyptic

language' rather than simply apocalyptic / apocalyptic literature. That seems to fit well with the material in Daniel and a strong case could be made to categorise the biblical corpus of apocalyptic material in this way. As a particular 'type' of prophecy, however, apocalyptic literature has a number of distinctive features / emphases.

(i) Focus on the unseen world

Apocalyptic literature takes us 'behind the scenes' to see the unseen world of spiritual warfare as God builds His everlasting Kingdom (e.g., the final prophecy in Chs. 10-12). We are also taken 'behind the scenes' to see significant events in salvation history, like the coronation of Jesus as King of God's everlasting Kingdom in the heavenly throne room (Ch. 7). There is a similar picture of the heavenly throne room in Revelation 4 and 5.

A key purpose in taking us 'behind the scenes' is to reveal where true power and authority lies. In the 'seen' world of history, power rests with human kingdoms and empires, whether Babylon, Medo-Persia, Greece, Rome (and their contemporary equivalents), and powerful individuals like Nebuchadnezzar and Alexander the Great (and their contemporary equivalents). And often in the 'seen' world of history they seem far more powerful than God and His people. Yet that is not true reality. Apocalyptic literature shows us where true power lies. God rules and is building His everlasting Kingdom. Human power and authority is transient, given and taken by God. In this respect, apocalyptic literature is a great encouragement to God's people, in whatever generation, as it reveals how things truly are.

(ii) Focus on times of difficulty for God's people

Apocalyptic literature has a particular focus on times of difficulty or stress for God's people. This is evident, for example, in that Daniel as a book about the Exile includes so much apocalyptic material. The Exile was an event of huge significance in the history of God's people calling into question their very existence. Within the book itself, the big-picture prophecies like Daniel 7 and 12 speak of the stress and difficulty experienced by God's people throughout history as they seek to live distinctively in light of God's rule. This is normal experience for God's people, in every generation. There will always be friction, opposition and struggle. There are times, however, when the opposition and stress are particularly intense. The detailed prophecies in Daniel 8 and 11 focus on an intense period of persecution for God's people in the second century B.C. And what is predicted in these detailed prophecies in a particular period of history is a pattern repeated at different times throughout history. Like the focus on the unseen world, this emphasis on times of difficulty for God's people is a great encouragement to endure. Through the toughest times, God rules, is with His people and is building His everlasting Kingdom.

(iii) Focus on the End Times

The focus on times of difficulty or stress for God's people is often expressed in apocalyptic literature in terms of an intense period of persecution before the end of history when the Lord Jesus returns and the everlasting Kingdom of God comes in its fullness in the New Creation. This intense period of persecution is the time of the Antichrist. The prophecies in Daniel 7, 11 and 12 refer to this period. Beyond this particular aspect of the end of history, apocalyptic literature has a broader relevance to the End Times. Daniel 12 is a good example with its focus on the return of Jesus, the 'time of distress', the resurrection of all people (and division) and the reign of God's people in the New Creation.

(4) Stylistic features of apocalyptic literature

(i) Use of symbolism

Apocalyptic literature uses a good deal of symbolism. A book like Daniel is full of it, for example: the four-part statue, rock and mountain (Ch. 2), Nebuchadnezzar's dream of a tree (Ch. 4), the writing on the wall at Belshazzar's feast (Ch. 5), the four beasts, ten horns, little horn, Ancient of Days and son of man (Ch. 7), the ram, goat with prominent horn, four horns, little horn (Ch. 8) and so on. The language is different, rather than difficult, and the explanations are all quite straightforward. We hope you will agree as you study the individual chapters!

(ii) Use of numbers

Another feature of apocalyptic language is the use of numbers. Numbers are used symbolically. Take for example, the number four, which suggests comprehensiveness. The four-part statue (Ch. 2) and the four beasts (Ch. 7) describe the full extent of human power throughout history. The number seven is used in the Bible to signify divine order or God's purposes. The number seven features most clearly in Daniel in chapter 9. Daniel prays in light of biblical prophecies that the Exile is to last for seventy years. And the vision Daniel receives as the answer to his prayer is of seventy weeks ('sevens').

Numbers are also used to refer to defined periods of time. So, for example, in Daniel we find references to 'time, times and half a time' (7:25, 12:7) and periods of '2,300 evenings and mornings' (8:14) and 1,290 and 1,335 days (12:11-12). In apocalyptic language these numbers signify a fixed period of time (determined by God), whether a short time or a longer time. And so in a detailed prophecy like Daniel 8 this kind of language can be taken to be referring to a short period of time (e.g. the persecution under Antiochus IV Epiphanes in the second-century B.C. which lasted three and a half years), whereas in the big-picture prophecies like Daniel 7 and the closing verses in the book in Daniel 12, it can be taken to be referring to a much longer period of time (e.g. the period between the time of Daniel and the time of the end or the period of intense distress that will happen before the end). In all cases, whether long or short, it is a fixed period of time, determined by God. Once again, this is profoundly reassuring for God's people during tough times. Periods of intense persecution will come, but God's sovereign rule means He will bring them to an end. All this points to the fact that God's rule will be seen in the reality that the whole of human history, which is characterised by the persecution of God's people, will come to an end and God's people will inherit the everlasting Kingdom of God in all its fullness.

(iii) Use of vivid language

In keeping with the use of symbolism and numbers, the language used in apocalyptic literature is vivid and dramatic. Illustrations of this would be the descriptions of the beasts in Daniel 7, particularly the terrifying fourth beast. The description of Antiochus' exploits and persecution of God's people in Daniel 8 and 11 is vivid and dramatic. Phrases like 'the abomination that causes desolation' (9:27; 12:11) sound as frightening as the facts they describe. Another example would be the description of the cross in 9:24 – 'Seventy "sevens" are decreed for your people and your holy

city to finish transgression, to put an end to sin, to atone for
wickedness, to bring in everlasting righteousness, to seal up
vision and prophecy and to anoint the Most Holy Place.'
Hopefully these brief reflections on the nature of apocalyptic
literature will help as you teach the material. We include a
lot more information / explanation in the detailed chapters
to guide you through the apocalyptic material.

Teaching apocalyptic literature – key principles
To summarise, here are three principles to help you teach
this material effectively.

(i) *Teach the big idea*
First, teach the big-idea. It is important not to get bogged
down or side-tracked by the detail. As you approach each of
the visions, try to get the big idea and make sure that drives
what you teach. For example, in the vision in Daniel 7 the
big idea is that God rules and is building an everlasting
Kingdom. All the details of the chapter – the identity of
the beasts, the horns, the little horn, the heavenly throne
room, the Ancient of Days and one like a son of man – are
embraced by / shed light on the big idea. In the detailed
vision in Daniel 11, the big idea is that God rules through
history, including stressful times. God will bring these
times to an end, and expects His people to trust Him and
live distinctively through these times. A vision like Daniel
11 is so detailed it would be very easy to lose sight of the
big idea.

(ii) *Use the detail*
All that said, you need to use the detail to illustrate the big
idea. The detail bring richness and colour. For example, the
detail concerning the persecution of God's people under

Antiochus (Chs. 8 and 11) brings a reality and realism to what is described. And in Daniel 11, before the vision focuses on Antiochus there is a detailed description of the machinations of human power, political intrigue and ambition. In chapter 9, the description of the cross is rich in detail (9:24). In Daniel 12, which focuses on the end of history, there is rich detail in the description of exactly what will happen, even in a single verse (12:1).

(iii) Engage the affections
When teaching apocalyptic literature it is important to feel / experience the impact of the text and convey that feeling / experience in the way you teach it. We need to work hard to convey the dramatic intensity of the visions, the vivid pictures of evil and sheer glory of God in His sovereign rule and divine power. Daniel's reaction to the revelation / visions is striking and makes this point powerfully. Daniel is deeply affected and humbled by the sober reality of what he sees (7:28; 8:27; 10:4-9; 10:15-11:1). That should be our reaction and the reaction we seek to convey.

I

Introduction to Daniel: God Rules
(Daniel 1:1-2)

Setting in context

Daniel is a complex book and getting our bearings at the start is important. An introductory study can be helpful in providing some basic navigation tools and in getting across the message of the book. The opening two verses of chapter 1 provide an appropriate text for such an introductory study. The verses are included here for ease of reference.

1. 'In the third year of the reign of Jehoiakim king of Judah, Nebuchadnezzar king of Babylon came to Jerusalem and besieged it.

2. And the Lord delivered Jehoiakim king of Judah into his hand, along with some of the articles from the temple of God. These he carried off to the temple of his god in Babylonia and put in the treasure house of his god.'

It would, of course, be perfectly appropriate to take these verses as the introduction to a study on the whole of Daniel 1 (which is the approach taken in the next chapter).

(1) Dating

The opening verse marks the beginning of the Exile. The 'third year of the reign of Jehoiakim' is 605 B.C. Nebuchadnezzar became king of Babylon in the same year (he reigned from 605–562 B.C.). This is the first show of strength by Nebuchadnezzar, and marked the beginning of the process that led to the eventual destruction of Jerusalem and the temple in 586 B.C. and the mass deportation of God's people into exile in Babylon.

While the events described in chapter 1 focus on the three-year training programme Daniel and his friends underwent in Babylon, the closing verse of the chapter provides an historical marker, denoting the fall of the Babylonian dynasty to the Medo-Persian kingdom under Darius the Mede and Cyrus the Persian. The 'first year of King Cyrus' (v. 21) is 539 B.C. and marked the end of the Exile.

(2) Context – structure of book

The book of Daniel is an historical account of the Exile. The first half of the book (Chs. 1–6) records a number of significant events that took place during the Exile. These events, which span the entire period of the Exile, focus both on God's dealings with His people and with the pagan kings of Babylon and Medo-Persia. The second half of the book (Chs. 7–12) records a number of prophetic visions Daniel received during the Exile (the final prophetic vision (Chs. 10–12) was just after the Exile ended). The prophetic visions point to a future when God's people will often be oppressed. But they also point to a glorious future, when God will establish His everlasting Kingdom with an all-powerful King, where one day God's people will reign with Him.

The opening verses of chapter 1 are an appropriate preface, both to the historical account that follows, and to the future orientation of the book.

(3) Context – message of book

The key message of the book is that *God rules and is building an everlasting Kingdom*. To God's people living in the world, it may not look or feel like it, but the fact is God rules. This message is particularly important in times of oppression for the people of God.

God calls His people to live distinctively in light of His rule. This is a key way God reveals His presence in the world of Babylon and advances His Kingdom. Living distinctively invariably results in conflict and oppression. God's people can also experience oppression as a direct consequence of their sinful disobedience. The Exile is a direct result of their sin and lack of distinctiveness. This is the outworking of God's covenant with His people. The covenant, with its guarantee of future blessing but also curses for disobedience, is key to understanding the Exile and to how God deals with His people throughout history.

Working on the text

Consistent with the structure and message of the book as a whole, these opening verses touch on some key themes. The following points can be identified.

(1) In spite of what it looks like and feels like God rules

(2) God's people experience oppression in the world of Babylon

(3) God's presence is inescapable, challenging other beliefs and worldviews

(1) In spite of what it looks like and feels like God rules

Verse 1 is a straightforward historical statement such as
might appear in a chronicle of events. History records the
might of the Babylonian kingdom under the powerful king
Nebuchadnezzar overpowering the weak king, Jehoiakim,
the city of Jerusalem and the people of Judah. The
language conveys a sense of dominance and subjugation
– Nebuchadnezzar 'came', 'besieged', 'carried off', 'put'. It
looked like the power was with Nebuchadnezzar. And it
would have felt like it for those who lived through it. Even
though the final destruction of the city and the temple
is still nearly twenty years in the future, the signs are
ominous. This is a defiant challenge to God's promises
about the covenant, the Davidic kingdom and the security
of Jerusalem.

If verse 1 is an historical record of what happened,
verse 2 is a theological explanation of what is really going
on. Whatever may have been the secondary causes of
the downfall of Jerusalem, such as the incompetence of
their later kings or the powerful new Babylonian king
Nebuchadnezzar, ultimately it was an act of God Himself.
God is in control. He gives His people into exile. He gives
the articles from His temple to be taken to the temple
of Nebuchadnezzar's god in Babylon. The verb 'gave'
(v. 2) (NIV 'delivered') is to be an important one in the
theology of the book. All power is given by God – the
great kingdoms and kings of this world, their power given
and taken by God, something that even Nebuchadnezzar
comes to recognise in the end (4:34-35).

Thus, in spite of what it looks like, the Exile is not
an event that disrupts God's plans. Rather, it is part of
God's plan. Nebuchadnezzar, Belshazzar and Cyrus are

all pawns on God's chessboard. What is God's plan? All these events are part of God's purpose to establish His everlasting Kingdom. In contrast to earthly kingdoms and kings which come and go (like the Babylonian kingdom and its kings) God will establish an everlasting Kingdom, with all power, authority and dominion given to God's anointed King. This is the main theme of the book, the dominant note sounded in every chapter. In the introductory segment 'Getting our Bearings' the section on the message of Daniel summarises how this theme is developed through the book. In this introductory study it might be helpful to give such an overview.

(2) *God's people experience oppression
       in the world of Babylon*

The book of Daniel could be described as 'A Tale of Two Cities' – Jerusalem, the city of God, and Babylon, the city of the world. Nebuchadnezzar, king of Babylon, attacks Jerusalem, and the people of God are taken from Jerusalem into exile in Babylon. Both are literal cities, capitals of their respective kingdoms, but both also stand for the abiding reality of God's people ('Jerusalem') living in a godless world ('Babylon'). In that regard, it is instructive to reflect on how the two names are used in Scripture.

Jerusalem (earlier Salem), first comes to prominence in Genesis 14 where Abraham meets its king, Melchizedek. Melchizedek is described as 'priest of God Most High' (Gen. 14:18). Already, therefore, Jerusalem is the place associated with the worship of the one true God. Much later Jerusalem is captured by David from the Jebusites (2 Sam. 5:6-15) and the Ark of the Covenant taken there (2 Sam. 6; Ps. 24). In the Psalms, the preferred name for

Jerusalem is Zion, a reference to Mount Zion, the hill on which the city stood. Yet Jerusalem is far more than a literal city. It is the people of God throughout history who gather on Mount Zion, the city of the living God (Heb. 12:22).

Babylon also first appears in Genesis 10 where it is associated with the sinister figure of Nimrod and the early Mesopotamian city states in Shinar (Gen. 10:9-12). While from the beginning of the Bible Jerusalem is associated with the worship of God, Babylon is associated with a warlord and pride in human achievement, which culminates in the Tower of Babel (Gen. 11:1-9). Later, the history of the region is marked by power struggles between Babylon in the south and Assyria in the north. As the book of Daniel begins, a long period of the supremacy of Assyria has come to an end with the fall of Nineveh, the Assyrian capital in 612 B.C. And now in 605 B.C., Babylon's vigorous new King, Nebuchadnezzar, had brought the city to the peak of its power. Yet like Jerusalem, Babylon is far more than a literal city. It is a symbol of the anti-God forces in history which battle with Zion (see e.g. Isa. 13-14 and Jer. 50-51). The language of 'Babylon' is used in the New Testament to make the same point. In his first letter Peter comments: 'She who is in Babylon, chosen together with you, sends you her greetings' (1 Pet. 5:13). Almost certainly Peter is referring to the Church ('she') in Rome ('Babylon'). The message of 1 Peter is that God's people are elect exiles (1 Pet. 1:1-2) called to live distinctively in the world (1 Pet. 2:11-12). In this world, they will experience suffering (1 Pet. 1:6-9) but there is a guaranteed glorious inheritance to look forward to in the future (1 Pet. 1:3-5). The final outcome of the battle is seen in Revelation 17 and 18 where Babylon is destroyed, followed by the coming down of the holy city, the New Jerusalem, in Revelation 21 and 22.

The clash of Jerusalem and Babylon – God's people living in a godless world – is a major theme in Daniel. Through the experience of Daniel and his friends living in Babylon we see how difficult it is for God's people to live distinctive lives in such an environment. They face constant pressure to conform and when they take a stand for God, opposition and persecution are inevitable. This is the focus of the conflict in chapters 1, 3 and 6. The pressure of living as God's people in a godless world is also a major focus of the apocalyptic material in Daniel and, in particular chapters 7, 8 and 11. Chapter 7 is a grand overview of history and the weight of worldly power which often opposes the people of God. Ultimately, however, God's power is greater, seen in the establishment of His everlasting Kingdom, which is His people's glorious inheritance. The more detailed prophecies in chapters 8 and 11 focus on an intense period of persecution under Antiochus Epiphanes in the second century B.C. The experience of oppression is an ever-present reality for the people of God. This will be the case until the Lord Jesus returns to bring in the New Jerusalem, the full and final fulfilment of God's everlasting Kingdom inaugurated with the first coming of Christ.

The oppression experienced by God's people arises from their calling to live distinctively in the world. But God's people will also experience oppression as a direct consequence of their sinful behaviour. The covenant between God and His people promises blessing for obedience but punishment for disobedience (e.g. Deut. 28). The Exile is a direct consequence of such sinful behaviour and loss of distinctiveness, warned of repeatedly in the

Prophets (e.g. Isa. 3, 5). But there is always purpose in God's punishment, to render His people distinctive again. God is totally committed to His people. They will inherit His everlasting Kingdom.

(3) God's presence is inescapable, challenging other beliefs and worldviews

What is the significance of the articles (vessels) from the temple that God delivered into Nebuchadnezzar's hand, which Nebuchadnezzar then put in the temple of his god in Babylon (v. 2)? These vessels will appear again in Chapter 5 where Belshazzar uses them at a drunken orgy. In Ezra we read of their return to Jerusalem where they are reinstated in the temple once it has been rebuilt (Ezra 1:7-11). In the same way that God gives His people into exile, God gives the articles into Nebuchadnezzar's hand. God is in control, all part of His plan.

The reference to Nebuchadnezzar's god is probably Marduk, head of the Babylonian pantheon. The placing of the articles from the temple of God in Jerusalem in the temple of Marduk is a deliberate and provocative statement as to the superiority of Marduk (and by association, Babylon and Nebuchadnezzar). In his recent book on Daniel, *Against the Tide*, John Lennox makes the insightful point that Nebuchadnezzar's actions are an attempt to relativize the absolute. The articles from the temple in Jerusalem representing the one true and living God are showcased along with the many gods of Babylon. When it came to gods the Babylonian worldview was relativism.

Such an arrogant challenge to God's authority raises the stakes. There are parallels with the incident in 1 Samuel 5 where the Philistines, having captured the Ark of the

Covenant at the battle of Ebenezer, place it in front of their god, Dagon, in his temple. When the people of Ashdod return to the temple, they find the statue of their god, Dagon, 'fallen on his face on the ground before the ark of the LORD' (1 Sam. 5:3-4). And, of course, in Babylon, when Belshazzar and his revellers use the temple vessels in his drunken party, God dramatically intervenes and both Belshazzar and the Babylonian kingdom fall.

In many ways the whole episode in 1 Samuel 4 and 5 foreshadows the Exile. God's people had attempted to use the Ark as a magical talisman to avoid defeat. The ark could not defend them and they were overpowered by the Philistines because of their idolatry and unbelief. Yet when the Philistines blasphemously desecrate the Ark before Dagon, God intervenes to demonstrate His rule and authority.

Earlier in biblical history, the events of the Exodus are a battle between God and the gods of Egypt. This is crystallised in Exodus 12:12 where God says: '...I will bring judgment on all the gods of Egypt. I am the LORD (Yahweh).' This is an emphatic answer to Pharaoh's question in Exodus 5:2: 'Who is the LORD, that I should obey him and let Israel go?'

There are also relevant passages in the Prophets. Particularly striking is Isaiah 46:

> 'Bel bows down, Nebo stoops low;
>   their idols are borne by beasts
>   of burden.
> The images that are carried about are
>   burdensome,
>   a burden for the weary.

> They stoop and bow down together;
>   unable to rescue the burden,
>   they themselves go off into captivity'
>   (Isa. 46:1-2).

Bel (or Lord) is Marduk, the chief Babylonian god, and Nebo, his son, the Babylonian god of wisdom. The reference is to the carrying of the images of these gods, along the Ishtar Way in Babylon to the temple of Marduk. Isaiah's point is to question what kind of 'gods' these really are which need to be carried? God, as Isaiah has already told us, is the one who carries us, His people (Isa. 40:11). Ultimately these false gods are just a heavy burden and will themselves be taken into captivity. This is probably a reference to the overthrow of the Babylonian kingdom, but ultimately the subjugation of all human power and wisdom to the sovereignty and power of God's everlasting rule.

Standing back from the detail of the text, the placing of the articles from the temple in Jerusalem in the temple in Babylon symbolise the presence of God in Babylon, challenging its beliefs and worldviews and building God's Kingdom. Through the book of Daniel, God's presence in the world of Babylon is seen in a number of different ways. We see it, for example, in His control of events, both the big picture (His control of the Exile) and in the detail. A number of details in chapter 1 illustrate. God influences Ashpenaz to show favour to Daniel. God gives Daniel and his friends good health and exceptional ability. All of this is with the intention of putting them into the heart of Babylon that God might build His Kingdom. God's control is also seen in His miraculous intervention, most evidently in the dramatic deliverance from the furnace (Ch. 3) and lions' den (Ch. 6). God's presence is also seen as He breaks into the world of Babylon with divine revelation, for example Nebuchadnezzar's dreams in chapters 2 and 4, and the writing on the wall in chapter 5. Although Nebuchadnezzar and Belshazzar do not understand what they have seen they are conscious of a higher authority and gripped by mortal fear. Understanding comes only when God gives the interpretation to Daniel. The collective wisdom of Babylon cannot shed any light on such ultimate realities. True knowledge and understanding only come when God breaks into our world bringing revelation. Again, this is a rich biblical theme, that finds its fulfilment in the revelation of God through Jesus Christ who came into the world to make God known (John 1:18). The content of the prophecies throughout the book reveal that God rules in the world (e.g. Chs. 2, 7, 12).

The presence of God in Babylon is also manifest through the distinctiveness of God's people. Nebuchadnezzar's strategy was to take the future leaders of God's people into Babylon and to put God out of their lives. Instead, Daniel and his friends lived distinctively in light of God's rule with the result that God put them into the heart of Babylon as His witnesses.

From text to message

(1) Get the message clear

i) Big idea
In spite of appearances, God rules and is building His Kingdom.

ii) Key questions
Preaching or teaching on this passage should answer the following questions:

- Who is in control of history?

- What is God's overarching plan for the world and His people?

- Why is oppression so often the experience of God's people?

- In particularly stressful times, why can God's people trust Him?

- In what ways is God's presence seen in the world?

(2) Engage the hearer

i) Point of contact

In his poem *The Second Coming*, Yeats wrote: 'Things fall apart, the centre cannot hold; mere anarchy is loosed upon the world.' This is how the people of Judah must have felt as the events of the Exile began to unfold.

Or the following from the experience of one of the authors: 'A number of years ago, my wife and I were on holiday in Keswick during one of the convention weeks. Between the meetings, we would spend our afternoons in the hills. The town of Keswick sits at the end of Derwent water, the lake surrounded by hills, forming a natural amphitheatre. On one particular afternoon, as part of the convention, the BBC were recording Songs of Praise in the open air at the edge of the lake. Although we must have been three or four miles away at the opposite end of the lake from the town, we could hear the singing clearly, echoed by the natural amphitheatre of the hills. The hymn being sung was *To God be the Glory* with the chorus:

> *Praise the Lord, praise the Lord!*
> *let the earth hear His voice;*

> *praise the Lord, praise the Lord!*
> *let the people rejoice:*
> *O come to the Father,*
> *through Jesus the Son*
> *and give Him the glory;*
> *great things He hath done!*

That day, in the splendour of God's creation, the earth heard the Lord's song. No one could escape it. No one could shut it out.' Inspiring as that was it is not a realistic picture of what it's like to live as God's people in the world. More often we find ourselves echoing the words of the Psalmist:

> *How can we sing the songs of the Lord*
> *while in a foreign land?* (Ps. 137:4)

The book of Daniel is a timeless message of encouragement and challenge to the people of God that answers, precisely, that question.

ii) Dominant pictures / illustrations

Pictures or illustrations that contrast the appearance of power with reality are helpful. For example, you could illustrate the power of Babylon in the Ancient World by showing a picture of the Ishtar Gate, the entrance to the Ancient City of Babylon. The gate has been reconstructed brick by brick in a museum in Berlin. Built both to impress and intimidate, the Ishtar Gate is an awesome sight (even in a museum), not only its sheer scale, but the striking blue and gold stonework with reliefs of bulls and dragons, the guardians of the gate and the city of Babylon. As you show a picture of this symbol of power you make the point that in spite of appearances God is in control. And of course, the Ishtar Gate is now a museum artefact, whereas God's

Kingdom endures. This pattern is repeated throughout history.

A more contemporary picture or illustration would be the Church today. In the Western world the powers of secularism dominate, the people of God feeling increasingly marginalised. Again that can be illustrated in a number of ways – both from a big-picture perspective, and the day to day reality of life.

(3) Work on application

- In spite of what it looks like and feels like God rules. This is a timeless principle of application. From our vantage point in salvation history we can look back and see how God has established His everlasting Kingdom with Jesus as His all-powerful King. Yet the Kingdom of God has not yet come in all its fullness. That will happen when Jesus returns. Until then, it will look like human power dominates. But God rules.

- Even when it looks like God has experienced a significant set-back He hasn't. Throughout history, again and again it seems God is on the back foot, His cause thwarted. But we should not be fooled. God's Kingdom is always going forward, His cause always advancing. Indeed, significant set-backs are often the catalyst for significant advance. This principle can be applied at a big-picture global level (e.g. the expulsion of missionaries from China in the 1950s that led to the growth of the indigenous Chinese Church) but also with respect to our local situations where set-backs in church life are used by God to advance the gospel. It can also be applied personally in the Christian life.

- God's control of history means that He uses nations and individuals to further His purposes. That was true in Daniel's day and it is true still. Again, we can see this happening on the big-scale but also in the details of our lives. This should not lead us to any sense of blind determinism or despair – that we are actors or puppets in a drama directed by God – but rather a quiet confidence that God is ultimately in control of everything. Also, as Christians, we should be interested and engaged as events unfold in the political life of our nation and world, but never unduly dismayed when things don't turn out as we would have wished. God has a purpose in it all and is in control.

- God sometimes lets it look like His cause has been defeated. In Daniel, allowing the articles from the temple to be taken into Babylon is a case in point. In the Western world today, to many observers it looks like God's cause has been defeated. It is a long time since God last brought revival to the Church in the West. But the truth is God is no less powerful, no less in control. There is purpose in His plans.

- As God's people we will experience oppression and difficulty living in the world. There are times when that is really intense. Part of God's plan in working towards this everlasting Kingdom is to reveal His purposes to His people through His Prophets. To that end, Daniel is God's prophetic

voice, strengthening the people of God in times
of difficulty and discouragement. The message of
Daniel would have provided such encouragement
for the people of God struggling to rebuild
Jerusalem and the temple after the Exile. Through
the inter-testamental period, and, in particular, the
intense persecution under Antiochus Epiphanes
in the late second century B.C. (the focus of the
detailed prophecies in Chs. 8 and 11), the message
of Daniel would have been a great source of strength
and encouragement. And for the people of God
today, there are parts of the world where things
are really difficult. And in the West there are signs
of difficult times ahead. The message of Daniel is
important.

• The oppression we experience is a consequence of
living distinctively as God's people in the world.
This will be a major focus of Daniel, both in the
narrative conflict chapters and in the prophetic
material. But oppression can also be a direct
consequence of sin and disobedience. God put
His people into exile because of their lack of
distinctiveness and idolatrous behaviour. As
the Church in the West finds itself increasingly
marginalised and under pressure, as God's people
we need to acknowledge this may be the result of sin
and disobedience. It can be equally true at a local
or personal level. Yet we need to remember there is
always purpose in how God deals with His people.
God put His people into exile to punish them, yes,
but also to purify them and render them distinctive

again. That is as true of the Church today. God is totally committed to His people.

• God's presence in the world is inescapable, challenging other beliefs and worldviews. In applying this today we might point to the witness of the local church, the distinctive witness of Christians living in the world testifying to God's rule, and the revelation of God in the words of Scripture.

Outline for a sermon or talk

While this outline focuses on verses 1 and 2, we suggest you read the whole of Daniel 1. These verses could also be incorporated as part of a sermon or talk on the whole of Daniel 1 (see next chapter).

Title: *Introduction to Daniel: God rules*
Text: *Daniel 1:1-2*

Structure:

(1) God's purposes are never defeated

   i) He controls history not simply reacts to it

   ii) He works towards the coming of His Kingdom

(2) God's people will be oppressed in the world

   i) He will punish their unbelief

   ii) He will be faithful to His covenant

(3) God's presence is inescapable

   i) He seems to allow His cause to be defeated

   ii) He vindicates His honour in the end

The sub-points above may or may not be used in the outline. They are included here simply to help with the flow of logical thought.

Bible study on Daniel 1:1-2

Again, while this study focuses on verses 1 and 2, it could be incorporated as part of a study on the whole of Daniel 1 (see next chapter).

Read Daniel 1

(1) Introduce the issues

   i) The message of the book of Daniel is that God rules, is building His Kingdom and therefore people should live in light of that fact. How do the opening verses of the book introduce this message?

(2) Study the passage

   i) Verse 1 is a straightforward record of what happened in history, verse 2 a theological commentary on the events. Why did God put His people into exile?

  ii) Why has God put His people into exile?

 iii) What is the significance of the articles from the temple being taken from Jerusalem into Babylon? Who is behind this and what's going on?

 iv) What is the biblical significance of the terms 'Jerusalem' and 'Babylon'?

  v) What are the ways God's presence is seen in Babylon?

(3) *Apply the passage*

i) Why is the principle taught in verses 1-2 so important in light of the reality of our experience living as Christians in a godless world? Illustrate this practically from your own experience of difficult situations, when truth about God's control of events has encouraged you.

ii) Do you think God punishes His people today for their disobedience and lack of distinctiveness? What signs are there of that happening in the Church today? And what is God's purpose in it?

iii) What are the ways God's presence is seen in the world today? How does this challenge other beliefs and worldviews?

(4) *Pray it through*

2

LIVING DISTINCTIVELY IN
LIGHT OF GOD'S RULE
(DANIEL 1)

Setting in context

Having dealt with the first two verses of chapter 1 separately as an introductory study to a series, we now come to consider the chapter as a whole. Even if verses 1-2 are taken separately, it makes sense to include them as a brief introduction to a study on the rest of the chapter.

(1) Dating

The events described in chapter 1 take place at the beginning of the Exile, and cover a three-year period. The Exile began in 605 B.C. (v. 1) when Nebuchadnezzar, at the beginning of his reign as king of Babylon, besieged Jerusalem and brought Daniel, Hananiah, Mishael and Azariah to Babylon as part of a group of young men in the first wave of the Exile (v. 4). They were to be trained for three years with a view to entering the king's service (v. 5). Verse 18 signals the end of that three-year period, when they entered the king's service as top graduates (v. 19). It's probable that their decision not to take the royal food and wine (v. 8) would have been at the beginning of the three-year training programme.

While the focus of the chapter is on events at the beginning of the Exile, the opening and closing verses serve as time markers for the entire duration of the Exile – 605 B.C. (v. 1) and the 'first year of king Cyrus' (v. 21), which is 539 B.C., the year Darius / Cyrus issued the decree to end the Exile.

(2) Context – structure of book

This is the first of three conflict chapters (Chs. 1, 3 and 6), focusing on Daniel, Hananiah, Mishael and Azariah as they live as exiles in Babylon. Here in chapter 1, the focus is on all four, although Daniel takes centre-stage. In chapter 3, the spotlight falls on Hananiah, Mishael and Azariah. And in chapter 6, Daniel alone is the focus.

The structure of the chapters is similar:

- They face pressure to conform.

- They make a decision to live distinctively, in spite of the consequences.

- God miraculously delivers them.

- God advances His Kingdom.

These three chapters span the entire period of the Exile: chapter 1 at the start; chapter 3, although not precisely dated, much later in Nebuchadnezzar's reign, sometime after the final destruction of Jerusalem and the temple in 586 B.C. and the mass deportation to Babylon; and chapter 6, which is precisely dated as 539 B.C., right at the end of the Exile. The fact that these recorded incidents are spread over such a long period brings perspective and realism to the way we teach the book of Daniel. Significant tests will come along, but most of the time steady, faithful, consistent witness is the order of the day.

(3) Context – message of book

If the message of the book as a whole is that *God rules*, the purpose of these conflict chapters is to show *how God's people are to live in light of the fact that He rules*. As exiles in the world, God calls His people to live distinctively. To live distinctively is costly, but God's people are to trust God. And as God's people live distinctively, God advances His Kingdom.

While the message of these conflict chapters is similar, there are important differences. For example, here in chapter 1, the tone is pretty low-key as Daniel politely asks the official for permission not to take the royal food and wine. Daniel takes the initiative, and the sense we get from the text is that these young men are looking for an opportunity to make their allegiance to God known, simply to be open and public about their faith. But in chapter 3, the situation is quite different. Hananiah, Mishael and Azariah face a direct and hostile challenge to their faith, necessitating a bold and courageous stand as they speak in open defiance to the king. They show great courage in the face of death. Similarly, in chapter 6, Daniel faces a direct and hostile challenge with great courage. The events of chapter 6 also reveal Daniel's consistency – faith that pervades every part of his life, lived out over many years.

The different ages and positions of influence held by Daniel and his companions are also worthy of comparison. Here in chapter 1 they're young men in their late teens enrolled in a training programme and with little or no influence. In chapter 3, Hananiah, Mishael and Azariah, probably in their late thirties / early forties, are established, successful and advancing rapidly up the political career ladder. By chapter 6, Daniel is an old man of eighty occupying a high profile position in the political and state life of the new regime under Darius. Looking at the chapters as a whole, God expects His people to make their allegiance known early on in their life, to keep faithful throughout life, and be vigilant to the fact that the toughest test may come late in life.

In each episode God miraculously delivers His people. That is most obvious with the furnace and the lions' den in chapters 3 and 6, but God's miraculous intervention is also evident here in chapter 1. God influences the officials, ensures Daniel and his friends come through the ten-day testing period looking healthier and better nourished than all the others and then gifts them with exceptional knowledge and understanding so that they graduate as top students.

Finally, in each of these episodes we observe that, as God's people live distinctively, God advances His Kingdom. Here in chapter 1, Daniel and his friends with their faith clear and strong graduate into positions of influence in Babylon. In chapter 3, Hananiah, Mishael and Azariah gain more promotion and influence. Furthermore, because of what he has witnessed, Nebuchadnezzar takes his first faltering steps to faith. And in chapter 6 the events conspire to bring about the end of the Exile.

To sum up, these differences, some obvious, others more subtle, mean that a careful handling of the text will bring a realism, richness and freshness to the way we teach and apply these 'conflict' chapters.

Working on the text

The structure of the chapter is as follows:

(1) In spite of what it looks like and feels like, God rules (vv. 1-2)

(2) The future leaders of God's people are enrolled in King Nebuchadnezzar's training programme and exposed to the pressure of Babylonian culture (vv. 3-7)

(3) Daniel makes his allegiance known, quietly and graciously, trusting in God (vv. 8-16)

(4) God gives Daniel, Hananiah, Mishael and Azariah exceptional knowledge and understanding, and they enter the king's service as top graduates (vv. 17-21)

The key to teaching narrative is to identify the turning point. The turning point is the main teaching point. In chapter 1, the turning point is verse 8, when Daniel resolves not to take the royal food and wine.

(1) *In spite of what it looks like and feels like, God rules (vv. 1-2)*

These opening verses in the book record factual history. King Nebuchadnezzar and his Babylonian Empire came to Jerusalem and besieged it, overpowering the weak King (v. 1). It looked like, and would have felt like, the power was with Nebuchadnezzar. His apparent dominance is symbolized by his taking the articles from the temple in Jerusalem and putting them in the treasure house of his god in Babylon (v. 2). While at one level these opening verses record factual history, the point the writer is emphasising is that while it looked like, and felt like, the power was with

Nebuchadnezzar, the reality is that God is in control. The key phrase is in the middle of the unit, the first half of verse 2: 'And the Lord delivered Jehoiakim king of Judah into his hand, along with some of the articles from the temple of God.' This is the key message of the book – God rules. God is in control, sovereign over the events described, the kingdoms of this world and the lives of individuals.

(2) *The future leaders of God's people are enrolled in King Nebuchadnezzar's training programme and exposed to the pressure of Babylonian culture (vv. 3-7)*

Nebuchadnezzar's tactics are astute. In this first wave of the Exile, he targets the future leaders of God's people (vv. 3-4). These young men, probably in their late teens, were the most able, gifted and connected of their generation. If Nebuchadnezzar could influence them, put God out of their lives, the effect would be felt for generations to come.

His strategy was to bring them to Babylon and enrol them in his elite training programme (v. 5) – if you like, King's College, Babylon. What was the world of King's College like? The text refers to 'the language and literature of the Babylonians' (v. 4) – a wholly different way of thinking, a different worldview. Babylon was a culture of many truths (relativism), many ways to live (moral relativism) and many gods (polytheism). The name 'Babylon' literally means 'gate of the gods'. Enter the world of Babylon and enter the world of many gods.

In such a culture, these young men faced significant pressure to conform. What kind of pressure? Not simply passive assimilation, Nebuchadnezzar's tactic was systematic indoctrination. He changed their location (v. 3), their language (v. 4b), their diet (v. 5a) and their names

(v. 7). The name changes are striking. Daniel (which means 'God is judge') is given the name Belteshazzar ('O lady, wife of the God Bel, protect the king'). Daniel's Babylonian name Belteshazzar is very similar to Belshazzar ('Bel protect the king'), the last ruler of the Babylonian Empire (Belshazzar's rule and demise are described in Ch. 5). Hananiah ('Yahweh is gracious') is named Shadrach ('command of Aku' – the moon god). Mishael ('Who is what God is?') is named Meshach ('Who is like Aku?'). And Azariah ('Yahweh is a helper') has his name changed to Abednego ('servant of the shining one' – Nebo). The point is clear. Their Hebrew names, all of which refer to the one true and living God, are changed to names that reflect the many gods of Babylon. Moreover, the Hebrew verb translated 'gave' in verse 7 ('The chief official gave them new names…') is literally 'put new names on them'. The verb is strong, associated with imposition and force, indicative of Nebuchadnezzar's desire to forcibly put God out of their lives.

While it is true that these young men faced significant pressure to conform, and would have been afraid and intimidated as they were taken down into Babylon, it is important to recognize the privileges and opportunities they were being offered – a place in King's College, the Ivy League of the ancient world, the fast-track into the Babylonian civil service. Mixed with fear, there must have been some sense of excitement and anticipation. For many in the group, particularly as time passed, the lure of all that Babylon offered would prove too great a temptation. In this regard, the phrase 'among these' at the beginning of verse 6 is significant. We cannot know for sure how many young men from Jerusalem were enrolled in Nebuchadnezzar's

training programme, but we can assume the group was of
a fair size, at least significantly more than Daniel and his
three friends. But from verse 6 onwards (signaled by the
phrase 'among these') and throughout the rest of the book,
the focus is on Daniel, Hananiah, Mishael and Azariah.
Why? Presumably because these were the young men
who were prepared to take a stand and live distinctively in
Babylon. Some of the larger group would have conformed
to the culture of Babylon, losing their distinctiveness as
God's people. Perhaps some others kept their faith, but it
was a secret faith, not lived out before the eyes of the world,
and therefore had little impact. Few then, and now, are
prepared to put their faith on the line and live distinctively
as God's people in an alien world.

(3) Daniel makes his allegiance known, quietly
and graciously, trusting in God (vv. 8-16)
Verse 8 marks the turning point in the text: 'But Daniel
resolved not to defile himself with the royal food and wine,
and he asked the chief official for permission not to defile
himself in this way.'

Daniel made a conscious decision to live distinctively and
make his allegiance to God known. The controlling verb in
verse 8 is the same as verse 7. In verse 7 the chief official 'put
new names on them' and here in verse 8 (a clear parallel is
intended) Daniel 'put it on his heart' not to defile himself.
Notice also that his decision immediately translates into
action as he asks the chief official for permission not to
defile himself in this way (v. 8). His allegiance was public
not private, spoken not silent. Moreover, at this stage, the
focus is on Daniel alone. Hananiah, Mishael and Azariah
will soon become involved (vv. 11-12), but initially it's

Daniel alone. Also, the clear inference from the text is that Daniel made his decision right at the start of their time in Babylon when they were first assigned the royal food and wine.

Why did Daniel make this decision? What motivated him? Daniel lived in light of the fact that his God rules. It may not have looked like it nor felt like it, but the fact is God rules, and Daniel trusted in his God and did what was right.

Notice a very important point. In considering what Daniel said 'no' to, we can easily fail to see what he said 'yes' to. He accepted his Babylonian name; he complied with the other aspects of the training programme and, over the next three years, excelled in his study of Babylonian language and literature. In time, he would accept the appointment as a 'wise man' of Babylon and serve with the magicians, enchanters, sorcerers and astrologers at court. Throughout the Exile he accepted increasing responsibility in matters of state, furthering the interests of the Babylonian Empire. He said 'yes' to all of that. God doesn't expect His people to fight every battle, but He does expect us to live distinctively, and sooner or later some issue or circumstance will arise affording us the opportunity to show where our true allegiance lies. For Daniel it was the royal food and wine. Was that because they had been sacrificed to pagan gods? Possibly, but we can't be sure. The vegetables and water might also have been sacrificed to the gods of Babylon. And there are contradictory examples, notably Queen Esther, who didn't draw a line on this particular issue. The point being made, therefore, is not so much about the particular issue, but about the principle of living distinctively, of publicly showing our allegiance to God. Circumstances and issues may vary, but the principle holds – God expects His people to live distinctively.

There is no doubt that what Daniel did took courage. At that stage he was a 'nobody' in Babylon and could easily have received swift and summary justice for even daring to question the king's orders. But notice also the manner in which Daniel takes his stand. He is gracious and shrewd. First, he asks the chief official Ashpenaz for permission (v. 8). In spite of the favour with which Ashpenaz viewed Daniel (v. 9), he will not grant the request, afraid of disobeying the orders of the king (v. 10). This is an entirely understandable reaction. Daniel, however, is not deterred and approaches the guard who has direct authority over the group (v. 11) and puts a proposal to him – to give them vegetables and water for ten days, compare them with the other young men, and then make a decision on the basis of what he sees (vv. 12-13). The guard agrees to their request (v. 14). It's striking that throughout the book, as we observe Daniel's courage, he is never foolhardy. He is shrewd, wise and diplomatic. For example, in chapter 2, we're told that Daniel speaks to Arioch, the commander of the king's guard, with 'wisdom and tact' (2:14). It is striking, also, how adept Daniel is in dealing with three very different rulers, Nebuchadnezzar, Belshazzar and Darius. Both courage and wisdom are commended by Daniel's example.

As Daniel and his friends make the decision to live distinctively, trusting in God, it is clear from the text that God is with them. For example, God's influence over Ashpenaz (v. 9) and, although the text does not explicitly say it, we can assume that the guard's agreement to Daniel's request (v. 14) had a divine influence behind it. Their health and vitality at the end of the ten-day testing period (v. 15) was not because of their choice of diet (we need to resist contemporary parallels to healthy diets here), but to the intervention of God. The result was they were allowed to continue on vegetables and water, presumably for the duration of the three-year training programme (v. 16).

(4) God gives Daniel, Hananiah, Mishael and Azariah exceptional knowledge and understanding, and they enter the king's service as top graduates (vv. 17-21)

Verse 17 is a summary of what happened during the rest of the training programme. God gifted the four of them with exceptional knowledge of Babylonian language and literature, and more besides. And Daniel was given the ability to understand visions and dreams, a gift he would use on a number of occasions (see Chs. 2, 4 and 5). They were able intellectually; they would have worked hard, but the text makes it clear that the excellence of their performance was due not so much to their ability, as to God's intervention. This is a very important point. Right through the chapter there are signals of God's control and divine intervention:

- 'And the Lord delivered Jehoiakim king of Judah into his hand, along with some of the articles from the temple of God' (v. 2).

- 'Now God had caused the official to show favour and sympathy to Daniel…' (v. 9).

- 'To these four young men God gave knowledge and understanding of all kinds of literature and learning. And Daniel could understand dreams and visions of all kinds' (v. 17).

In addition to these explicit references in the text it is likely that, as with Ashpenaz, God caused the guard appointed over them to agree to their request (vv. 11-14). And the fact that they looked healthier and better nourished than the others at the end of the ten-day testing period (v. 15) says more about God's intervention than their healthy diet.

Daniel, Hananiah, Mishael and Azariah graduate with distinction and enter the king's service (vv. 18-19). Although, at this stage, Nebuchadnezzar did not perceive the hand of God in this, he is left in no doubt as to the superiority of these four compared with the other graduates – not just a bit better, but ten times better (v. 20). Verse 21 is a time marker for the duration of the Exile, but also a marker for Daniel's role throughout the Exile, at the heart of the political and cultural life of Babylon. There's an obvious irony. Nebuchadnezzar wanted to take the future leaders of God's people and make them future leaders of Babylon. That was his way of putting God out of their lives and out of their future. He got what he wanted. The future leaders of God's people did become future leaders of Babylon. But there was one glitch in his plan. Instead of putting God out of them, they put God into the heart of Babylon, and by God's amazing grace, ultimately into the heart of Nebuchadnezzar himself. God has the upper hand. God rules.

From text to message

(1) *Get the message clear*

i) *Big idea*
In light of the fact that God rules, God expects His people to live distinctively, showing their allegiance to Him.

ii) Key questions

Preaching or teaching on this passage should answer the following questions:

- What kinds of pressure to conform do we experience as Christians living in the world today?

- What does God expect from us?

- Over what issues should we take a stand and show our allegiance to God?

- How should we go about it?

- In such circumstances, what can we expect from God?

(2) Engage the hearer

i) Point of contact

A helpful way to start the sermon or Bible study would be to show a picture of the Ishtar Gate, the entrance to the ancient city of Babylon. The gate has been reconstructed brick by brick in a museum in Berlin. It was usual for captives to be brought into Babylon through the Ishtar Gate and, almost certainly, Daniel and his friends would have entered the city this way. Built both to impress and intimidate, the Ishtar Gate was an awesome sight, not only its sheer scale, but the striking blue and gold stonework with reliefs of bulls and dragons, the guardians of the city. Passing through the gate, captives entered the tunnel-like atmosphere of the Ishtar Way with its high walls and reliefs of lions joining the bulls and dragons. These young men would have been left in no doubt as to the sheer power of Nebuchadnezzar's Babylon and the pressure to conform.

Yet while they would have been afraid and intimidated, the magnificence of their surroundings would surely have sparked some sense of excitement and anticipation at the opportunities that lay before them. After all, they weren't being taken to some dungeon, but to the King's College, the Ivy League of the Ancient World and the fast track to the Babylonian civil service.

ii) *Dominant pictures / illustrations*

The dominant picture is of some young people living in an alien culture making the decision to live distinctively and show their public allegiance to God. What they did took courage, for sure, but we need to be careful of giving the impression that Daniel and his friends are exceptional believers, super-heroes of the faith. They're just lads, university freshers! Moreover, there's a danger of suggesting the events described were more dramatic than they were. It's all pretty low-key, away from public scrutiny, with Daniel and his friends having no influence / prominence at this stage.

Another striking feature of the account is that while they said 'no' to the food and wine they said 'yes' to lots of other things. Moreover, Daniel was not only gracious, but shrewd in the way he worked. Here is a picture of a believer who doesn't look to fight every battle, who doesn't fight them loudly, and who has plenty savvy about him.

In summary, the dominant pictures suggested by the text may be different from some cherished stereotypes of Daniel.

(3) *Work on application*

In this first of the three 'conflict' chapters, we will include extensive notes on application, some of which will also be relevant to chapters 3 and 6.

- As Christians living as exiles in the world
  (1 Pet. 1:1), we are exposed to a culture that
  challenges our faith. The worlds of Babylon then
  and today share striking similarities. Many truths
  (relativism), many ways to live (moral relativism)
  and many gods (polytheism) are the touchstones
  of secular culture today. Think, for example, of
  the university campus. Many truths – different
  ideas, ideologies all with equal validity. The
  idea of one true explanation of the world and
  humanity (objective absolute truth) is regarded as
  intellectually naïve, arrogant and socially divisive.
  In the world of many truths there are many ways to
  live – secular morality advocates freedom of lifestyle
  choice, governed by generally accepted parameters
  (which are becoming increasingly blurred). And a
  culture of many gods. The view that there is one
  true God, a unique Saviour, is anathema in our
  culture. This climate is not of course unique to the
  university campus; it is everywhere, the pervasive
  atmosphere of our modern secular world, the air
  we breathe. Yet this is nothing new. The similarities
  with the Ancient World of Babylon are striking.

- The pressure we face to conform, at least in the
  Western world, is more about assimilation than
  forced authoritarian compliance (although we
  are seeing the very first signs of the latter). Peer
  pressure, particularly for the young, is a major
  factor, especially in an increasingly secular culture,
  where being a Christian means we are increasingly
  different. The shame or stigma associated with

being a Christian is a check to many from living
distinctively.

- As Christians, God expects us to live distinctively
  in the world – not to withdraw from it, or be
  compromised by it, but to live distinctively in it.
  This principle is articulated very clearly in a letter
  like 1 Peter (see esp. 1 Pet. 2:11-12). The dual
  risks of withdrawing from the world (a greater
  risk perhaps for older Christians?) or being
  compromised by the world (maybe more of an issue
  for younger Christians?) are real, and need to be
  spelt out.

- Living distinctively in the world will mean saying
  'yes' to some things. As Christians we are not
  called to fight every battle. But inevitably situations
  will present where we need to say 'no' and come
  clean about our convictions and show where our
  true allegiance lies. The particular issues and
  circumstances will vary and giving careful thought
  to a range of applications will be helpful in this
  regard. For example, issues relevant to young people
  might include drinking, relationships, internet use
  etc. One fruitful line of application would simply
  be to encourage people not to be secret about their
  Christian faith. For many Christians, their friends,
  work colleagues, neighbours or classmates are
  unaware that they are Christians.

- In showing our allegiance to God, it is important to
  be open about why we are doing it. So, for example,
  a young Christian who draws a line about alcohol

needs to tell her friends why she won't get drunk – not because it's bad for her health, but because she's a Christian. Making that connection is important for gospel witness. In pressing home this application, however, we need to be sensitive and understanding about how hard this is.

- God is the hero of the story, not Daniel. While Daniel is undoubtedly an example and inspiration, the reason Daniel lived the way he did was because of his trust and confidence in God. Daniel knew that in spite of appearances, God rules, and he lived his life in light of that fact. God was Daniel's inspiration, and God, not Daniel, needs to be our primary inspiration. In this regard, we need to be careful of painting the picture of Daniel as an exceptional believer. He is an example to us all.

- Depending on our circumstances, living distinctively might mean standing alone. A Christian who is the only believer where they work, or in their family, or in a sports team may well experience this isolation.

- While chapter 1 is, of course, relevant to Christians of any age, there is an obvious application to young people. Don't be afraid to give weight to this age group in your applications (there's plenty of opportunity in Chs. 3 and 6 to balance things up). Impress on young Christians the importance, early on in the Christian life, of taking the decision to live distinctively and being open about their faith. Key transitions in life are important in this regard, for example, a young person moving to secondary school, or a student going to university. Evidence suggests that if a stand is not taken quickly, it is far less likely to be taken at all. If you are teaching or studying chapter 1 with a group of predominantly older Christians, then encourage them to pray for and disciple young believers.

- The manner in which Daniel took his stand is instructive. He was shrewd and gracious. This is not a license for subtle manipulation, but a warning against a foolhardy attitude, and taking a principled position which is communicated with a lack of grace and humility. The primary attribute of Christian character in all circumstances is humility.

- To live distinctively is risky and costly, but we are to trust God. As we find ourselves under pressure for our faith, God may intervene in striking ways. He will certainly give us grace sufficient for the circumstances we face. When Peter writes to the Christians in Asia Minor who are suffering for their faith he exhorts them to stand fast in God's grace (1 Pet. 5:12).

- As we live distinctively as Christians showing our allegiance to God, God is advancing His Kingdom. How God advances His Kingdom through our witness is for Him to determine. He may put us in a position of influence or not. He may use us significantly or not. It is pertinent to say, however, that God puts us where we are (e.g. as a Christian teacher, plumber, doctor or student) for a purpose, and therefore we should be alert to opportunities as they arise, willing to be used by God to advance His Kingdom.

Outline for a sermon or talk

This outline focuses on the whole of Daniel 1. Verses 1-2 could be taken separately as an introductory study to the book (see previous chapter). If that is what you decide to do, we suggest you also include the verses here in the study of Daniel 1. Verses 1-2 not only function as an introduction to the book as a whole, but also to Daniel 1.

The structure of the chapter is relatively straightforward, and we would suggest an outline that reflects this structure.

Title: Living distinctively in light of God's rule
Text: Daniel 1

Structure:

(1) Remember God rules (vv. 1-2)

(2) Living in the world (vv. 3-7)

    i) Secular culture

    ii) Pressure to conform

(3) Living distinctively (vv. 8-16)

    i) Not to withdraw, not to compromise, but to live distinctively in the world

    ii) Discerning the issue

    iii) How to go about it

(4) Trusting God (vv. 17-21)

    i) God's grace is sufficient

    ii) God's Kingdom advances

The sub-points above may or may not be used in the outline. They are included here simply to help with the flow of logical thought.

Bible study on Daniel 1

This Bible study covers the whole of Daniel 1. For an introductory Bible study, based on verses 1-2, see the previous chapter.

Read Daniel 1

(1) Introduce the issues

   i) As Christians we live as exiles in the world (1 Pet. 1:1). In light of the fact that God rules, God expects us to live distinctively, showing our allegiance to Him.

     From a first reading of the chapter, how are we encouraged and inspired to do that?

(2) Study the passage

   i) Verses 1 and 2 are key. What is the principle taught in these verses?

   ii) What was Nebuchadnezzar's tactic in bringing these young men to his training college in Babylon? (vv. 3-4)

   iii) Living in Babylon, Daniel and his friends were exposed to a culture that challenged their faith (vv. 3-7). What particular pressures to conform did they face? What opportunities were they being offered?

   iv) The phrase 'among these' at the beginning of verse 6 is significant. Of the group of young men taken to Babylon, how do you think the group divided in terms of their allegiance to God?

v) Daniel took the decision to be open about his faith, making his allegiance clear (v. 8). What do we make of the fact that he said 'no' to the royal food and wine, but said 'yes' to a number of other things (e.g. his place in the training programme and his change of name)?

vi) Daniel was well aware of the risks, but what motivated him to make his allegiance to God known?

vii) Having made his decision not to take the royal food and wine, how did Daniel go about it in terms of his dealings, first with Ashpenaz, and then the guard appointed over them? (vv. 9-16)

viii) What evidence is there in the text of God's intervention? (vv. 9, 15-16, 17)

ix) How does God advance His Kingdom through these events? (vv. 18-21)

(3) *Apply the passage*

i) Why is the principle taught in verses 1-2 so important in light of the reality of our experience living as Christians in a godless world? Illustrate this practically from your own experience of difficult situations, when truth about God's control of events has encouraged you.

ii) As Christians, what pressures to conform do we face in our culture today? What particular (and increasing) pressures are young Christians experiencing today?

iii) God expects us to live distinctively, showing our allegiance to Him. What's our motivation for doing this? What stops us doing it?

iv) Part of what it means to show our allegiance to God is simply being open about the fact that we are Christians. How open are you about your faith with work colleagues, classmates etc.?

v) Practically, what does living distinctively and showing our allegiance to God look like in terms of what we say 'yes' and 'no' to? How do we know where and when to draw the line?

vi) Having made his decision not to take the royal food and wine, the way Daniel went about it is striking. What can we learn from his manner and approach?

vii) Living distinctively, showing our allegiance to God, can be costly in terms of the consequences we face. What can we expect from God?

viii) If we live distinctively and show our allegiance to God, how will God use our witness to advance His Kingdom?

(4) Pray it through

3

GOD REVEALS THAT HE RULES
(DANIEL 2)

Setting in context

(1) Dating

The events described in chapter 2 follow on immediately from chapter 1. Daniel and his friends have entered King Nebuchadnezzar's service after completing their three-year training programme. The apparent discrepancy in dates – chapter 2 verse 1 refers to 'the second year of his reign' – is explained by the fact that Nebuchadnezzar's accession year (605–604 B.C.) would not have been counted in the years of his reign (a Babylonian convention).

(2) Context – structure of book

While chapter 2 is part of the narrative section of the book (Chs. 1–6) describing events that took place during the Exile, Nebuchadnezzar's dream is prophetic vision. There are strong parallels with the prophetic vision in chapter 7 (Chs. 7–12 contain four prophetic visions Daniel received during the Exile). Fig. 1 shows the parallels between chapters 2 and 7.

Fig. 1 Parallels between chapters 2 and 7

Chapter 2	**Chapter 7**
Nebuchadnezzar's dream	**Daniel's vision**
Four-part statue	*Four beasts*
Head of gold	Lion
Chest and arms of silver	Bear
Belly and thighs of bronze	Leopard
Legs of iron, feet of iron and clay	Fourth beast
	Ten horns
	Little horn
	Ancient of Days
....	
Rock cut not with human hands which smashes the statue and becomes a great mountain that fills the whole earth	Coronation of son of man as King of God's everlasting Kingdom

The four-part statue (Ch. 2) corresponds to the four beasts (Ch. 7). The rock cut not with human hands which becomes a great mountain that fills the whole earth (Ch. 2) corresponds to one like a son of man crowned as King of God's everlasting Kingdom. The parallels are striking.

Chapters 2 and 7 are not only similar in content; they begin and end the section of the book written in Aramaic.

- Ch. 1:1–2:3   Hebrew

- Ch. 2:4–7:28   Aramaic

- Ch. 8:1–12:13   Hebrew

Aramaic was the court language of Babylon and the lingua-franca of the ancient world. The use of Aramaic indicates that the content of these chapters is of universal significance, a message for unbelievers as well as for believers. The Hebrew chapters, in particular 8–12, deal with matters concerned with the future of God's people.

The Aramaic section has a clear chiastic structure, reflecting its structural and thematic cohesion (Fig. 2).

Fig. 2 Chiastic structure of Aramaic section

a Ch. 2   Prophetic vision of four-part statue, rock and mountain

   b Ch. 3   God delivers His people from the furnace

      c Ch. 4   God saves Nebuchadnezzar

      c Ch. 5   God judges Belshazzar

   b Ch. 6   God delivers Daniel from the lions' den

a Ch. 7   Prophetic vision of four beasts, Ancient of Days and son of man

A final note on structure. Chapter 2 is the first of three consecutive chapters tracing Nebuchadnezzar's journey to faith. Nebuchadnezzar is shown in all his power as king of Babylon, but on each occasion he is confronted by a greater power, the God of heaven who rules and who eventually humbles Nebuchadnezzar to bring him to saving faith. In chapters 2 and 4, God's revelation to Nebuchadnezzar comes through interpreted dreams. In chapter 3, Nebuchadnezzar sees first-hand the miraculous deliverance of Shadrach, Meshach and Abednego from the furnace.

(3) Context – message of book

The message of Daniel is that *God rules, is building an everlasting Kingdom, and calls people to live in light of that fact.* This chapter covers the breadth of this message. In the introductory section 'Getting our Bearings' we categorised the prophetic material as big-picture and detailed prophecies. Chapters 2 and 7 are examples of the former. They take a big-picture, wide-angled view of the future.

God's Kingdom and King stand in stark contrast to earthly kingdoms and kings which rise and fall. This is an important message for the people of God, especially in times of difficulty and pressure. It is also an important message for the unbelieving world (hence the Aramaic). With the spotlight on Nebuchadnezzar and the beginning of his journey to faith, the message of the chapter is that there is no greater power than the power of God, and therefore all people need to submit to Him and live in light of His rule.

The chapter, however, is not simply concerned with the content of what is revealed (that God rules), but with the nature of revelation itself. In contrast to the futility of human power and wisdom, God alone knows and reveals truth.

The beginning of Nebuchadnezzar's journey to faith (and the material in the chapters that follow) reflects the point that all people are to live in light of God's rule.

Working on the text

It is a long chapter, but the story is told in an exciting and dramatic way, a great chapter to teach. Here's a suggested structure to take us through the text.

(1) Nebuchadnezzar's dream exposes the futility of human power and wisdom (vv. 1-13)

(2) Daniel's shrewdness in a time of crisis and conviction that God alone can reveal the mystery (vv. 14-23)

(3) Daniel tells Nebuchadnezzar that God has revealed the mystery (vv. 24-30)

(4) Nebuchadnezzar's dream of a four-part statue, a rock and a great mountain (vv. 31-35)

(5) The interpretation of the dream – earthly kings and kingdoms will rise and fall, but God will establish an everlasting Kingdom with His all-powerful King (vv. 36-45)

(6) Nebuchadnezzar acknowledges the sovereignty of God and promotes Daniel, Shadrach, Meshach and Abednego (vv. 46-49)

[Note – this structure helpfully brings out the dual emphasis that God reveals (the nature of revelation) and that God rules (the content of revelation).]

(1) Nebuchadnezzar's dream exposes the futility of human power and wisdom (vv. 1-13)

These verses are a brilliant anatomy of the ultimate futility of human power and wisdom. Nebuchadnezzar is having bad dreams, his mind is troubled and he can't sleep (v. 1).

Outwardly, at the peak of his ambition and power with the world at his feet, and yet none of that can prevent mortal fear and dread coming upon him. His military and political power cannot help in a situation where dark imaginings rob him of sleep and leave him afraid and perplexed at mysteries he cannot even visualize, much less handle. Human power is formidable when dealing with other manifestations of human power. There was no military rival in the field and no political machinations that Nebuchadnezzar needed to fear. Yet for all that, he is a mere mortal and cannot escape the restlessness emanating from fear of the unknown. This remains true for the powerful and self-sufficient today, as then.

What does Nebuchadnezzar do? Where does he look for an explanation? He summons the 'magicians, enchanters, sorcerers and astrologers' to tell him the dream and interpret it for him (vv. 2-3). This group represents the collective wisdom of Babylon – worldly wisdom. In response to the king's request, they ask Nebuchadnezzar to tell them the dream so that they can interpret it (v. 4). Whether or not Nebuchadnezzar has some recollection of the dream we cannot be sure (the text is ambiguous). Perhaps he did remember, but suspected that if he told them the dream they would give an interpretation favourable to him? Perhaps he doubted their wisdom, their ability? Whatever the reason, the one sure way of testing their credentials was to ask them to tell him the dream as well as interpret it.

As the narrative plays out (vv. 5-13), Nebuchadnezzar becomes more and more aggressive and irrational, his wise men more and more desperate: threats of horrific punishment are made in the same breath as the promise of lavish gifts (vv. 5-6); further appeals made to the king to tell them the dream so they might interpret it (v. 7);

accusations of time wasting and conspiracy (vv. 8-9). Matters come to a head when the wise men conclude (rightly) that human power and wisdom are incapable of doing what the king asks: 'What the king asks is too difficult. No-one can reveal it to the king except the gods, and they do not live among men' (v. 11). In their own words they acknowledge the limitations and futility of human wisdom, and conclude that the answers Nebuchadnezzar is looking for will only come through divine revelation. With dramatic irony the narrative sets up what will follow later in the chapter. Nebuchadnezzar's response is irrational and cruel. In a fit of rage he orders the execution of all the wise men of Babylon (v. 12). The scene concludes with the king's men despatched to look for Daniel and his friends to put them to death along with the rest of the wise men (v. 13).

Dangerous times – Nebuchadnezzar is volatile and insecure, ready to punish severely all those who fail to do what he expects and demands. We will see a similar response from Nebuchadnezzar in chapter 3 when Hananiah, Mishael and Azariah refuse to worship his golden image. We might explain all this away by concluding that Nebuchadnezzar's response is unusual and exaggerated. But that is to miss the point. What is being exposed here is the total emptiness of the pretensions of the whole court establishment and the inherent futility of human power and wisdom.

(2) *Daniel's shrewdness in a time of crisis and conviction that God alone can reveal the mystery (vv. 14-23)*

In contrast to the frenetic atmosphere of the preceding verses, with Daniel's appearance there is order and calm. Some have questioned why Daniel was ignorant of the decree since he is one of the wise men threatened with death. A plausible explanation is that not all the wise men had been summoned at first. Probably only the most senior were present. Remember that Daniel was a young man, having only recently graduated and entered the king's service, at this stage not particularly prominent.

Daniel's approach, manner and speech are in stark contrast to the panic, fretfulness and helplessness of his fellow wise men, and the irrational fury of King Nebuchadnezzar. His manner with Arioch, the commander of the king's guard is striking: 'Daniel spoke to him with wisdom and tact' (v. 14). This is reminiscent of his approach with Ashpenaz, chief of the court officials, in chapter 1. Daniel's diplomacy with Arioch here in chapter 2 is seen in his questioning, not so much the severity, as the haste of the king's decree (v. 15). The NIV translation 'harsh' is better rendered as 'peremptory'. The upshot of this meeting with Arioch is an audience with the king (v. 16). Once again, Daniel's diplomacy is evident as he asks the king for time so that he might interpret the dream for him. It is striking to note that just a few verses before, Nebuchadnezzar had reacted angrily to the wise men when he perceived they were trying to stall for time (v. 8). Why did Nebuchadnezzar accede to Daniel's request for more time? Possibly because Nebuchadnezzar had calmed down, regretting his injudicious command? Possibly because Daniel had indicated that he could interpret the dream? Possibly because Nebuchadnezzar remembered that when he had interviewed Daniel and his friends at the end of their training, in matters of wisdom and understanding they were ten times better than all the rest (1:20)? It's unlikely, though, at this stage, that Nebuchadnezzar knew about the particular gift God had given Daniel to understand visions and dreams (1:17); but he was about to find that out. Whatever the reason (and, of course, God's influence was behind it all), Nebuchadnezzar granted Daniel's request for time.

More important is how Daniel uses the time. He returns to his house, and having explained the matter to Hananiah, Mishael and Azariah, urges them to pray with him that God might reveal the mystery. Daniel knows that God alone is able to reveal these things, and so he pleads with God in prayer. A number of points are worthy of note. They pray to the 'God of heaven' (v. 18). This title of God is used frequently, for example, in Ezra and Nehemiah. As a title, it draws attention to that central affirmation of Israel's faith: 'Our help is in the Name of the Lord who made heaven and earth' (Ps. 115:15; 121:2; 124:8). In contrast to the Babylonian gods, who were as impotent as the wise men of Babylon, Daniel and his friends confidently pray to the God of heaven believing He can and will reveal the mystery. The fact that Daniel 'urged' his friends to pray (v. 18), shows the importance he placed on prayer (both individually and corporately). Prayer features prominently in Daniel's life and throughout the book (Chs. 6, 9, 10), connecting God's people to the unseen world and the outworking of the will of God. It's also noticeable that Daniel urges his friends to pray that God might reveal the mystery, so that they might not be executed with the rest of the wise men of Babylon (v. 18). Daniel does not relish martyrdom and will do all he can to avoid it. But in the last analysis he realises that only God can protect them.

During the night God reveals the mystery to Daniel (v. 19). What follows (vv. 20-23) is an extended prayer of praise and thanksgiving from Daniel. Including this prayer in the text makes the point, emphatically, that God alone is able to reveal what is hidden (v. 22). Again, a number of the details are worthy of note. It is a prayer of praise to the 'name of God' (v. 20a), which as Exodus 6:3 states, is known only to those to whom He reveals it. Praise is due to God for His greatness, wisdom and activity in history and the created order. Wisdom and power (v. 20b) are a frequent combination in the Wisdom Literature (e.g. Job 12:13), showing that the Lord's power is no mere arbitrary sovereignty, but flows from His all-embracing wisdom. God controls the various phases of history – 'times and seasons' (v. 21a) – whether times of prosperity or adversity. The reference to setting up kings and deposing them (v. 21b) roots the prayer in the situation of the Exile (see e.g. 1:1-2; 21; Ch. 5). Since God alone is wise, all wisdom on earth is a gift from Him (v. 21c). Notice in verses 21-22 that 'he' is emphatic: 'he changes'; 'he sets up'; 'he gives'; he reveals'; 'he knows'. Verse 23 moves from thanksgiving to praise as Daniel acknowledges the faithfulness of God in granting him heavenly wisdom. The phrase 'God of my fathers' (v. 23a) emphasises continuity and the enduring nature of God's covenant with His people (e.g., Deut. 1:21; 6:3; 12:1). This is a confession of faith, a sense of awe and wonder that God has answered their prayer so clearly and specifically.

(3) Daniel tells Nebuchadnezzar that God has revealed the mystery (vv. 24-30)

The point that Daniel has stressed in verse 20-23 – that God alone is able to reveal what is hidden – is reiterated as Daniel goes to Nebuchadnezzar and explains that God has revealed the mystery. Why the delay in explaining the dream and giving the interpretation? Simply because Daniel is at pains to emphasise, both to Nebuchadnezzar and to the reader, that the revelation comes from God. Naturally, Arioch and Nebuchadnezzar assume that Daniel, as a wise man, is claiming to be able to reveal the mystery (vv. 25-26). Daniel eschews any desire for self-advancement or promotion and humbly makes the point that God has revealed the mystery to him (vv. 27-30). Again, one or two details are striking. Arioch introduces Daniel to the king as 'a man among the exiles from Judah' (v. 25). Verse 26 refers to Daniel by his Babylonian name. Moreover, Nebuchadnezzar's question to Daniel (obscured by the English translation) is expressive of his incredulity. Verse 26 could be paraphrased: 'Are you really telling me you can do this?' These details make the point that things are not what they seem. While it looked like the power was with Nebuchadnezzar, the reality is that the power is with God. God's people may appear weak and marginalised, they may experience disdain, but God is in control, God is with them and God uses them.

There is another strand running through verses 27-30, the repeated reference to the fact that God has revealed these things for Nebuchadnezzar's benefit. This is most clearly expressed in verse 30: 'this mystery has been revealed to me [Daniel]…so that you, O king, may know the interpretation and that you may understand what went through your mind.' Such revelation to Nebuchadnezzar is an act of grace and mercy from God, which ultimately will lead him to a saving knowledge of God (described in Chs. 3 and 4).

(4) Nebuchadnezzar's dream of a four-part statue, a rock and a great mountain (vv. 31-35)

Before we look at the detail of the dream, a comment on the phrase in verse 28, which the NIV translates as 'in days to come'. The phrase literally means 'in the latter days' and is common in the Prophets and elsewhere in Scripture. Some wish to take this as simply meaning at some unspecified time in the future, but the intended meaning (and the content of the prophetic material in the rest of the book would endorse this conclusion), is a reference to the End Times and the coming of the Kingdom of God in its fullness. The whole of history is moving to its end. In prophetic literature there is always that dimension: the great crises of history anticipate the End; the judgements in history point to the judgement on history when the Kingdom of God finally comes in its fullness.

The art of the storyteller has kept us in suspense for thirty verses. Only now are we told Nebuchadnezzar's dream. His dream is of a large statue, both frightening and awe-inspiring in appearance (v. 31). Colossal statues of gods were common in the Ancient World. The statue is of human form (vv. 32-33). There are four parts:

(i)   *the head made of pure gold;*
(ii) *the chest and arms of silver;*
(iii) *the belly and thighs of bronze;*
(vi) *the legs of iron and feet a mixture of iron and baked clay.*

The fact that the statue is in four parts suggests worldwide scope like the four rivers of Eden (Gen. 2:10-14). Gold and silver stand for wealth and bronze and iron for power. The mixture of clay and iron in the feet, however, suggests a fatal weakness. In spite of the great strength of iron these elements are incompatible. As the dream continues, a rock cut not by human hands strikes the feet of the statue (the part of the statue made with a mixture of iron and clay) and smashes them (v. 34). The whole statue comes tumbling down, shattered into tiny pieces like chaff that the wind blows away without leaving a trace (v. 35a). All that is left is the rock that struck the statue which becomes a huge mountain that fills the whole earth (v. 35b). Numerous scriptural parallels come to mind. The stone which becomes a huge mountain recalls the mountain of the Lord (Isa. 2:2 and Micah 4:1) and the 'filling of the earth' recalls Habakkuk 2:14: 'the earth will be filled with the knowledge of the glory of the Lord, as the waters cover the sea'.

(5) *The interpretation of the dream– earthly kings and kingdoms will rise and fall, but God will establish an everlasting Kingdom with His all-powerful King (vv. 36-45)*

It is important to realise that this dream needed to be interpreted. The dream is not in itself revelation but raw material for revelation. If Daniel had simply recounted the dream to Nebuchadnezzar he would probably have thought that he (Nebuchadnezzar) was the rock, which had already broken the other nations and gained universal dominion. We shall see a similar principle operating in chapters 4 and 7 (vision and interpretation). This point is underlined in verse 45 where Daniel notes that both the dream and interpretation are from God and therefore can be trusted.

The four-part statue represents four kingdoms (vv. 36-43). Nebuchadnezzar and his Babylonian kingdom are represented by the head of gold (vv. 36-38). The interpretation acknowledges the might and power of Nebuchadnezzar and his kingdom, but makes it clear that great as that power / dominion is, it is given by God. This echoes the point made earlier in Daniel's prayer that God 'sets up kings and deposes them' (v. 21a). Following Nebuchadnezzar and his Babylonian kingdom, there will be another kingdom, but less powerful (v. 39a). This second kingdom is represented in the statue by the chest and arms of silver. Next, a third kingdom, one of bronze, will rule over the whole earth (v. 39b). The fourth kingdom is described in verses 40-43. This fourth kingdom is represented in the statue by the legs of iron and the feet of iron and clay. As iron and clay do not mix, this kingdom will be a divided kingdom.

What are these kingdoms? Given the identification of the head of gold as Nebuchadnezzar and his Babylonian kingdom (625–539 B.C.), it seems logical to conclude that the other kingdoms are those which followed Babylon in world history, namely Medo-Persia (539–331 B.C.), Greece (331–63 B.C.) and Rome (63 B.C.–A.D. 476). Such specific interpretation is appropriate. That said, however, we shouldn't limit the interpretation to specific kingdoms, and a general interpretation to all human kingdoms throughout history is also appropriate (a similar specific and general interpretation is also suggested by the vision in Ch. 7).

The interpretation now moves to the rock and the mountain (vv. 44-45). The God of heaven will set up a kingdom that will never be destroyed or succeeded. In fact it will crush all other kingdoms and bring them to an end (v. 44). The rock which smashes the base of the statue (in the time of Rome) is Jesus Christ. The fact that the rock is not cut by human hands reveals His divine origin. The rock becomes a great mountain which is the everlasting Kingdom of God inaugurated with Christ's coming. The reference to the mountain filling the whole earth points forward to the end of time when Jesus will return and the Kingdom of God will come in its full and final form in the New Creation.

Until then God is building His Kingdom throughout the world as people submit to God's King, the Lord Jesus. When that building work is complete, when all people have had the opportunity to acknowledge His rule, God's King, Jesus, will return and God's Kingdom will be fully and finally complete.

Some have argued that four kingdoms cannot be successive since they are all destroyed at once. But prophetic material like this does not work on purely literalistic lines. These kingdoms, like all others in history, eventually come to an end by violence, decay or popular desire for change, but the final deathblow to human power happened when the Kingdom of God came in the person of Jesus. Through His death and resurrection He destroyed the tyranny of sin and its dominion in the world. Fig. 3 summarises.

Fig. 3 Interpretation of dream

Nebuchadnezzar's dream Four-part statue	Interpretation
Head of gold	Babylonian kingdom (625–539 B.C.)
Chest and arms of silver	Medo-Persian kingdom (539–331 B.C.)
Belly and thighs of bronze	Greek kingdom (331–63 B.C.)
Legs of iron, feet of iron and clay	Roman kingdom (63 B.C.–A.D. 476)
Rock cut not with human hands which smashes the statue and becomes a great mountain that fills the whole earth	Jesus Christ inaugurates the everlasting Kingdom of God. God's Kingdom will come in its fullness when Jesus returns.

(6) Nebuchadnezzar acknowledges the sovereignty
of God and promotes Daniel, Shadrach,
Meshach and Abednego (vv. 46-49)

Nebuchadnezzar is now as intemperate in his gratitude as
he had been in his threats (v. 46). His whole demeanour
and attitude suggest relief that he was the head of gold, and
that consequently there is no immediate threat to him. He
does make some acknowledgment of God's sovereignty,
although his praise is directed as much toward Daniel as
to Daniel's God (vv. 46-47). Nonetheless, this is his first
faltering step in a long journey to faith.

Nebuchadnezzar's comment in verse 47 underlines a key
message of the chapter – that God reveals what is hidden.
Such 'summarising comments' are a recurring feature in
these narrative chapters, usually from the lips of pagan
kings. Nebuchadnezzar summarises here, and again in
chapters 3:28 and 4:34b-35. In chapter 6 Darius provides
the summary (6:26-27).

The chapter closes with Nebuchadnezzar making Daniel
ruler over the entire province of Babylon and in charge of all
the wise men (v. 48). One can imagine that, at least for now,
Daniel would have been a very popular leader with the rest
of the wise men, grateful for his (as they saw it) intervention
in saving their lives. Moreover, at Daniel's request (another
example of Daniel's shrewdness) he asks the king to appoint
Hananiah, Mishael and Azariah administrators over the
province (v. 49). Nebuchadnezzar agrees.

Remember Nebuchadnezzar's tactics. He wanted to
take the future leaders of God's people and make them
future leaders of Babylon. That was his way of putting God
out of their lives. He got what he wanted. The future leaders
of God's people did become future leaders of Babylon.

Barely a few years into the Exile, Daniel was in charge of the whole province and chief of the wise men, with Hananiah, Mishael and Azariah as high ranking officials. It looked like Nebuchadnezzar has succeeded. That is reiterated by the fact that Daniel's friends, referred to earlier in the chapter by their Hebrew names (v. 17), are referred to here by their Babylonian names. But the text is rich in irony. While they furthered the interests of Babylon, their primary calling was to serve as God's faithful, distinctive witnesses at the heart of this pagan world. And Daniel, one of Nebuchadnezzar's closest political advisors was a believer. In spite of appearances, God is clearly in control. It may not look like it, or feel like it, but God rules.

From text to message

(1) Get the message clear

i) Big idea

God alone reveals absolute truth. What God reveals is that He rules and is building an everlasting Kingdom.

ii) Key questions

Preaching or teaching on this passage should answer the following questions:

- What are the deepest questions facing humanity?
- To what extent can human wisdom and knowledge answer these questions?
- What can God alone reveal?
- How does God reveal?
- What is God's everlasting Kingdom?
- Has God's everlasting Kingdom come?

- How should humanity respond to the fact of God's rule?

(2) *Engage the hearer*

i) *Point of contact*

A helpful way to start the sermon or Bible study might be a comment on Nebuchadnezzar's bad dreams and disturbed sleep. What he dreams is something we can all identify with, the stuff of nightmares. Sometimes we wake up in a cold sweat, fretful and disturbed, unable to remember what we have dreamt.

Another point of contact might be to illustrate the array of contemporary human wisdom on offer today. For example, a survey of the 'Mind, Body and Spirit' section of a bookshop or search online raises obvious questions: 'Where do you look?' 'What can you believe?' 'Will it lead to truth or will it, in the end, be found wanting and disappoint, leaving a sense of emptiness, bitterness and anger?' In making such a point (which is valid), however, you need to be careful of sounding naïve or arrogant, particularly if you are speaking to people who are not Christians.

ii) *Dominant pictures / illustrations*

The dominant picture is of contrasts. On the one hand, Nebuchadnezzar is a mighty king; on the other hand he is mere flesh and blood, disturbed by his dreams and searching for answers. Then there is the contrast between human wisdom and divine revelation. Human wisdom is ultimately futile. The search for truth, answers to the deep mysteries of life leads to a dead end. By contrast, God alone is able to reveal what is hidden. God alone has the answers to the meaning of life and the purpose of humanity. Another major contrast drawn in the chapter is between human and divine power. Human power is transient, given and taken by God. Human kingdoms and kings come and go. By contrast, God's power is absolute, universal and everlasting, seen most clearly in the fact that God establishes an everlasting Kingdom in Christ.

The prophetic material here expressed in apocalyptic language engages the senses and emotions. It will be helpful to bring that out in the way we preach or teach the chapter.

(3) *Work on application*

- This chapter exposes the ultimate futility of human power and wisdom. Many people, including the most powerful and wealthy, come to a point of crisis when they search for answers to fundamental questions about life, death and meaning. Often some circumstance or event raises such questions. People search for answers in all sorts of places, whether philosophy, spirituality or popular culture, but ultimately human wisdom cannot provide the answers.

- The futility of human power is also evident in the irrational response and actions of Nebuchadnezzar. The well-known saying is true: 'Power corrupts, but absolute power corrupts absolutely.'

- Only God is able to reveal what is hidden, and answer such fundamental questions. God is a revealing God who speaks. As Christians, we are in the privileged position that God has revealed Himself fully and finally in the person of His Son (John 1:1-18), and in the Word of God contained in the Scriptures of the Old and New Testaments. This is full, sufficient and authoritative revelation (2 Tim. 3:14-17).

- What God reveals is that He rules. God's rule is seen in His sovereignty over nations and individuals. Human power, whether on an international scale, a national scale, or in a host of other smaller ways, is transient. Power is given and taken away. The great kingdoms and rulers of history, ancient and modern, have passed into the annals of time. The political power of today is the political history of tomorrow.

- God's rule is evidenced supremely in the fact that He is building an all-powerful Kingdom. In applying the passage it is important to note that what is prophesied in Daniel (the rock that became a mountain) has happened. The Lord Jesus (the rock) has come, establishing God's Everlasting Kingdom (the mountain).

- In this regard, it is also important to convey the 'now' and 'not yet' dimension to the Kingdom of God. With Jesus' first coming, His Kingdom is established and the power of evil in the world conquered, but until He returns, opposition and strife will continue. The age of proclamation will be the age of opposition. When Jesus returns He will establish a New Creation, where His people will live and reign with Him for eternity.

- God's judgement on those who oppose Him and His people is seen throughout history. But that judgement is merely a pointer to the full and final judgement that will occur at the end of history when Christ returns.

- While the message and application of the chapter is for believers, it is also relevant to unbelievers. Chapter

2 begins the Aramaic section, with its universal applicability, both to believers and unbelievers. The pattern and progress of world history are set. With the first coming of Christ, God has inaugurated His Everlasting Kingdom which will be fully and finally established with His return at the end of history. All people will be raised on that day. Those who have submitted to the rule of God's King in this life will receive the glorious inheritance of this Kingdom, but those who have not submitted to His rule will be judged for eternity. Encourage people to submit to God's rule now, while there is time.

- It is important to remember that God's revelation here is, in part at least, for the benefit of Nebuchadnezzar as an individual. This is part of God's purpose to bring Nebuchadnezzar to saving faith. It will be a long journey to faith, as the events of chapters 3 and 4 make clear, but in the end God will humble Nebuchadnezzar to the point of saving faith. In applying this chapter to unbelievers, emphasise that God deals with us as individuals and also the extent of His grace (Nebuchadnezzar had no right to expect salvation).

- While these are the key applications from the chapter, there is also a good deal we can learn from Daniel's example. His reaction to the crisis is telling. In his dealings with Arioch and then Nebuchadnezzar, Daniel is wise and diplomatic. Having asked the king for time, he returns home and gathers his friends together to pray. Faced with another crisis in chapter 6, again Daniel's response

is to pray (6:10). After God reveals the content of
Nebuchadnezzar's dream and the interpretation,
Daniel is at pains to point away from himself to
God as the one who reveals. Daniel makes this
point by recording his prayer of thanksgiving, and
then the extensive dialogue with Nebuchadnezzar
which follows. Here is a picture of the true servant
of God who points away from self to God. Daniel is
the model believer, committed to living a distinctive
life, ready and willing to be used by God. God used
Daniel to advance His purposes. As a result of these
events Daniel and his friends (at Daniel's request) are
promoted – more influence at the heart of Babylon.
While the principle is true – that God uses us to
advance His Kingdom – how God uses us is for
Him to determine. Our mind-set should always be
that God has put us where we are for a purpose and
therefore we should be ready and willing to be used.

Outline for a sermon or talk

We would suggest an outline that reflects the structure of
Daniel 2.

Title: **God reveals that He rules**
Text: **Daniel 2**

Structure:

(1) **Futility of human power and wisdom (vv. 1-13)**

(2) **God alone reveals truth (vv. 14-30)**

 i) *Daniel's reaction to the crisis*

 ii) *God reveals the dream and the interpretation*

(3) God reveals that He rules (vv. 31-45)

    i) Dream – four-part statue, rock and mountain

    ii) Interpretation – earthly kingdoms rise and fall, but God will establish an Everlasting Kingdom that will fill the whole earth

(4) God advances His Kingdom (vv. 46-49)

    i) Nebuchadnezzar's 'acknowledgement' of God

    ii) God's Kingdom advances

The sub-points above may or may not be used in the outline. They are included here simply to help with the flow of logical thought.

Bible study on Daniel 2

Read Daniel 2

(1) Introduce the issues

    i) From a first reading of the chapter, what do you think is the key message for believers?

    ii) From a first reading of the chapter, what do you think is the key message for unbelievers?

    iii) What are some of the features of the prophetic material / apocalyptic language that you notice from this chapter? What impression does this kind of literature make on you?

(2) Study the passage

    i) What do we learn from the text about human power and wisdom (vv. 1-13)?

ii) What qualities, already evident in chapter 1, are seen in the way Daniel reacts to the crisis (vv. 14-23)?

iii) What do we learn about God from Daniel's prayer of praise and thanksgiving (vv. 20-23)?

iv) What is the point of the extended dialogue between Daniel, Arioch and Nebuchadnezzar in verses 24-30?

v) What is the meaning of the dream (vv. 31-35; 36-45)?

vi) What do you make of Nebuchadnezzar's reaction (vv. 46-48)?

(3) *Apply the passage*

i) What are the deepest questions facing humanity?

ii) In our culture today, where do people search for answers to life's questions?

iii) What lessons about prayer do we learn from Daniel and how would these make a difference to how we pray individually and as a church?

iv) A key message of the chapter is that God alone can reveal truth. From our perspective as Christians how has God revealed Himself to us?

v) What God reveals is that He will build an everlasting Kingdom. From our perspective as Christians to what extent has this promise been fulfilled?

vi) How does the message of this chapter encourage you in evangelism?

vii) What do we learn from Daniel about how we should live as Christians and, in particular, how we should react in difficult or crisis situations?

(4) Pray it through

4

LIVING COURAGEOUSLY IN
LIGHT OF GOD'S RULE
(DANIEL 3)

Setting in context

(1) Dating

Although not precisely dated, it is likely that the events described in chapter 3 happened much later in Nebuchadnezzar's reign, sometime after the final destruction of Jerusalem and the temple in 586 B.C. and the mass deportation to Babylon. A date around 580 B.C. seems plausible. Nebuchadnezzar would have been at the height of his power. Shadrach, Meshach and Abednego (their Babylonian names are used throughout Ch. 3) are probably in their late thirties / early forties.

(2) Context – structure of book

This is the second of three conflict chapters (Chs. 1, 3 and 6) focusing on Daniel, Shadrach, Meshach and Abednego as they live as exiles in Babylon. In chapter 1 the focus is on all four, although Daniel takes centre stage. In chapter 6 it is only Daniel, while here in chapter 3 the spotlight falls on Shadrach, Meshach and Abednego.

The structure of the chapters is similar:

- They face pressure to conform.

- They make a decision to live distinctively, in spite of the consequences.

- God miraculously delivers them.

- God advances His Kingdom.

The three chapters span the entire period of the Exile: chapter 1 at the start; chapter 3 well into the Exile; and chapter 6, dated as 539 B.C., right at the end. The fact that these recorded incidents are spread over such a long period brings perspective and realism to the way we teach the book of Daniel. Significant tests will come along, but most of the time steady, faithful, consistent witness is the order of the day.

As well as being the second of the three conflict chapters (along with Chs. 1 and 6), Daniel 3 is the second of three consecutive chapters (Chs. 2, 3 and 4) describing God's progressive revelation to Nebuchadnezzar, leading to his eventual conversion. God's revelation to Nebuchadnezzar in chapters 2 and 4 comes through interpreted dreams (the 'dream of the four-part statue' and the 'dream of the tree'), while here in chapter 3 he is an eye-witness to the power of God.

There is also a structural link to chapter 2, where the image of gold Nebuchadnezzar constructs (Ch. 3) resembles the statue in his dream (Ch. 2).

(3) Context – message of book
If the message of the book as a whole is that *God rules*, the purpose of these conflict chapters is to show *how God's people are to live in light of the fact that He rules*. As exiles in

the world, God calls His people to live distinctively. To live distinctively is costly, but God's people are to trust God. And as God's people live distinctively, God advances His Kingdom.

While the message of these conflict chapters is similar, there are important differences. In chapter 1, for example, the sense we get is of Daniel and his friends looking for an opportunity to make their allegiance to God known. Daniel's approach is quiet and gracious as first he politely asks Ashpenaz' permission not to take the royal food and wine, and then, having failed to persuade Ashpenaz, he puts a reasoned proposal to the guard appointed over them. It is all pretty low key. But here in chapter 3, the situation is quite different. Shadrach, Meshach and Abednego face a direct and hostile challenge to their faith – bow down and worship the statue or die! Nebuchadnezzar's bold and brutal decree necessitates a bold and courageous stand in open defiance to the king.

Moreover, the young men of chapter 1, teenagers studying in King's College, Babylon, are now in their late thirties / early forties, established, successful and rapidly advancing up the political career ladder. Having entered into the king's service as top graduates (1:19), within a very short time they received rapid promotion as regional administrators in the province of Babylon, with Daniel as ruler over the entire province (2:48-9). Here in chapter 3, we read of their continued influence as 'leaders' in Babylon (3:12). They had a great deal to lose in defying the king's command, and because of their position their defiance was sure to be high profile. Incidentally, we should beware of reading anything into the fact that Daniel does not figure in this episode. The most likely explanation is that he simply wasn't there, perhaps away on the king's business. Certainly, there is no suggestion that he compromised.

Given that chapter 3 is in the Aramaic section of the book (Chs. 2–7), that suggests there is also a message here for unbelievers. As noted above, chapters 2, 3 and 4 describe Nebuchadnezzar's journey to faith. In each chapter, Nebuchadnezzar's power, great as it is, is confronted by a greater power: the God of heaven who reveals, who rules, who delivers His people and who saves even the likes of Nebuchadnezzar. Here in chapter 3, the power on display is God's miraculous deliverance of Shadrach, Meshach and Abednego from the furnace. One of the striking points in this episode is that God made sure Nebuchadnezzar saw what happened. Moreover, it is not only God's miraculous deliverance that is challenging to unbelievers, but the faithfulness, courage and confidence in God of His people. Through these Aramaic chapters the consistent message to the unbeliever is to bow in worship, not to a golden statue or any other idol, but to the one true living God, the God of heaven.

Working on the text

The structure of the chapter is as follows:

(1) Shadrach, Meshach and Abednego face a direct and hostile challenge to their faith (vv. 1-12)

(2) Shadrach, Meshach and Abednego make a bold and courageous stand, in spite of the consequences (vv. 13-18)

(3) God delivers Shadrach, Meshach and Abednego from the furnace (vv. 19-27)

(4)   Nebuchadnezzar acknowledges the sovereignty of
      God and promotes Shadrach, Meshach and Abednego
      to positions of greater influence in Babylon (vv. 28-30).

The turning point in the text is Shadrach, Meshach and
Abednego's defiant statement of faith (vv. 16-18). The
turning point is the main teaching point.

(1) Shadrach, Meshach and Abednego face a direct and hostile challenge to their faith (vv. 1-12)

Immediately the parallels with chapter 2 are evident.

> 'You looked, O king, and there before you stood a large
> statue – an enormous, dazzling statue, awesome in
> appearance. The head of the statue was made of pure
> gold...' (2:31-32a)

> 'King Nebuchadnezzar made an image of gold, ninety
> feet high and nine feet wide, and set it up on the plain of
> Dura in the province of Babylon.' (3:1)

Daniel's interpretation of Nebuchadnezzar's dream of the
statue in chapter 2 had made it clear to the king that while
earthly kings and kingdoms come and go (including his
Babylonian kingdom represented by the golden head of the
statue), God will establish an everlasting Kingdom. This was
a prophetic prediction (for the benefit of Nebuchadnezzar)
of the coming of Christ and the inauguration of His
everlasting Kingdom. We saw in chapter 2 the faltering
start of Nebuchadnezzar's journey to faith in response to
this revelation (2:46-49), but just how faltering it was is now
evident. The revelation that the head of gold on the statue
was Nebuchadnezzar and his Babylonian empire (2:36-38)
had gone to his head, swelling his pride and self-confidence.

As the years passed, with his ever increasing dominion and power, he had forgotten that God rules and that all he had was given by God (2:37). Moreover, the prophetic prediction in chapter 2 about the overthrow of the Babylonian kingdom 'in the future' (2:45b) would have made Nebuchadnezzar complacent. It is amazing that Nebuchadnezzar's refusal to heed the warning of chapter 2 does not prevent God's further revelation to him, both here in chapter 3 and in chapter 4. This is evidence of God's amazing grace.

The construction of this image of gold is rampant idolatry on the part of Nebuchadnezzar – symbolizing the elevation of himself and his kingdom as the focus of worship. The image of gold reflects the statue in chapter 2, except that this image is made entirely of gold (only the head of the statue in chapter 2 was made of gold, representing king Nebuchadnezzar and his Babylonian empire). The fact that the entire statue is of gold indicates Nebuchadnezzar's supreme arrogance in thinking that his Babylonian kingdom is unassailable.

The entire civil and state bureaucracy is summoned to the dedication of the image (v. 2). This would have included Shadrach, Meshach and Abednego as provincial officials (2:49). It must have been an impressive sight as they all stood before the golden image (v. 3). The decree that is then pronounced (vv. 4-6) is all-encompassing ('O peoples, nations and men of every language…') and uncompromising ('Whoever does not fall down and worship will immediately be thrown into a blazing furnace.'). This is the worst extreme of a totalitarian state, total subjugation under human authority and power.

In verses 8-12, we read that some of the astrologers (wise men of Babylon) 'denounced the Jews' (v. 8b).

Shadrach, Meshach and Abednego are reported in person to the king for their refusal to worship the image. The NIV translation 'denounced' perhaps loses something of the Aramaic expression, which means literally 'tear and eat the flesh'. At one level, it is reasonable to conclude that the astrologers were motivated by jealousy, probably because Shadrach, Meshach and Abednego, along with Daniel, had been promoted above them. We will see this again in chapter 6 when the administrators and satraps plot against Daniel, once again, it seems, because of his prominence and the favour shown to him by King Darius. The underlying principle, however, is that God's people will be oppressed, precisely because they are the people of God.

A final observation in this section. Note verse 5: 'As soon as you hear the sound of the horn, flute, zither, lyre, harp, pipes and all kinds of music, you must fall down and worship the image of gold that king Nebuchadnezzar has set up.' This is repeated a number of times in the chapter (vv. 7, 10, 15). What is the purpose of this repetition? The music is intended (we can assume) to create the appropriate mood to encourage worship of this image; the repetition of this phrase in the text is intended to convey something of the hypnotic, manipulative effect of the music, exposing the sinister nature of what is happening.

(2) Shadrach, Meshach and Abednego make a bold and courageous stand, in spite of the consequences (vv. 13-18)

Verse 13 begins with Nebuchadnezzar's reaction to the fact that Shadrach, Meshach and Abednego refuse to worship the golden image. He is described as 'furious with rage' (v. 13). This arrogant man is outraged at their disobedience and defiance. We have already observed this reaction in chapter 2, when he decrees that all the wise men of Babylon be put to death because they are unable to tell the king his dream and its interpretation (2:12). Nebuchadnezzar thinks and acts irrationally. The shift to a more conciliatory tone in verses 14 and 15 is merely a stay of execution. He asks whether the accusation is true (v. 14), gives them another chance to fall down and worship the image (v. 15a), and then explains again the consequences should they disobey (v. 15b). His final words are striking: 'Then what god will be able to rescue you from my hand?' (v. 15c) This defiant statement, almost a challenge, precipitates the turning point, Shadrach, Meshach and Abednego's defiant statement of faith (vv. 16-18).

In contrast to Daniel's approach – his gracious request to the chief official (1:8), his reasoning with the guard (1:11-13), his wisdom and tact and request for time (2:14-16) – Shadrach, Meshach and Abednego's approach here is direct and bold. Notice the logic of what they say. They do not need to defend themselves before Nebuchadnezzar because they have a higher authority, the God of heaven (v. 16). They trust God, confident that He is able, if He so wills, to deliver them from the furnace (v. 17). After all, they had seen God's miraculous intervention in the early days of the Exile (1:15-17). And they had seen God reveal to Daniel Nebuchadnezzar's dream and its interpretation, saving them from execution (2:17-19). They had every confidence that God could deliver them again. But their courage and conviction were such that even if it meant they had to die for their faith they would not compromise. God would deliver them in the end, even if that meant through death. The high point of their statement of faith is in verse 18: 'But even if he does not [deliver us], we want you to know, O king, that we will not serve your gods or worship the image of gold you have set up.'

(3) God delivers Shadrach, Meshach and
Abednego from the furnace (vv. 19-27)

On hearing their bold statement of faith, and seeing their courage, Nebuchadnezzar, burning with anger, orders the furnace to be heated seven times hotter than usual (v. 19), so hot in fact that the soldiers responsible for binding the three men and throwing them into the furnace are killed by the flames (v. 22). The details in the text are important. Shadrach, Meshach and Abednego are bound and thrown into the furnace fully clothed (v. 21).

Verses 24 to 27 are powerful drama. Nebuchadnezzar's reaction is one of shock and amazement at seeing not three, but four men walking around in the fire, unbound and unharmed (vv. 24-25). His own description of the fourth man is someone who 'looks like a son of the gods' (v. 25b). Who is this fourth person? Commentators discuss at length whether this is an angel (that's the description attributed to Nebuchadnezzar (v. 28)) or a physical appearance of Jesus before His incarnation (a Christophany). It is difficult to be emphatic either way. What we do know is that God is present, in the person of a divine being, with His people in the furnace. This is a fulfilment of the Lord's promise in Isaiah 43:2-3:

> 'When you walk through the fire,
>   you will not be burned;
>   the flames will not set you ablaze.
> For I am the Lord, your God,
>   the Holy One of Israel, your
>   Saviour...'
>   (Isa. 43:2c-3a)

At Nebuchadnezzar's command, Shadrach, Meshach and Abednego walk out of the fire (v. 26) and the satraps, prefects, governors and royal advisers crowd around them (v. 27). Their interest is perfectly natural, but the writer intends us to recall the similar list in verse 2. Earlier in the chapter these state officials were summoned to the dedication of the image of gold. And now they crowd around the people of God miraculously delivered from the furnace. Quite a contrast! We are told what they saw. Shadrach, Meshach and Abednego were unharmed, not a single hair singed, their clothes not burned and not even the smell of fire around them (v. 27b). We are not told what the crowd made of it all; the focus, rather, is on Nebuchadnezzar's reaction.

(4) Nebuchadnezzar acknowledges the sovereignty of God and promotes Shadrach, Meshach and Abednego to positions of greater influence in Babylon (vv. 28-30)

God's grace to Nebuchadnezzar is astonishing. Remember that Nebuchadnezzar's intention was to destroy the people of God. And yet God, in His mercy, revealed to Nebuchadnezzar (Ch. 2) that any power and dominion he has is given by God, and that while his earthly kingdom will pass away, God will establish an everlasting Kingdom. Why did God do that? He did it, not primarily to teach Nebuchadnezzar a lesson in humility, but to lead him to saving faith and worship of the one true and living God. This is the amazing grace of God, intent on saving men such as Nebuchadnezzar.

In verses 46-49 of chapter 2 we observed the first faltering steps of Nebuchadnezzar's journey to faith. The passing years and the events of chapter 3 reveal just how faltering it was. But having witnessed the strength of faith and conviction of God's people, and God's miraculous intervention in delivering them from the furnace, Nebuchadnezzar takes another step on his long journey to faith. Yet his statement in verse 28, praising the God of Shadrach, Meshach and Abednego and acknowledging their strength of faith, while sincere, is still some way from personal faith. Nebuchadnezzar's decree in verse 29 is in stark contrast to the earlier decree in verses 4-6. Both are addressed to the peoples, nations and men of every language, the first to bow down to a golden image, the second to acknowledge the God of heaven. Finally, he promotes Shadrach, Meshach and Abednego, the people of God more and more at the heart of Babylon, pointing the unbelieving world to God (v. 30).

From text to message

(1) Get the message clear

i) Big idea
In light of the fact that God rules, God expects His people to live distinctively, showing their allegiance to Him. There are times when that requires a bold and courageous stand.

ii) Key questions
Preaching or teaching on this passage should answer the following questions:

- What kinds of direct and hostile challenges to our faith do we face as Christians today?

- In such circumstances, what does God expect from us?

- What can we expect from God?

- What is the significance of the events described here for unbelievers?

(2) Engage the hearer

i) Point of contact

A helpful way to start the sermon or Bible study would be to convey some sense of the scale and splendour of the golden image Nebuchadnezzar set up. One way to do that might be to bring to mind the sight of impressive buildings. The city of London, for example, like every major city in the world, has its fair share of iconic buildings. Dominating London's skyline are the Swiss Re skyscraper (affectionately known as the 'Gherkin'), the newer and taller 'Shard of Glass' south of the river on London Bridge, and now under construction the Pinnacle (affectionately known as the Helter-Skelter) which will dwarf them all. They are magnificent buildings, indicative of the best of human achievement in design, engineering, aesthetic impact and commercial success. Undeniably impressive, the sight of them invokes a sense of awe, especially when you stand close up at the foot of these great towers reaching to the sky. In the Ancient World, the image of gold, ninety feet high and nine feet wide, set up by Nebuchadnezzar on the plain of Dura in the province of Babylon, would have been an equally impressive sight. The magnificence of the city of Babylon epitomized by its Ishtar Gate and Hanging Gardens was surpassed by this magnificent golden statue, dedicated as an object of worship to the might of King Nebuchadnezzar and his all-conquering empire.

ii) Dominant pictures / illustrations

In contrast to chapter 1, which was pretty low key, the events described here are high profile and dramatic. The TV crews would be camped out on the plain of Dura covering these events! It is high intensity right through the chapter: the manipulation and control to force people to worship the statue; the denouncing of Shadrach, Meshach and Abednego; the fury of Nebuchadnezzar; their defiant stand; the nature of their punishment; the heating up of the furnace; the sight of the divine being in the furnace; their dramatic deliverance.

(3) *Work on application*

- As Christians living as exiles in the world (1 Pet. 1:1) we are exposed to a culture that challenges our faith. In some parts of the world, Christians face intense pressure and persecution, the worst extremes of totalitarianism. In such contexts, the kind of forced compliance we read of here in Daniel 3 is not uncommon. Studying this chapter, it is helpful to draw attention to the Persecuted Church in the world, informing people of what is happening and encouraging them to pray.

- In the West, the pressure we face to conform is more about assimilation of a prevailing secular culture than direct authoritarian compliance. That said, however, we are beginning to see the first signs of direct pressure being put on Christians to conform to a secular agenda. Also, orthodox churches that are part of major denominations are coming under increasing pressure as the denomination pursues a liberalising or revisionist agenda that mirrors the culture. While we should be alarmed at these trends, we should not be surprised. In the West, for centuries we have enjoyed an 'abnormal' situation where the prevailing culture has been Christian. The change to a prevailing secular culture is returning us to what is 'normal' Christian experience – opposition, maybe even persecution for those who hold to orthodox Christian convictions. This opposition will come from outside but also from inside the Church.

- We also need to apply this in much more mundane ways, but no less pressing and real for the individuals involved. For example, a Christian forced to comply with some practice at work which compromises their faith. Or in the realm of friendships, relationships, family, there are times when Christians come under concerted pressure to compromise their faith and convictions, or even to abandon their faith.

- While Daniel 3 is, of course, relevant to Christians of any age, there is an obvious application to people at a stage of life where they are established, successful, advancing in their careers and with a lot to lose. The cost of standing courageously is real. It may mean being looked over for promotion, losing your job, or just losing friendship or face with peers.

- In these conflict chapters, it is important to remember that God is the hero of the story, not Shadrach, Meshach and Abednego or Daniel. While they are undoubtedly an example and inspiration, the reason they acted the way they did was because of their trust and confidence in God. They knew that in spite of appearances, God rules, and therefore lived and acted in light of that fact. God was their inspiration. And God, not Shadrach,

Meshach and Abednego, needs to be our primary inspiration. They should not be seen as exceptional believers but rather examples we can all aspire to.

- The manner in which Shadrach, Meshach and Abednego take their stand is instructive. In contrast to Daniel's approach in chapters 1 and 2, their approach is bold and defiant. We need to beware evaluating the relative merits of these approaches. Both have their place. God-given wisdom is necessary to discern which is appropriate given the circumstances. There are certainly occasions when faced with a direct and hostile challenge to our faith, the appropriate response is a bold and courageous stand in open defiance.

- Shadrach, Meshach and Abednego took their stand trusting in God's promise of deliverance. While the principle is true, and we are to trust in God's promised deliverance, how God delivers us is for Him to determine. He will certainly give us grace sufficient for the circumstances we face. He may intervene in dramatic ways to deliver us from a particular situation of conflict. Ultimately, of course, God's promised deliverance is from death to eternal life. The Christian, trusting in God's promised deliverance, is safe and secure, even if they lose their lives for the sake of the gospel.

- As we live distinctively as Christians showing our allegiance to God, His Kingdom advances. Again, while the principle is true, how God advances His Kingdom through our witness is for Him to determine. He may put us in a position of influence or not. He may use us significantly or not. We should always remember that God puts us where we are for a purpose and never think that God will not use a stand that we take for Him to advance His Kingdom. Invariably God uses ordinary people to advance His Kingdom.

- In applying this passage to unbelievers, a key point to make is that the events described are factual history in the same way that the miracles in the Gospels are factual history. Ask people what they make of the events described. Confront people with the fact that the mighty King Nebuchadnezzar and his Babylonian kingdom are now consigned to the annals of history. All that remains is artefacts to be viewed in museums.

Outline for a sermon or talk

The structure of Daniel 3 is relatively straightforward, and we would suggest an outline that reflects this structure.

Title: Living courageously in light of God's rule
Text: Daniel 3

Structure:

(1) Remember God rules

(2) Living in the world (vv. 1-12)

   i) Secular culture

   ii) Pressure to conform – direct challenge

(3) A bold and courageous stand (vv. 13-18)

   i) Courage

   ii) Conviction

(4) Trusting God (vv. 19-27)

    i) *God's grace is sufficient*

    ii) *God's promised deliverance*

(5) God's Kingdom advances (vv. 28-30)

    i) *God uses His people*

    ii) *God works in the hearts of unbelievers*

The first point, while not directly from the text of the chapter, sets the material in the context of the key message of the book as a whole – God rules.

The sub-points above may or may not be used in the outline. They are included here simply to help with the flow of logical thought.

Bible study on Daniel 3

Read Daniel 3

(1) Introduce the issues

    i) As Christians we live as exiles in the world
    (1 Pet. 1:1). In light of the fact that God rules,
    when faced with a direct and hostile challenge
    to our faith, God expects us to take a bold and
    courageous stand.

       From a first reading of the chapter, how are we
    encouraged and inspired to do that?

(2) Study the passage

    i) Shadrach, Meshach and Abednego face a direct
    and hostile challenge to their faith. What is it and
    what lies behind it? (vv. 1-12)

    ii) How did they react to the king's decree and
    what does their statement to Nebuchadnezzar

reveal about their faith and confidence in God?
(vv. 13-18)

[You might find it helpful to compare with
Daniel's approach in Chs. 1 and 2.]

iii) What did God do? (vv. 19-27)

iv) How did Nebuchadnezzar react to what he had
seen God do? (vv. 28-30)

(3) *Apply the passage*

i) What kind of direct and hostile challenges to
their faith do Christians face in the world today?
Are there circumstances when we face such direct
challenges?

ii) God expects us to live distinctively, showing our
allegiance to Him. What's our motivation for
doing this? What stops us doing it?

iii) The way Shadrach, Meshach and Abednego took
their stand is striking. What can we learn from
their manner and approach? [Again, comparison
with Daniel in Chs. 1 and 2 might be helpful.]

iv) Taking a bold stand against a direct and hostile
challenge can be costly in terms of the consequences
we face. What can we expect from God?

v) If we take a bold and courageous stand for God, how
will He use our witness to advance His Kingdom?

vi) What are the implications of the events described
for unbelievers?

(4) *Pray it through*

5

GOD RULES IN SALVATION: NEBUCHADNEZZAR'S CONVERSION (DANIEL 4)

Setting in context

(1) Dating

Chapter 4 is the testimony of Nebuchadnezzar's conversion, written in his own hand. Whether these are his actual words, included in the book at this point, or written by Daniel from Nebuchadnezzar's perspective, it hardly matters. This is a remarkable testimony to God's gracious intervention in Nebuchadnezzar's life.

The events described take place over at least an eight-year period. Following the dream and its interpretation by Daniel, a period of twelve months passes (v. 29) before the dream is fulfilled. If we assume that the 'seven times' (vv. 16, 23) are seven years, Nebuchadnezzar's humbling to the point where he is brought to faith lasts seven years. Nebuchadnezzar reigned from 605–562 B.C. If the events of chapter 3 take place sometime after the destruction of Jerusalem and the temple in 586 B.C. (we suggested at a date of around 580 B.C.), then that would put the events here in chapter 4 sometime in the period 580–562 B.C., and probably earlier rather than later in this period, since following his conversion, Nebuchadnezzar was restored to his throne and became even greater than before (v. 36).

(2) Context – structure of book

Chapters 4 and 5 are at the heart of the Aramaic section of the book (Fig. 1). The Aramaic section is of universal significance, a message for all people, unbelievers as well as believers.

Fig. 1 Chiastic structure of Aramaic section

   a Ch. 2   Prophetic vision of four-part statue, rock and mountain

     b Ch. 3   God delivers His people from the furnace

       c Ch. 4   God saves Nebuchadnezzar

       c Ch. 5   God judges Belshazzar

     b Ch. 6   God delivers Daniel from the lions' den

   a Ch. 7   Prophetic vision of four beasts, Ancient of Days and son of man

There are clear structural parallels between chapters 4 and 5 (Fig. 2).

Fig. 2 Parallels between chapters 4 and 5

Ch. 4 Nebuchadnezzar's conversion	Ch. 5 Belshazzar's judgement
Dream (vv. 4-18)	Writing on the wall (vv. 5-16)
Interpretation (vv. 19-27)	Interpretation (vv. 17-28)
Fulfilment (vv. 28-33)	Fulfilment (vv. 29-31)

Chapter 4 concludes three consecutive chapters where the power of Nebuchadnezzar has been confronted by a greater power, the God who rules. In chapters 2 and 4 God's revelation to Nebuchadnezzar comes through interpreted dreams. In chapter 3, he sees the power of God in delivering Shadrach, Meshach and Abednego from the furnace.

(3) Context – message of book

The message of Daniel is that *God rules, is building an everlasting Kingdom, and calls people to live in light of that fact.* A key aspect of God's rule is His sovereignty in salvation, powerfully demonstrated here in Nebuchadnezzar's conversion. In chapter 5 we see God's judgement on Belshazzar.

God's revelation to Nebuchadnezzar is to lead the king to repentance and faith. In 2:46-49, following Daniel's interpretation of the dream, Nebuchadnezzar makes some acknowledgement of God's sovereignty, although his praise is directed as much toward Daniel as to God. The events of chapter 3 and the construction of the image of gold which he requires people to worship, indicate just how faltering his journey to faith really was. Following his sight of the dramatic deliverance of God's people in chapter 3, Nebuchadnezzar's statement of faith (3:28) evidences a greater understanding, yet is still far from genuine repentance and saving faith. Through it all, God is gracious and patient with Nebuchadnezzar.

Working on the text

The structure of the chapter is as follows:

(1) Introduction to Nebuchadnezzar's testimony of his conversion (vv. 1-3)

(2) Nebuchadnezzar's dream exposes the futility of
     human power and wisdom (vv. 4-8)

(3) Nebuchadnezzar recounts to Daniel his dream of the
     tree (vv. 9-18)

(4) Daniel interprets the dream and calls
     Nebuchadnezzar to repent (vv. 19-27)

(5) The dream is fulfilled and Nebuchadnezzar is
     brought to repentance (vv. 28-33)

(6) Nebuchadnezzar's psalm of praise following his
     conversion, and his restoration (vv. 34-37)

*(1) Introduction to Nebuchadnezzar's
      testimony of his conversion (vv. 1-3)*

Verses 1-3 function like an introduction or preface. Nebuchadnezzar is addressing 'the peoples, nations and men
of every language, who live in all the world' (v. 1). This
mode of communicating was not uncommon for rulers like
Nebuchadnezzar in the Ancient Word, attested by many
parallels from his own times and in the later Medo-Persian
period (see a similar pattern in Esther). The significance
of what he has to say to all people reflects the universal
significance of the message of Daniel. While the mode of
communicating is not surprising, the content of what he
says certainly is.

In the introduction he seems to be recalling the earlier
dream and its interpretation (Ch. 2) and the experience
of the blazing furnace (Ch. 3). As we have seen, while
these events made a strong impression on him at the time
(2:46-49; 3:28), the effect was temporary. The statue and
furnace in chapter 3 seem to have denied what he learned

in chapter 2. The reference in 4:4 to his contentment and prosperity was after the events of chapter 3. Again, the impression seems to have been fleeting. This is true to human experience. Impressions, even deep ones, tend to fade and old patterns of behaviour return. And yet, in spite of this, God is determined to bring Nebuchadnezzar to true repentance and faith.

Nebuchadnezzar realises that 'the Most High God' (v. 2) is the most powerful, whose Kingdom is eternal. The language (also 4:34-35) echoes the Psalms (for example, Ps. 145:13). Some commentators have expressed the view that a pagan king would simply not write in that way. This ignores the powerful influence Daniel had on Nebuchadnezzar and, in time, Darius (see his similar testimony in 6.25-27) and the fact these pagan kings were converted.

(2) Nebuchadnezzar's dream exposes the futility
of human power and wisdom (vv. 4-8)

Nebuchadnezzar begins his testimony ('I, Nebuchadnezzar …' (v. 4)), describing events that happened over an eight-year period that eventually led to his conversion. At the start he is in his palace contented and prosperous (v. 4). The Aramaic word translated 'prosperous' is used metaphorically to describe a flourishing tree, its use here intended to point forward to Nebuchadnezzar's dream. God breaks into his life with another dream and Nebuchadnezzar is terrified by what he sees (v. 5). We saw a similar reaction to the earlier dream (2:1) but here his fear is heightened. As before he summons the wise men of Babylon to interpret the dream (v. 6). We might have thought he would have learned his lesson from his previous experience. Again, though, this is consistent with human experience and behaviour. We struggle to learn. Nebuchadnezzar explains the dream to them but they could not interpret it (v. 7). Finally Daniel comes and Nebuchadnezzar tells him the dream (v. 8a). Back in chapter 1, we recall how God had given Daniel, as a young man, the ability to interpret visions and dreams (1:17b). Daniel had interpreted Nebuchadnezzar's dream in chapter 2, making it clear that the revelation had come from God, not Daniel (2:24-30). Nebuchadnezzar had struggled to grasp this, attributing the ability to Daniel himself (2:46-47). The way Nebuchadnezzar refers to Daniel here in chapter 4 – 'Belteshazzar, after the name of my god, and the spirit of the holy gods is in him' (4:8b) – indicates he is a long way from understanding. This interpretation is given further credence by the fact that in chapter 5 both the queen mother (5:11) and Belshazzar (5:14) use this expression of Daniel – 'the spirit of the holy gods is in him.'

(3) Nebuchadnezzar recounts to Daniel his dream of the tree (vv. 9-18)

Recognising Daniel's gift (although not as yet the source of his gift), Nebuchadnezzar tells Daniel his dream (v. 9). The dream is of 'a tree in the middle of the land. Its height was enormous. The tree grew large and strong and its top touched the sky; it was visible to the ends of the earth. Its leaves were beautiful; its fruit abundant, and on it was food for all. Under it the beasts of the field found shelter, and the birds of the air lived in its branches; from it every creature was fed' (vv. 10b-12). This image is not unique to the book of Daniel. In Ezekiel, the prophet speaks of Pharaoh (and Assyria) as a cedar (Ezek. 31:1-9). It is a picture of power and prosperity.

The tone changes in verse 13 as a messenger, a holy one, comes down from heaven. This is reminiscent of a number of biblical passages, for example, God coming down from heaven to destroy the tower of Babel (Gen. 11:1-9). The word 'messenger' used here in Daniel 4 might better be translated as 'watcher'. Zechariah speaks of 'the eyes of the Lord which range throughout the earth' (Zech. 4:10). God sees all. The watcher commands the tree to be cut down, but the stump and roots are to be left in the ground so that it can grow again (vv. 14-15a). The once great tree is reduced to a pitiable shadow of its former self 'in the grass of the field' (v. 15a). The change from 'it' to 'him' in verse 15b suggests the dream is about an individual. The individual is to be deprived of his dignity and sanity, living with the animals with the mind of an animal 'till seven times pass by for him' (v. 16). 'Times' is generally taken to mean years although the word can have a more general sense of 'seasons'.

Verse 17 announces the certainty of the judgement. It is a 'decision' (perhaps better understood as a 'decree') and also a revelation 'so that the living may know.' The whole thrust of the book is that 'the Most High is sovereign over the kingdoms of men.' Yet that is seen only through the eyes of faith and Nebuchadnezzar still doesn't see. The section concludes with Nebuchadnezzar asking Daniel to interpret the dream for him (v. 18).

(4) Daniel interprets the dream and calls Nebuchadnezzar to repent (vv. 19-27)

Again, Daniel's courtesy and tact are evident (v. 19). The words 'perplexed' and 'terrified' are not Daniel fearing for his own life, rather his distress at what was to happen to

Nebuchadnezzar. This is more than courtesy. One can imagine Daniel had a real affection for and loyalty to Nebuchadnezzar. This is evidenced in the favourable and restrained account Daniel gives of the dream (vv. 20-22). In the earlier dream Nebuchadnezzar had been identified with the head of gold (2:38). He is now identified with the tree (v. 22). The tree represents Nebuchadnezzar (and his Babylonian kingdom) at the height of his power. Moreover the image is one of a benevolent ruler, not a dictator. This description makes no reference to the king's pride and could be read as a celebration of the positive and beautiful aspects of Babylonian civilisation. So far so good.

Yet the ominous details of verse 23 about the messenger from heaven saying the tree should be cut down prepare us for the solemn words in verses 24-27. In verse 24 we are reminded this is 'the decree the Most High has issued'. It is God's decision to deal with Nebuchadnezzar in this way. Nebuchadnezzar will be driven away from his people and live with the wild animals (v. 25a). This will be for a period of 'seven times' (seven years) until he acknowledges the sovereignty of God (v. 25b). The stump of the tree and the roots that were left mean that once Nebuchadnezzar has acknowledged that God rules, his kingdom will be given back (v. 26). Daniel's interpretation concludes with a call to Nebuchadnezzar to repent of his sins (v. 27a), not just words, but a changed life and behaviour (v. 27b). Daniel here is at one with prophets like Amos in his insistence that true worship must be accompanied by justice and mercy. These are the evidences of genuine repentance and faith. While it is clear what Nebuchadnezzar must do God will always have the last word: 'It may be then that your prosperity will continue' (v. 27c).

(5) The dream is fulfilled and Nebuchadnezzar is brought to repentance (vv. 28-33)

The dream is fulfilled, but not until twelve months later (v. 29). Through that twelve-month period there is no mention of repentance. Nebuchadnezzar is complacent rather than repentant. The text emphasises his prosperity and sense of power: 'Is not this the great Babylon I have built as the royal residence, by my mighty power and for the glory of my majesty?' (v. 30) Nebuchadnezzar's voice (the voice from earth) is immediately contrasted with the voice from heaven (v. 31a). The judgement pronounced (v. 31b) is carried out swiftly (vv. 32-33). The mighty king Nebuchadnezzar is utterly humbled – his power, dignity, sanity, humanity taken from him. Commentators discuss at length what particular illness or condition affected Nebuchadnezzar. A credible suggestion is a type of madness called lycanthropy. The precise diagnosis of his condition matters less than the fact that God humbled him.

(6) Nebuchadnezzar's psalm of praise following his conversion, and his restoration (vv. 34-37)

The phrase 'At the end of that time' (v. 34) emphasises an important theme in the book – God's control of times and seasons. When God's judgement on Nebuchadnezzar had achieved its intended purpose, it is not prolonged needlessly. 'At the end of that time, I, Nebuchadnezzar, raised my eyes towards heaven, and my sanity was restored' (v. 34a). He is no longer looking down over the city, surveying all he has power over (vv. 29-30), he is looking up toward heaven to the one who has power over him. The upward look reveals a change of heart, repentance

and faith. This is followed by a wonderful hymn of praise
to God (vv. 34b-35):

> 'Then I praised the Most High; I honoured and
>   glorified him who lives for ever.
>   His dominion is an eternal dominion;
>   his kingdom endures from
>   generation to generation.
>   All the peoples of the earth
>   are regarded as nothing.
>   He does as he pleases
>   with the powers of heaven
>   and the peoples of the earth.
>   No-one can hold back his hand
>   or say to him: "What have you done?".'
>
>   (4:34b-35)

The language here echoes the Psalms (e.g. Ps. 145:13;
115:3) and the great Prophets (e.g. Isa. 14:27; 40:17). It is
the testimony of a man who has clearly been converted. It
is a paraphrase of the message of the book of Daniel – God
rules, is building an everlasting Kingdom, and calls people
to live in light of that fact.

Having come to recognise that God rules, Nebuchadnezzar's sanity, honour and splendour are restored to him,
his power and kingdom even greater than before (v. 36).
Nebuchadnezzar's final words in the book are a powerful
testimony from a changed man: 'Now I, Nebuchadnezzar,
praise and exalt and glorify the King of heaven, because
everything he does is right and all his ways are just. And
those who walk in pride he is able to humble' (v. 37). They
are a greater testimony to the God who changed him, the
God who rules in salvation.

From text to message

(1) Get the message clear

i) Big idea

God rules in salvation, bringing Nebuchadnezzar to saving faith.

ii) Key questions

Preaching or teaching on this passage should answer the following questions:

- What is God's power like?
- What is human power like?
- Why did God save Nebuchadnezzar?
- What does this tell us about God?
- How does God save Nebuchadnezzar?
- How long did it take to save Nebuchadnezzar?
- What does true conversion mean?

(2) Engage the hearer

i) Point of contact

We live in a celebrity culture, in the Church (sadly) as well as in the world. We love to parade celebrities at evangelistic events and hear the stories of their conversion. Footballers, film stars or ex-criminals are certain to draw a crowd. At one level it is a great witness to the transforming power and purposes of God to have clear Christians in prominent roles. Yet there is always the danger that the focus is more on the celebrity than the Saviour.

In Nebuchadnezzar we have the ultimate celebrity conversion, yet the text of Daniel keeps the spotlight firmly on God. As we reflect on who Nebuchadnezzar was, how he opposed God and His people, the astonishing events that led to his conversion, the relentlessness of God's grace, we learn much about God's rule in salvation. Like Saul's conversion in the New Testament, God is powerful to save and His purposes will not be hindered by anyone.

ii) Dominant pictures / illustrations

The dominant picture is of the impossibility (humanly speaking) of Nebuchadnezzar's conversion. The fact that someone so opposed to God and His people was converted is remarkable. How could God change his heart and why would He want to?

Another dominant picture is the contrast between human power and God's power (a recurring theme through the book). The fragility of human power and pretentions is exposed. This is true of individuals, institutions, companies, governments, kingdoms and nations. As individuals (the focus here is on Nebuchadnezzar) building our careers, houses, bank balances can bring a false sense of security. We can become complacent and proud of our achievements and empires we build, however large or small. God can take it all from us in an instant. In contrast to the fragility of human power and pretentions stands God in His awesome power. The picture of God here is frightening. He sees all and will have His way.

In terms of the specifics of Nebuchadnezzar's conversion there are some interesting perspectives, not least the length of time. God's timing is rarely our timing.

Nebuchadnezzar's humbling is a powerful picture of the true nature of repentance. Having repented and believed Nebuchadnezzar looking to heaven is a powerful picture of the orientation of true faith.

(3) *Work on application*

- The key application is God's sovereignty in salvation. Nebuchadnezzar's conversion reveals God's sovereign power. This mighty king is humbled before Almighty God.

- God's sovereignty in salvation means that He is powerful enough to save anyone. Nebuchadnezzar ranks among the chief antagonists to God and His people, yet God saved him. Saul in the New Testament is similar – the principal antagonist to the gospel became the principal evangelist. This gives us confidence in our evangelism. Even the most unlikely people, family and friends who are opposed to the gospel, can be converted.

- God has the right to choose who He converts. In our personal evangelism we should not limit God to who we would choose as converts.

- God sees the big picture and works on a timescale that is often much longer than we would like. We also need to be patient allowing God to work in people's lives in His time.

- God will build His Kingdom, and nothing and no-one will stop that. When individuals oppose God and His people He can convert them to advance His cause. Sometimes this happens in very dramatic ways like Nebuchadnezzar and Saul. In the life of a local church, God can convert the most implacable opponents to the gospel. God can convert people to advance His cause. God can also judge them and remove them as we'll see in chapter 5.

- God's kindness and mercy in saving people is an important application. Nebuchadnezzar did not deserve salvation. In truth, none of us do. It might be helpful in application to work through the book tracing God's dealings with Nebuchadnezzar in order to build a picture of God's rule in salvation and the extent of His grace. In this regard it will be important to summarise all that Nebuchadnezzar did to oppose God and His people as well as the different ways God revealed the truth to Nebuchadnezzar.

- In applying the passage it is important to alert people to the fragility of human power. Power leads to complacency, pride and a sense of self-reliance. Human power is fragile, however, and can be taken from us in an instant. Sometimes God does that to humble us. In the end it happens for everyone when they die. We take nothing from this life except faith in Jesus or none. In preaching or teaching on this passage we want to impress on people the need to acknowledge God's rule now while there is time. We want to warn people against complacency and the fact that possessions and power blind us from recognising the truth.

- It is important to emphasise the futility of human wisdom when it comes to understanding ultimate truth. Only God can reveal ultimate truth.

- With an eye to what follows in chapter 5, we want to warn people of the dangers of presuming on God's grace or putting off making a decision. God may keep giving them opportunities to repent or be swift in His judgement. God rules in salvation. God rules in judgement.

- This passage helps us understand and explain the true nature of conversion – humility before God and genuine repentance. Becoming a Christian is not a lifestyle choice. It is a sober realisation of sin under the conviction of the Holy Spirit that leads to repentance and faith. We need to be clear on what the gospel is and what we tell people.

Outline for a sermon or talk

We suggest two possible ways of preaching Daniel 4. The first outline takes a thematic approach tracing God's dealings with Nebuchadnezzar through the book culminating with his conversion here in Daniel 4.

The second outline follows the structure of Daniel 4, focusing on Nebuchadnezzar's testimony.

An outline is included in the next chapter that takes Daniel 4 and 5 together.

Outline 1

Title: God rules in salvation: Nebuchadnezzar's conversion
Text: Daniel 4

Structure:

(1) God and Nebuchadnezzar (Chs. 1–3)

    i) Nebuchadnezzar's opposition to God / God's people

    ii) God's revelation to Nebuchadnezzar

(2) Nebuchadnezzar's conversion (Ch. 4)

    i) His pride

    ii) His humbling

iii) His repentance and conversion

iv) His restoration

(3) God rules in salvation

Under the third point you would draw out a number of applications.

Outline 2

Title: A testimony of conversion
Text: Daniel 4

Structure:

(1) Introduction (vv. 1-3)

(2) Awareness of God but still relying on superstition (vv. 4-8)

Nebuchadnezzar is genuinely interested in God but is looking in the wrong places.

(3) Seeing God's purposes (vv. 9-27)

Nebuchadnezzar sees clearly God's purposes and what he must do.

(4) Ignoring God's warning and suffering the consequences (vv. 28-33)

Nebuchadnezzar's complacency will not lead him to repentance and he is humbled by God.

(5) Bowing to God and accepting His grace (vv. 34-37)

Nebuchadnezzar is brought to true repentance, conversion and restoration.

The notes in the outline are included by way of explanation.

Bible study on Daniel 4

A Bible study is included in the next chapter that takes Daniel 4 and 5 together.

Read chapter 4

(1) Introduce the issues

    i) From a first reading of the chapter, what do you think is the key message for believers?

    ii) From a first reading of the chapter, what do you think is the key message for unbelievers?

(2) Study the passage

    i) Trace God's dealings with Nebuchadnezzar up to this point in the narrative.

    ii) Given his previous experience, why does Nebuchadnezzar summon first the wise men of Babylon (magicians, enchanters, astrologers and diviners)? (vv. 4-8)

    iii) What is the meaning of the dream? (vv. 9-27)

    v) Why does Nebuchadnezzar do nothing for a year? (vv. 28-30)

    vi) What happens to Nebuchadnezzar? (vv. 31-33)

    vii) How does the passage describe his repentance and faith and what does he testify about God? (vv. 34-37)

(3) Apply the passage

    i) What do we learn from this chapter (and God's dealings with Nebuchadnezzar throughout the book) about God's sovereignty in salvation?

ii) How does this encourage us in terms of the
advance of God's Kingdom?

iii) How does this encourage us in evangelism?

iv) What do we learn about human power and pride?

v) What do we learn about human wisdom?

vi) What do we learn about the true nature of
conversion?

(4) *Pray it through*

6

GOD RULES IN SALVATION:
BELSHAZZAR'S JUDGEMENT
(DANIEL 4 AND 5)

Setting in context

(1) Dating

The focus of Daniel 5 is Belshazzar. The text refers to 'Nebuchadnezzar his father' (v. 2). Belshazzar's father was Nabonidus and Nebuchadnezzar his father (i.e. Belshazzar's grandfather). This is not a textual error. The Bible, and other ancient texts, often use 'father' and 'son' in the sense of descendants.

Nebuchadnezzar reigned from 605–562 B.C., his son Nabonidus from 556–539 B.C., with Belshazzar as co-regent with his father from 552–539 B.C. The events described in this chapter take place on the last night of Belshazzar's life and the Babylonian dynasty. Verse 30 is a date marker: 'That very night Belshazzar, king of the Babylonians, was slain, and Darius the Mede took over his kingdom at the age of sixty-two.' The year is 539 B.C., the same year Cyrus decreed that the Exile should come to an end (2 Chron. 36:22-23; Ezra 1:1-4; Isa. 45:1). We assume that Darius / Cyrus is the same person.

(2) Context – structure of book

Chapters 4 and 5 are at the heart of the Aramaic section of the book (Fig. 1). The Aramaic section is of universal significance, a message for all people, unbelievers as well as believers.

Fig. 1 Chiastic structure of Aramaic section

  a Ch. 2   Prophetic vision of four-part statue, rock and mountain

    b Ch. 3   God delivers His people from the furnace

      c Ch. 4   God saves Nebuchadnezzar

      c Ch. 5   God judges Belshazzar

    b Ch. 6   God delivers Daniel from the lions' den

  a Ch. 7   Prophetic vision of four beasts, Ancient of Days and son of man

There are clear structural parallels between chapters 4 and 5 (Fig. 2).

Fig. 2 Parallels between chapters 4 and 5

Ch. 4 Nebuchadnezzar's conversion	Ch. 5 Belshazzar's judgement
Dream (*vv. 4-18*)	Writing on the wall (*vv. 5-16*)
Interpretation (*vv. 19-27*)	Interpretation (*vv. 17-28*)
Fulfilment (*vv. 28-33*)	Fulfilment (*vv. 29-31*)

(3) Context – message of book

The message of Daniel is that *God rules, is building an everlasting Kingdom, and calls people to live in light of that fact*. A key aspect of God's rule is His sovereignty in salvation. In Daniel 4 God's sovereignty in salvation is seen in Nebuchadnezzar's conversion. That is contrasted here in Daniel 5 with God's judgement on Belshazzar.

Daniel 5 also marks the end of the Babylonian dynasty. God rules over nations and kingdoms. Human kingdoms and rulers rise and fall but God will build an everlasting Kingdom under the rule of His all-powerful King.

While Daniel was at the heart of political life in Babylon during the reign of Nebuchadnezzar, and had seen Nebuchadnezzar wonderfully converted, the reign of Belshazzar was very different. Daniel was marginalized for over twenty years, until he is recalled here right at the end of Belshazzar's reign to interpret the writing on the wall. He is remembered by the Queen Mother, but forgotten by Belshazzar (vv. 11-12). The call to God's people to live distinctively is just as much for the years of obscurity in the background, as it is in the days of prominence when the major tests come. This is the realism of a book like Daniel.

The reign of Belshazzar was a bleak time for Daniel and God's people. Two of the prophetic visions recorded in Daniel 7-12 were received at the beginning of Belshazzar's reign (Chs. 7 and 8).

Working on the text

The text is carefully constructed. It begins with Belshazzar's arrogance and ends with his downfall, with the bulk of the text explaining the reasons for his demise. The structure is as follows:

(1) Belshazzar's blasphemous pride (vv. 1-4)

(2) The writing on the wall exposes the futility of human power and wisdom (vv. 5-9)

(3) Daniel, marginalized under Belshazzar, is brought to his attention (vv. 10-12)

(4) Daniel brings the word of God to Belshazzar, indicating that his time for repentance is past (vv. 13-24)

(5) Daniel interprets the writing on the wall, pronouncing judgement on Belshazzar and the Babylonian kingdom (vv. 25-28)

(6) Belshazzar is slain and the Babylonian kingdom falls (vv. 29-31)

(1) *Belshazzar's blasphemous pride (vv. 1-4)*

Verse 1 describes a great banquet. The writer's reference to drinking is intended to convey the drunken revelry of the scene. A contrast is immediately drawn with Nebuchadnezzar (at least the Nebuchadnezzar of Daniel 4). Moreover, Belshazzar's irresponsibility as a ruler is implied. If his Babylonia kingdom fell to the Medo-Persian kingdom that night (v. 30), they must have been encamped at the city gates. A drunken party is hardly appropriate. Belshazzar is a feckless and unworthy king.

What is described in verses 2-4 is far worse than revelry. It is blasphemy and sacrilege. Belshazzar has the articles (vessels) that were taken from the temple in Jerusalem at the start of the Exile (1:2) brought out so they can drink from them. As they drink they praise the pagan gods of gold and silver, of bronze, iron, wood and stone. It is easy to imagine the ribald laughter. After all, Jerusalem is a desolate ruin and any 'god' who allowed that cannot be much of a god! As they praised the pagan gods, there is a clear connection in the writer's mind with the materials in the statue in chapter 2. God brought that crashing down. And God will bring Belshazzar down. Nebuchadnezzar's words at the end of Daniel 4 echo powerfully: 'And those who walk in pride he is able to humble' (4:37b).

A comment about the articles from the temple and their significance in Daniel. Nebuchadnezzar had taken the vessels from the temple in Jerusalem and put them in the temple of his god in Babylon (1:2). It was an arrogant statement from Nebuchadnezzar that he was more powerful than God. And that's what it looked like. The vessels were in his temple in Babylon. Jerusalem, the city of God, and its temple lay in ruins. Yet appearances mask reality. The key phrase at the beginning of the book 'the Lord delivered' (1:2) applies not only to God's people but to the articles from the temple. It is God who delivered the vessels into Nebuchadnezzar's hand. It is God who delivered His people into exile. God is in control. God rules. Therefore, the presence of the articles in the temple in Babylon symbolises God's presence in Babylon, challenging its beliefs and worldviews, building His Kingdom and revealing His absolute authority.

(2) *The writing on the wall exposes the futility of human power and wisdom (vv. 5-9)*

What happens next is dramatic. Verse 5: 'Suddenly the fingers of a human hand appeared and wrote on the plaster of the wall, near the lampstand in the royal palace. The king watched the hand as it wrote. His face turned pale and he was so frightened that his knees knocked together and his legs gave way' (vv. 5-6). This reads like an eye-witness account. The finger / hand of God is referred to a number of times in Scripture, for example in Exodus 8:19. Belshazzar's reaction (vividly described) is terror as the finger of God writes the verdict on his life (v. 6). He summons the wise men of Babylon promising great rewards if they can read the writing and tell him what it means (v. 7). These enchanters, astrologers and diviners (human wisdom) have appeared throughout the book, summoned by the kings to interpret dreams and visions (2:1-13; 4:4-8). Belshazzar's promise of lavish rewards is reminiscent of a similar promise made by Nebuchadnezzar in 2:6. Belshazzar's reference to 'the third highest ruler in the kingdom' (v. 7b) is an accurate statement of historical fact – Belshazzar ruled as co-regent with his father Nabonidus. As on previous occasions, the wise men of Babylon are unable to interpret (v. 8). Their abject failure on each occasion exposes the futility of human wisdom in matters of ultimate truth. They are baffled and Belshazzar is terrified (v. 9).

(3) Daniel, marginalized under Belshazzar, is brought to his attention (vv. 10-12)

The impasse is broken by the intervention of a new character who takes charge with calm authority (v. 10). This cannot be Belshazzar's queen, for his wives are mentioned in verse 3. The word 'queen' could just as accurately be translated 'queen mother'. She is clearly a senior figure whose memory goes back to the early years of Nebuchadnezzar's reign. It may be that she was the wife of Nabonidus and thus Belshazzar's own mother. In any case she was someone who could enter the royal presence uninvited.

Her words are a reminder of the earlier chapters and Daniel's significant role (vv. 11-12). She speaks of Daniel's outstanding abilities and educational achievements, but most importantly of his God-given power to 'interpret dreams, explain riddles and solve difficult problems' (v. 12). The queen's dignity, wise advice and air of quiet authority is in sharp contrast to the drunken, discredited court. We are left wondering whether she knew the true God, but the spotlight quickly passes from her and focuses again on Daniel.

(4) Daniel brings the word of God to Belshazzar, indicating that his time for repentance is past (vv. 13-24)

So far the narrative has moved rapidly. The pace now slows as Daniel interprets not only the writing, but the wider significance of the events that have led to God's judgement on Belshazzar. Verses 13-15 remind us of some of the earlier detail. This is not simply repetition, but a further insight into Belshazzar's world-view. He refers to Daniel in a similar way to the queen, with one important difference. Belshazzar refers to Daniel as one of the 'exiles' brought from Judah (v. 13). This is revealing. Belshazzar has no understanding of where true power lies and that human power is given by God. It may be that he had known about Daniel all along (although he pretended not to) and only turned to him because he was desperate. He promises the same rewards to Daniel as he did to the wise men (v. 16). He still thinks he is the one who gives power even though his power is about to be taken from him (along with the Babylonian kingdom) by the ultimate power and authority – God.

In Daniel's dealings with Nebuchadnezzar he was courteous and gracious (2:16, 26-28; 4:19-27). His manner with Belshazzar is brusque (v. 17). It is judgement time. This is similar to Elijah's words to Ahab in 1 Kings 21:20-24 and

Amos' pronouncement of judgement on Israel: Then the Lord said to me, 'The time is ripe for my people Israel; I will spare them no longer.' (Amos 8:2)

Daniel also makes it clear that God's wisdom cannot be bought (see also Num. 22:15-18 and the story of Balaam).

From verse 18, Daniel compares Belshazzar with Nebuchadnezzar. This makes explicit the intended link between chapters 4 and 5, as these two kings are presented in contrasting ways. Daniel's summary of the reign of Nebuchadnezzar focuses first on the greatness of the power God gave him (vv. 18-19), but then, because of his arrogance and pride how God humbled him leading to his eventual repentance and conversion (vv. 20-21). Again, this is not repetition without good reason. It emphasises the key message of the book – God rules and calls all people to live in light of that fact.

Belshazzar is judged because he knew all this about Nebuchadnezzar and yet refused to humble himself before God (v. 22). He had ample opportunity to repent, but refused. And now that opportunity has gone. In spite of what he knew, Belshazzar has set himself against God. His final act of defiance taking the vessels from the temple, drinking from them and praising the gods of silver and gold, bronze, iron, wood and stone, seals his fate (v. 23). These gods are dead, but the living God of heaven, whom he would not honour, holds his life in His hands.

(5) Daniel interprets the writing on the wall,
    pronouncing judgement on Belshazzar and
    the Babylonian kingdom (vv. 25-28)

Once again, the art of the storyteller is superb at building suspense. Although the reader is aware of what is at stake, only now are we told what was written on the wall and its meaning. The inscription, written in Aramaic is MENE, MENE, TEKEL, and PARSIN (v. 25). The meaning is given in verse 26.

Mene refers to the 'numbering' or 'appointing' of Belshazzar's days. The God of heaven who has numbered the days of his reign is about to bring them to an end. Many scriptural references come to mind, for example, Psalm 90: 'Teach us to number our days aright, that we may gain a heart of wisdom.' (Ps. 90:12)

Tekel means that weighed in God's scales, Belshazzar's life was weightless and amounted to nothing. Weighing on scales suggests that a just judgement is being imposed. Belshazzar is a perfect illustration of Psalm 62: 'if weighed on a balance, they are nothing; together they are only a breath.' (Ps. 62:9) Belshazzar is accountable to God and without excuse having ignored repeated warnings and continued in arrogant defiance to the end.

Peres means 'shared, divided out' and signals the end of the Babylonian kingdom. It will fall to the Medo-Persian kingdom. The alert reader will notice the familiar word 'given'. Power is given to the Medo-Persian kingdom. They are God's agent in bringing down Babylon. And in time they too will fall.

(6) Belshazzar is slain and the Babylonian kingdom falls (vv. 29-31)

The chapter ends with Belshazzar rewarding Daniel (v. 29), the death of Belshazzar that very night (v. 30) and the fall of Babylon to the Medo-Persian kingdom. Verse 29 is striking. We might have expected some sense of repentance or realisation from Belshazzar, yet there is none. He behaves as if he is still the powerful ruler. 'That very night' (v. 30) indicates the swiftness of God's judgement. The tiny detail of Darius' age confirms this is fact, not fiction (v. 31).

The fall of Babylon to the Medo-Persian kingdom is prophesied in Isaiah 13 and 14. Similarly, Jeremiah speaks of enemies from the north (Jer. 50:9) and the destruction of the city (Jer. 51:54ff). In Daniel, the dream of the four-part statue (Ch. 2) and the vision of the four beasts (Ch. 7) are being fulfilled as the second kingdom (Medo-Persia) replaces the first (Babylon).

The fall of Babylon to the Medo-Persian kingdom would bring about the end of the Exile. God's people will return to Jerusalem and the articles will be returned to the temple. No individual or kingdom will prevent God building His Kingdom. God rules.

From text to message

(1) Get the message clear

i) Big idea
God rules in salvation, judging Belshazzar, taking his life, and giving the Babylonian kingdom to the Medo-Persians.

ii) Key questions
- What is God's power like?
- What is human power like?
- Why did God judge Belshazzar?
- What does this tell us about God?
- What opportunity did Belshazzar have to repent?

(2) Engage the hearer

i) Point of contact

One of the attractions in Stratford upon Avon was 'The Elizabethan Experience' in a building opposite the Royal Shakespeare Theatre. It was a brilliantly conceived and executed multi–media display using colour, speech, music and drama that brought to life Elizabethan England, especially a visit of Queen Elizabeth I to Kenilworth, passing through Stratford when Shakespeare was a boy. As the show came to an end, the lights dimmed one by one, with the final scene an eerie, haunting darkness in which echoed the last words of the great speech on the seven ages of man in *As You Like It*: 'mere oblivion, sans teeth, sans eyes, sans taste, sans everything'. In such an atmosphere little imagination was needed to be acutely conscious of the uncertainty and brevity of life. That is the atmosphere which broods over Daniel 5 as Belshazzar and his Babylonian kingdom meet their end.

ii) Dominant pictures / illustrations

The events described in Daniel 5 have captured the imagination of artists like Rembrandt and musicians such as Walton. The drama is intense and frightening.

The dominant picture is of the decisiveness and finality of God's judgement – from a scene of drunken indulgence and flagrant idolatry to death and destruction in one night.

The writing on the wall and the interpretation is a powerful picture of God numbering our days, weighing our lives on the scales of justice and pronouncing His verdict.

Another dominant picture is the contrast between human power and God's power (a recurring theme through the book). The fragility of human power and pretentions is exposed. Whether individuals, institutions, companies, governments, kingdoms or nations, this can lead to complacency, arrogance and pride. God can take it all from us in an instant. His purposes may be to save us or to judge us. That is His sovereign prerogative. In contrast to the fragility of human power and pretentions stands God in His awesome power. The picture of God here is frightening. He sees all and will have His way.

(3) Work on application

- The key application is God's sovereignty in salvation. God's judgement on Belshazzar reveals God's sovereign power. This arrogant king is judged by God who rules.

- Belshazzar's judgement is in sharp contrast to Nebuchadnezzar's conversion. God may save those who oppose Him, but He may judge them. This reveals God's sovereignty.

- God will build His Kingdom, and nothing and no-one will stop that. When individuals oppose God and His people He can convert them to advance His cause (like Nebuchadnezzar) or He can judge them and remove them (like Belshazzar). Likewise with institutions, regimes and dynasties, God can remove them, change power structures as He controls the progress of history. The same is true of the Church. Churches that are faithful to His word and the gospel He will use to further His Kingdom; those that are not, in the end He will judge.

- The chapter teaches us that God will hold us accountable for what we have seen and heard.

For example, if someone grows up in a Christian home or a living church, or perhaps attends a living church for a while and hears the gospel, God will hold them accountable.

- God's kindness and mercy in saving people is an important application of the previous chapter. God's severity in judgement is an important application here. In the end God will judge all those who reject Him and refuse to repent. In applying the passage we need to warn people of the dangers of presuming on God's grace or putting off making a decision. God may keep giving them opportunities to repent or be swift in His judgement. In Nebuchadnezzar (Ch. 4) we see a man who was nearly lost but in the end repented and believed. In Belshazzar (Ch. 5) we have a sober warning that people can go too far in rejecting God and pass a point of no return. Paul's frightening words in Romans 1 come to mind as God 'gave them over' (Rom. 1:24, 26, 28).

- In applying the passage it is important to alert people to the fragility of human power and pretentions. Power leads to complacency, pride and a sense of self-reliance. Human power is fragile, however, and can be taken from us in an instant. In the end it happens for everyone when they die. We take nothing from this life except faith in Jesus or none. In preaching or teaching on this passage we want to impress on people the need to acknowledge God's rule now while there is time. We want to warn people against complacency and the fact that possessions and power blind us from recognising the truth.

- It is important to emphasise the futility of human wisdom when it comes to understanding ultimate truth. Only God can reveal ultimate truth.

- Teaching this chapter should impress on people urgency in evangelism.

Outline for a sermon or talk

The outline is based on the structure of Daniel 5. A second outline takes Daniel 4 and 5 together.

Outline 1

Title: **God rules in salvation: Belshazzar's judgement (or The writing on the wall)**

Text: **Daniel 5**

Structure:

(1) A blasphemous party (vv. 1-4)

  i) *Human recklessness*

  ii) *Blasphemy*

(2) A terrifying portent (vv. 5-12)

  i) *God breaks in*

  ii) *Futility of human wisdom*

  iii) *Where the answer is to be found*

(3) A devastating judgement (vv. 13-31)

  i) *A lifetime of opportunity*

  ii) *A hard heart*

  iii) *God's judgement pronounced*

  iv) *God's judgement executed*

Outline 2 (Dan. 4 and 5 together)

Title: *God rules in salvation*
Text: *Daniel 4 and 5*

Structure:

(1) God saves (Ch. 4)

    i) Nebuchadnezzar's life

    ii) God saves him

(2) God judges (Ch. 5)

    i) Belshazzar's life

    ii) God judges him

(3) God rules

    i) His sovereignty in salvation

    ii) His Kingdom advances

    iii) Acknowledge His rule

The notes in the outline are included by way of explanation.

Bible study on Daniel 5

Read chapter 5

(1) Introduce the issues

    i) From a first reading of the chapter, what do you think is the key message for believers?

    ii) From a first reading of the chapter, what do you think is the key message for unbelievers?

(2) Study the passage

    i) What is the significance of Belshazzar using the vessels from God's temple in his party (vv. 1-4)?

    ii) What can the wise men of Babylon do for Belshazzar (vv. 7-9)? What does this teach us about human wisdom?

    iii) How do the queen and Belshazzar view Daniel? (vv. 10-16)

    iv) How does Daniel address Belshazzar and what is the significance of this? (v. 17)

    v) What is the background to Belshazzar's judgement? (vv. 18-24)

    vi) What does the writing on the wall mean? (vv. 25-28)

    vii) What do you make of Belshazzar's response? (v. 29)

    viii) God's judgement is swift and final. Do you think it is fair? (vv. 30-31)

(3) *Apply the passage*

    i) What do we learn from this chapter (and God's dealings with Belshazzar) about God's sovereignty in salvation?

    ii) What do we learn about human power and pride?

    iii) What do we learn about human wisdom?

    iv) How does God hold people accountable?

    v) Why will people not repent?

    vi) What does God's judgement mean in the end?

    vii) How does this motivate us in evangelism?

(4) *Pray it through*

Bible study on Daniel 4 and 5

Read chapters 4 and 5

(1) *Introduce the issues*

   i) From a first reading of Daniel chapters 4 and 5, what do we learn about God's sovereignty in salvation?

(2) *Study the passage*

   i) Chapter 4 records the culmination of Nebuchadnezzar's journey to faith. Trace how God reveals Himself to Nebuchadnezzar throughout his life (in Chs. 1, 2, 3 and now here in Ch. 4).

  ii) Why do you think God chooses to save Nebuchadnezzar?

 iii) Verses 34-37 of chapter 4 are a powerful description of 'conversion'. What are the notable features of his 'conversion'?

 iv) In chapter 5, how does Belshazzar defy God? What's the significance of what he does?

  v) God's judgement of Belshazzar is swift and final. Is God fair (compare His dealings with Belshazzar and Nebuchadnezzar)?

(3) *Apply the passage*

   i) Having studied the chapters in detail, consider again question 1 (above) – what do we learn about God's sovereignty in salvation?

   ii) What lessons can we draw from these chapters
      about evangelism?
      a) about God's role and ours
      b) about the importance of evangelism

  iii) What do you think the difference is between
      someone who professes to be a Christian (but
      isn't) and someone who is converted? Think of the
      difference between Nebuchadnezzar's response
      to God's revelation in chapters 1, 2 and 3 with his
      response here in chapter 4.

(4) *Pray it through*

7

LIVING CONSISTENTLY IN
LIGHT OF GOD'S RULE
(DANIEL 6)

Setting in context

(1) Dating

The events described in this chapter take place in 539 B.C., a significant year in the context of the book of Daniel. This is the first year of Darius and the end of the Exile (1:21). The Babylonian kingdom under Belshazzar has fallen to the Medo-Persian kingdom under Darius (5:30-31). We understand Darius / Cyrus to be the same person (6:28). It is possible that the decree referred to in 6:26 is the decree that marked the end of the Exile, allowing the people of God to return to Jerusalem and rebuild the temple (2 Chron. 36:22-23; Ezra 1:1-4; Isa. 45:1). Daniel's prayer in chapter 9 that the Exile would come to an end is also dated as 539 B.C. (9:1). These different events – the change of dynasty, Daniel's return to prominence under Darius, his dramatic deliverance from the lions' den, his prayer for restoration – are all connected in God's plan to bring the Exile to an end.

(2) *Context – structure of book*

As well as the links with chapters 5 and 9, in terms of the chronology of events, chapter 6 is the third of three conflict chapters (Chs. 1, 3 and 6) focusing on Daniel, Hananiah, Mishael and Azariah as they live as exiles in Babylon. In chapter 1 the focus is on all four, in chapter 3 on Hananiah, Mishael and Azariah, but here in chapter 6 the spotlight falls on Daniel.

The structure of the chapters is similar:

- They face pressure to conform.

- They make a decision to live distinctively, in spite of the consequences.

- God miraculously delivers them.

- God advances His Kingdom.

Looking at the three conflict chapters together, they span the entire period of the Exile: chapter 1 at the start; chapter 3 well into the Exile; and chapter 6 right at the end. Significant tests like these come along rarely. For most of the time God's people are called to steady, faithful, distinctive witness. But when the tests do come, the challenge is not to be found wanting.

(3) *Context – message of book*

If the message of the book as a whole is that *God rules*, the purpose of these conflict chapters is to show *how God's people are to live in light of the fact that He rules*. As exiles in the world, God calls His people to live distinctively. To live distinctively is costly, but God's people are to trust God. And as God's people live distinctively, God advances His Kingdom.

While the message of these conflict chapters is similar, there are important differences. In chapter 1, the tone was pretty low key as Daniel and his friends look for an opportunity to make their allegiance known and be open about their faith. Chapters 3 and 6 are much more dramatic. In both cases, God's people face a direct and hostile challenge to their faith: bow down and worship a golden image or be thrown into a furnace (Ch. 3); do not pray to any god or man except Darius or be thrown into a lions' den (Ch. 6). In refusing to comply, Daniel, Hananiah, Mishael and Azariah display great courage. There are, however, a number of subtle differences between chapters 3 and 6. In chapter 3, the antagonist is King Nebuchadnezzar, while in chapter 6 Daniel faces a malicious and devious attack from his fellow state officials. In contrast to Nebuchadnezzar, King Darius does all he can to save Daniel from the lions' den, but is unable to do so. Also, the conspiracy against Daniel in chapter 6 reveals his consistency. His faith pervades every part of his life. His consistency is also evidenced by the fact that he is now a mature man of eighty. Behind him lies a life of faithful, consistent, prayerful witness. This is seen in the way he responds to the king's decree. Quietly and without any fuss he just carries on doing what he has always done. As a man of eighty, it is striking that what is arguably Daniel's greatest test comes along late in life. This is an important message for older Christians to finish well.

Given that chapter 6 is in the Aramaic section of the book (Chs. 2–7), there is also a message here for unbelievers. Like Nebuchadnezzar before him, Darius is an eye-witness to the power of the God of heaven. The power on display here is the miraculous deliverance of Daniel from the lions' den. Not only that, but also the strength of Daniel's faith. Darius must have been powerfully convicted by

Daniel's reaction to the crisis and his confidence in God. The progressive revelation of God to Nebuchadnezzar in chapters 2, 3 and 4 led to his eventual conversion. Here in chapter 6, when King Darius witnesses the power of God in miraculously delivering Daniel from the lions' den, he acknowledges the sovereignty of God in what reads like a psalm of praise (6:25-27) and, in all probability, issued the decree that brought about the end of the Exile.

(4) Parallels with the Gospels

In the Introductory Material 'Getting our Bearings in Daniel' we made the point that we do not consider Daniel a type of Christ in the way that, for example, Joseph, Moses and David are. Daniel is God's Prophet and a model believer who shows what it means to live distinctively in the world. Here in chapter 6, however, there are a number of pointers to / parallels with the passion narratives in the Gospel. First, the parallels between Darius and Pilate. Darius sees that what is happening to Daniel is unjust, yet is unable to save him. Pilate sees that Jesus has committed no crime and yet is constrained from preventing Him going to His cross. Both Daniel and Jesus are innocent, and suffer unjustly. Both maintain silence before their accusers. Both face death, Daniel in the lions' den and Jesus on the cross. Daniel is sealed in the lions' den with a stone. The Lord Jesus, having given His life on a cross, was sealed in a tomb with a stone. At the first light of dawn, Darius hurries to the lions' den. At the first light of dawn, the women hurry to the tomb of Jesus. Daniel walks out of the den unharmed. The Lord Jesus, on resurrection morning, walks out of the tomb, raised to life, having defeated death.

These parallels point us to Christ, and remind us that if we suffer as believers, we are participating in the fellowship of Christ's sufferings (Phil. 3:10). Whatever the cost, whatever suffering we must endure for the sake of the gospel, we can trust in God's promised deliverance. While the principle is true, how God delivers us is for Him to determine. He will certainly give us grace sufficient for the circumstances we face. He may intervene in dramatic ways to deliver us from a particular situation of conflict, or He may not. Ultimately, of course, God's promised deliverance is from death to eternal life. The Christian, trusting in God's promised deliverance, is safe and secure, even if they lose their lives for the sake of the gospel.

Working on the text

The structure of the chapter is as follows:

(1) Daniel faces a malicious and devious attack, the actions of those who oppose him revealing a lifetime of consistent distinctiveness (vv. 1-9)

(2) Daniel continues to do what he has always done, in spite of the consequences (vv. 10-16)

(3) God delivers Daniel from the lions' den (vv. 17-24)

(4) Darius' decree acknowledges the sovereignty of God (vv. 25-28)

The turning point in the text (the key teaching point) is Daniel's reaction to the king's decree (v. 10).

(1) Daniel faces a malicious and devious attack, the actions of those who oppose him revealing a lifetime of consistent distinctiveness (vv. 1-9)

The end of chapter 5 records a change of dynasty. With the death of Belshazzar, the Babylonian dynasty falls to the Medo-Persian kingdom under Darius (5:30-31). A new kingdom, a new king, a whole regime change, and Daniel once more finds himself in a position of authority and influence. Throughout the reign of Belshazzar, Daniel had been marginalized until he was summoned at the queen mother's request to interpret the writing on the wall at Belshazzar's banquet (5:10-12). These events may have brought him to the attention of Darius, but whatever the reason Daniel is back at the heart of political life. Darius appoints 120 satraps (regional governors) with three administrators (provincial governors) over them, one of whom is Daniel (6:1-2). The function of these administrators was to ensure 'that the king might not suffer loss' (6:2). Daniel's job was to safeguard the king's economic prosperity, a job in which, compared to the other administrators and satraps, he so distinguished himself by his exceptional qualities, that Darius planned to set him over the whole kingdom as prime minister (6:3). There are resonances here of chapter 1, where God gifted Daniel and his three friends with exceptional knowledge and ability, such that they stood out in comparison with the others (1:17-20). Daniel's promotion, then and now, was achieved not through political maneuvering, deceit, spin or compromise, but through God-given ability and God-inspired integrity.

Darius' plan to appoint Daniel over the other administrators and satraps met with a hostile reaction from his colleagues. Fuelled by jealousy, they seek to undermine and discredit him. Their first tactic is to find grounds to bring charges against him in respect of his public duties (v. 4a). Their investigation, we can be sure, would have been thorough. Had there been even the slightest hint, or suggestion, of dirt on Daniel, they would have dug it up!

But they can find nothing. Verse 4b is a striking testimony to Daniel's character: 'They could find no corruption in him, because he was trustworthy and neither corrupt nor negligent.' They couldn't touch him in his public and political life, and so there begins to form in their minds a plan they knew would find Daniel out; they would get him on his faith (v. 5). Their plan was to trap him, to force him to choose between his loyalty to his king or to his God. They knew where his ultimate allegiance lay. They knew what he would do. Even in their smug confidence, their absolute certainty that their plan would be a success, they bear testimony to Daniel's conviction. All they had to do was dupe the king. And that was easy. With Darius they played their trump card; they flattered him, playing on his pride. Verse 6: 'So the administrators and the satraps went as a group to the king and said: "O King Darius, live for ever! The royal administrators, prefects, satraps, advisers and governors have all agreed (Daniel, of course, had not agreed, but Darius' pride blinds him to what is going on) that the king should issue an edict and enforce the decree that anyone who prays to any god or man during the next thirty days, except to you, O king, shall be thrown into the lions' den"' (vv. 6-7). And so the decree is issued and, under the laws of the Medes and Persians, cannot be repealed (vv. 8-9). The behaviour of the conspirators stands in stark contrast to Daniel's: his trustworthiness matched by their deceitfulness; his exceptional qualities by their burning, consuming jealousy.

While, at one level, Daniel's colleagues were motivated by jealousy, their tactics reveal the deeper issue. God's people will be oppressed and face hostility precisely because they are the people of God. And the agent of opposition is the Devil himself, the prince of this world, whose power controls fallen humanity. In the New Testament Peter writes: 'Be self-controlled and alert. Your enemy the Devil prowls around like a roaring lion looking for someone to devour. Resist him, standing firm in the faith…' (1 Pet. 5:8-9a). The clear sense we get from the text is of these men prowling around, scheming, manipulating and hunting as a pack (like lions). The recurrent phrase in the text – they 'went as a group' (vv. 6, 11, 15) – is telling. By contrast, Daniel stands against them, alone. Again, this reminds us of Daniel 1 where the young Daniel stands alone (initially at least) (1:8).

(2) Daniel continues to do what he has always done, in spite of the consequences (vv. 10-16)

Verse 10 marks the turning point in the text. As a turning point, it is strikingly un-dramatic! 'Now when Daniel learned that the decree had been published, he went home to his upstairs room where the windows opened towards Jerusalem. Three times a day he got down on his knees and prayed, giving thanks to his God, just as he had done before.' (6:10) His actions reveal his habits, that quiet, faithful, consistent witness throughout his life in Babylon. He simply carries on doing what he has always done. Daniel's mind and heart remained in Jerusalem, not in Babylon, his allegiance to his God never compromised. It is evident, from here and elsewhere, how important prayer is in Daniel's life. His reaction to the crisis in chapter 2 is to ask Nebuchadnezzar for time that he might pray (2:16-17). Here in chapter 6, we observe his daily practice of prayer. And then in chapter 9 (dated in the same year as the events here in chapter 6), we are given an extended example of

Daniel's prayer life. All of this indicates the importance of prayer in his life.

While Daniel simply carries on doing what he has always done, his actions are, of course, in breach of the decree issued by Darius. Daniel was well aware of that and of the penalty, but he would not compromise. For Daniel, it was an expression of where his ultimate allegiance lay. To have ceased to pray to his God, for one day, let alone thirty days, was a line he was not prepared to cross, even if it cost him his life. To have done so would have shifted his allegiance from the King of heaven and His kingdom to the kingdom of this world and its gods. To have done so would have discredited his testimony, his faithful consistent witness over many years. This, of course, is the Devil's tactic. If he could discredit Daniel's testimony now, it would call into question and undermine all that had gone on before.

The conspirators knew where to find Daniel (v. 11), indicative of the fact that his prayer life was not secret, but open. His allegiance to God was a public allegiance. Having observed him at prayer, they report him to the king (vv. 11-16). Notice that they refer to him as 'one of the exiles from Judah' (v. 13) (this is how Belshazzar refers to Daniel in 5:13), indicating their resentment towards Daniel, not because of his political position, but because of his faith. God's people will be oppressed, precisely because they are the people of God. The extended dialogue in these verses between Darius and the conspirators describes the king's attempts to save Daniel. He realizes his mistake, but there is nothing he can do, since the decree has been put in writing, and stands. His final words to Daniel as he is thrown into the lions' den: 'May your God, whom you serve continually, rescue you!' (v. 16b). Although very different in tone, these words echo Nebuchadnezzar's challenge to Shadrach, Meshach and Abednego in 3:15b. Once again the gauntlet is thrown down. How powerful is Daniel's God? Will He be able to rescue him?

(3) God delivers Daniel from the lions' den (vv. 17-24)

Daniel is in the lions' den. Unlike the fiery furnace, we do not see inside the lions' den. What we see is the agitation of King Darius. He returns to his palace, spends the night without eating or entertainment, and cannot sleep (v. 18). Like Nebuchadnezzar in 2:1, Darius is both disturbed and sleepless. He was, we can infer, conscious to some extent at least of a greater power at work. To say that he was under the conviction of God is perhaps going too far, but there is something there, a troubled spirit. At first light of dawn, he hurries to the den and cries out in an anguished voice: 'Daniel, servant of the living God, has your God, whom you serve continually, been able to rescue you from the lions?' (v. 20). Wonderfully, the answer is yes, as Daniel answers from the den that he has been protected by an angel sent from God, who shut the mouths of the lions (vv. 21-22a). Notice the reason Daniel gives. God delivers him because he was found innocent in the sight of God (v. 22b). That is the primary reason for his deliverance, the fact of his innocence before King Darius is secondary. Overjoyed, Darius orders that Daniel be lifted out of the den and he is found to be unharmed, without even a scratch, because he had trusted in his God (v. 23b). The parallels with chapter 3 are clear, with God's servants miraculously delivered, unharmed.

The fate of those who had falsely accused Daniel (v. 24) is sobering.

(4) Darius' decree acknowledges the sovereignty of God (vv. 25-28)

Darius' reaction (vv. 25-28) is similar to Nebuchadnezzar's reaction in chapter 2 (vv. 46-49), chapter 3 (vv. 28-30) and chapter 4 (vv. 34-35) – some recognition of, and humility before, the sovereignty of God, and the reward of God's servants. In both chapters 3 and 6, the kings' initial decrees, indicative of the futility of human wisdom and human power (the decree to worship the image of gold in chapter 3, and the decree to worship no other man or god but Darius, here in Ch. 6) are replaced with decrees calling on all people to fear and show reverence to the God of Daniel. As indicated earlier, it is possible that the decree referred to here in 6:26, is the decree that marked the end of the Exile, allowing the people of God to return to Jerusalem and rebuild the temple. Darius' psalm of praise to God (6:26b-27) is very similar to Nebuchadnezzar's in 4:34-35. Both kings acknowledge God's eternal dominion and His total sovereignty. It is remarkable that these testimonies come from the lips of pagan kings. God's rule is powerfully evident in bringing these people to faith.

From text to message

(1) Get the message clear

i) Big idea
In light of the fact that God rules, God expects His people to live distinctively, showing their allegiance to Him. There are times when that requires a bold and courageous stand. Living a consistent life will enable us to do so.

ii) Key questions
Preaching or teaching on this passage should answer the following questions:

- What does it mean for a Christian to live a consistent life?

- What kind of opposition, hostility and malicious attacks do we face as Christians from those who seek to undermine us?

- What kind of direct and hostile challenges to our faith do we face as Christians today?

- In such circumstances, what does God expect from us?

- What can we expect from God?

(2) Engage the hearer

i) Point of contact

Famously remembered for his gold medal in the quarter-mile at the 1924 Paris Olympic Games, Eric Liddell's success was all the more prominent because of his refusal to run in his favoured event, the 100 yards, because the heats were on a Sunday. A newspaper at the time reported an interview with Liddell, where he was asked the secret of his success in the quarter-mile. His answer: 'For the first two hundred yards I run as hard as I can. The next hundred, with God's help, I run harder. The final stretch, I set my sights on the line, looking neither to the left, nor the right, until I break the tape. One glance sideways on the closing straight and the race is lost!' One of the important messages in this chapter is for older Christians to keep on running the race and finish well.

ii) Dominant pictures / illustrations

The events in Daniel 6 take place in the year 539 B.C., nearly seventy years after Daniel and his friends were taken, as teenagers, into exile in Babylon. Daniel is therefore an old man of eighty, and not the young lad depicted in so many children's Bibles sitting down next to the cuddly lions! He's a mature man, a mature believer, with a lifetime of unbroken testimony behind him. And now he is faced with perhaps the greatest test of his life. Where does his true allegiance lie? Will his testimony remain intact, or will he flinch and compromise? Will he finish well?

(3) Work on application

- The Devil's tactics are timeless. He prowls around looking to devour us, to discredit our testimony and witness (1 Pet. 5:8). It is important to emphasise that the Devil is real. He is a powerful divine being, directing the opposition and persecution we face as Christians. His attack may be directed at any area of our life – our work, our personal life, our family life, our spiritual life.

- Both here and in chapter 3, Daniel and his companions face a direct challenge to their faith: bow down to the golden image or die (Ch. 3); do not pray to any god or man except King Darius or die (Ch. 6). While the pressure we face in the West is more about assimilation of the culture than direct authoritarian compliance, our Christian brothers and sisters in the Persecuted Church around the world do face this kind of persecution. And in the West we are beginning to see the first signs of direct pressure being put on Christians to conform to a secular agenda, pressure from outside the Church and pressure from inside the major denominations.

- The conspiracy against Daniel reveals his consistency, a powerful example of someone whose faith pervades every aspect of their life. This is an important line of application, encouraging Christians to live out their faith in every area. To live distinctive lives in the world (1 Pet. 2:11-12) embraces our work, social lives, family lives as well as church life.

- Another aspect of Daniel's consistency is his lifetime of steady, faithful witness. It will be helpful in application to reflect briefly on his biography: his decision as a young man to make his allegiance to God known; his faithful witness during the reign of Nebuchadnezzar; his faithfulness during the years he was marginalized under Belshazzar, which meant that when the time came for God to use him he was ready; his faithfulness as an old man of eighty not to compromise when the tough test came.

- Daniel's prayer life is also revealing. There is evidence of this throughout the book, for example in chapters 2 and 9. But here in chapter 6 it is his daily devotional habits that we see, where three times a day he prayed (v. 11). The discipline of daily devotions, the regularity of quiet times, is important for every Christian.

- While Daniel 6 is, of course, relevant to Christians of any age, there is an obvious application to older Christians. For Daniel the toughest test came late in life. Surely it is too much to expect a man of Daniel's age to make such a costly and courageous stand? If Daniel had compromised, his lifetime of consistent witness would have been discredited. Encourage older Christians to keep on running the race and finish well (Phil. 3:13-15).

- Again, it is important to remember that God is the hero of the story, not Daniel. For sure, Daniel is a great example and inspiration, but the reason he acted the way he did was because of his trust and confidence in God. Daniel lived in light of the fact that God rules. God was Daniel's inspiration, and Daniel's God, not Daniel, should be our primary inspiration. We should not be too quick to view Daniel as an exceptional believer, but rather as someone who is an example for us all to follow.

- The manner in which Daniel took his stand in defiance of the king's decree is striking. In contrast to Hananiah, Mishael and Azariah in chapter 3, whose approach was bold and defiant in the face of the king, Daniel's reaction to the decree is simply to carry on doing what he has always done and go to his room to pray (v. 10). Again, we need to beware evaluating the relative merits of these approaches. Both have their place; neither is more courageous than the other. God-given wisdom is necessary to determine which is appropriate given the circumstances.

- Daniel took his stand trusting in God's promise of deliverance. While the principle is true, and we are to trust in God's promised deliverance, how God delivers us is for Him to determine. He will certainly give us grace sufficient for the circumstances we face.

He may intervene in dramatic ways to deliver us from a particular situation of conflict. Ultimately, of course, God's promised deliverance is from death to eternal life. The Christian, trusting in God's promised deliverance is safe and secure, even if they lose their lives for the sake of the gospel.

- As we live distinctively as Christians showing our allegiance to God, His Kingdom advances. Again, while the principle is true, how God advances His Kingdom through our witness is for Him to determine. He may put us in a position of influence or not. He may use us significantly or not. It is striking that the events here transpire to bring about the end of the Exile. This dramatic change in the circumstances of the people of God (a time of renewal / revival) is brought about by Daniel doing what he has always done, praying to his God. The point is that God calls His people to consistent faithfulness. How God chooses to use our witness is for Him to determine.

- In applying this passage to unbelievers, a key point to make is that the events described are factual history in the same way that the miracles in the Gospels are factual history. Use these events to point forward to Jesus and the greatest miracle of all, His resurrection from the dead. Ask people what they make of the events described.

Outline for a sermon or talk

Once again, the structure of Daniel 6 is relatively straight-forward, and we would suggest an outline that reflects this structure.

Title: Living consistently in light of God's rule
Text: Daniel 6

Structure:

(1) Remember God rules

(2) A malicious attack reveals a consistent life (vv. 1-9)

　i) *The Devil's tactics*

　ii) *Consistency*

　iii) *Pressure to conform*

(3) A steady and courageous response (vv. 10-16)

　i) *Courage*

　ii) *Steadiness*

(4) Trusting God (vv. 17-24)

　i) *God's grace is sufficient*

　ii) *God's promised deliverance*

(5) God advances His Kingdom (vv. 25-28)

　i) *God uses His people*

　ii) *God works in the hearts of unbelievers*

　iii) *God dramatically advances His Kingdom*

The first point, while not directly from the text of the chapter, sets the material in the context of the key message of the book as a whole – God rules.

The sub-points above may or may not be used in the outline. They are included here simply to help with the flow of logical thought.

Bible study on Daniel 6

Read chapter 6

(1) Introduce the issues

    i) As Christians we live as exiles in the world (1 Pet. 1:1). In light of the fact that God rules, He expects us to live consistent lives, so that when a tough test comes we will not be found wanting and will stand courageously.

        From a first reading of the chapter, how are we encouraged and inspired to do that?

(2) Study the passage

    i) Chapter 6 gives an insight into Daniel's life. What do we learn about the way he lived and how his faith impacted his life? (vv. 1-9)

    ii) What tactics did those who sought to undermine Daniel employ? (vv. 4-9, 11, 15) Who lies behind this?

    iii) What direct and hostile challenge to his faith did Daniel face?

    iv) How did Daniel react to the king's decree and what does this reveal about him? (vv. 10-16) [You might find it helpful to compare Daniel's approach here with his approach in chapter 1, and Shadrach, Meshach and Abednego's in chapter 2].

    v) What did God do? (vv. 17-23)

    vi) How did Darius react? What did he do? (vv. 24-28)

    vii) What parallels are there between the events described here and the Gospels? What is the significance of this?

(3) *Apply the passage*

    i) What lessons from Daniel's life can we take from this chapter? Think of his age, the long years between the events recorded in the book, his private life, his public life, his devotional life.

    ii) Is it harder taking a stand when you are an older or a younger Christian?

    iii) What kinds of tactics does the Devil use to undermine our faith and witness?

    iv) What kind of direct and hostile challenges to their faith do Christians face in the world today? Are there circumstances when we face such direct challenges?

    v) God expects us to live distinctively, showing our allegiance to Him. What's our motivation for doing this? What stops us doing it?

    vi) The way Daniel took his stand is striking. What can we learn from his manner and approach? [Again, comparison with Chs. 1 and 3 might be helpful.]

    vii) Taking a bold stand against a direct and hostile challenge can be costly in terms of the consequences we face. What can we expect from God?

    viii) If we stand for God, how will He use our witness to advance His Kingdom?

ix) What are the implications of the events described in this chapter for unbelievers?

(4) *Pray it through*

8

GOD'S UNIVERSAL RULE
(DANIEL 7)

Setting in context

Chapter 7 begins the second part of the book, where we move from largely narrative to prophetic visions, with its emphasis on the unseen world. Visions and heavenly messengers are prominent, numbers with symbolic significance abound, and the conflict raging in the heavenly realms and how this relates to events on earth, is central.

(1) Dating

The vision is dated as 'the first year of Belshazzar king of Babylon' (v. 1). The year is 552 B.C., some fifty years into the Exile, Daniel aged in his late sixties. Power has passed from Nebuchadnezzar to Belshazzar. While Daniel had been at the heart of political life in Babylon during the reign of Nebuchadnezzar and had seen Nebuchadnezzar wonderfully converted, the reign of Belshazzar was very different. Daniel was marginalized for over twenty years until he was recalled right at the end of Belshazzar's reign (remembered by the Queen Mother, but forgotten by Belshazzar (5:11-12)) to interpret the writing on the wall.

Daniel receives this vision, therefore, at the beginning of a bleak and discouraging time for the people of God, when they lived under the rule of someone who set himself against the Lord of heaven (5:23). In such circumstances, this revelation of the true meaning and direction of history under God's sovereign control would have been a great encouragement to Daniel, then, and to the people of God ever since, especially when they are living through difficult times.

(2) Context – structure of book

Chapters 7–12 record four visions (Fig. 1). Each vision is precisely dated, allowing us to relate the visions to particular times and events described in the narrative chapters 1–6.

Fig. 1 Prophetic visions Daniel received during the Exile

Vision	Reference	Description	Dating
Vision 1	Ch. 7	Ram, goat, four horns, little horn, Ancient of Days, son of man	552 B.C. 'first year of Belshazzar' (7:1)
Vision 2	Ch. 8	Ram, goat, four horns, little horn	550 B.C. 'third year of Belshazzar' (8:1)
Vision 3	Ch. 9	Daniel's prayer and vision of seventy weeks	539 B.C. 'first year of Darius' (9:1)
Vision 4	Chs. 10–12	Spiritual warfare, kings of south and north, king who exalts himself, End Times	536 B.C. (after Exile ends) 'third year of Cyrus' (10:1)

Notes:

i) The first two visions are dated at the beginning of
    Belshazzar's reign, with the third and fourth at the end of
    the Exile (the decree to end the Exile was in 539 B.C.).

ii) We take Darius and Cyrus to be the same person.

All the prophetic material (the four visions, Nebuchadnezzar's dreams and the writing on the wall) conveys the
main theme of the book – God rules and is building an
everlasting Kingdom. Within this broad framework, some
prophecies take a big-picture, wide-angled view of the
future, while others focus on the detail with more of a zoom-
lens approach. Chapters 2, 7, 9 and 12 are the big-picture
prophecies, with chapters 8 and 11 focusing on a particular
period in the second century B.C. when God's people
suffered an intense period of persecution under Antiochus
IV Epiphanes, who reigned from 175–164 B.C.

Chapters 2 and 7 bracket the Aramaic section of the book
which contains material of universal significance – a message
for all people. The Aramaic section has a clear chiastic structure, reflecting its structural and thematic cohesion (Fig. 2).

Fig. 2 Chiastic structure of Aramaic section

  a Ch. 2   Prophetic vision of four-part statue, rock
              and mountain

    b Ch. 3   God delivers His people from the furnace

      c Ch. 4   God saves Nebuchadnezzar

      c Ch. 5   God judges Belshazzar

    b Ch. 6   God delivers Daniel from the lions' den

  a Ch. 7   Prophetic vision of four beasts, Ancient of
              Days and son of man

Reflecting this structure there are strong parallels between chapters 2 and 7 (Fig. 3).

Fig. 3 Parallels between chapters 2 and 7

Chapter 2	Chapter 7
Nebuchadnezzar's dream	**Daniel's vision**
Four-part statue	*Four beasts*
Head of gold	Lion
Chest and arms of silver	Bear
Belly and thighs of bronze	Leopard
Legs of iron, feet of iron and clay	Fourth beast
	Ten horns
	Little horn
	Ancient of Days

....

| Rock cut not with human hands which smashes the statue and becomes a great mountain that fills the whole earth | Coronation of son of man as King of God's everlasting Kingdom |

The four-part statue (Ch. 2) corresponds to the four beasts (Ch. 7). The rock cut not with human hands which becomes a great mountain that fills the whole earth (Ch. 2) corresponds to one like a son of man crowned as King of God's everlasting Kingdom. The parallels are striking.

Finally in terms of structure, the prominence of chapter 7, concluding the Aramaic section, and beginning the section containing the four visions, suggests that it functions as the key chapter in the book, not simply through its location at the mid-point, but the centrality of its message.

(3) Context – message of book

The message of Daniel is that *God rules, is building an everlasting Kingdom, and calls people to live in light of that fact.*

Daniel 7 is a big-picture prophecy covering the breadth of this message. With its panoramic survey of world history, the vision concerns God's universal rule. God is in control of history. In contrast to human kingdoms and kings which rise and fall (under God's sovereign control), God will build an everlasting Kingdom under the rule of His all-powerful King. God's people, often opposed throughout history, will inherit this everlasting Kingdom. Those who oppose God and His people will be judged, His judgements throughout history a sign of His full and final judgement at the end of history. This is an important message for the people of God, but also for the unbelieving world (remember this chapter concludes the Aramaic section of the book with its message of universal significance). In the end, all peoples, nations and men of every language will bow before God's King (7:14).

Big-picture prophecies (like Daniel 7) embrace the detailed prophecies in chapters 8 and 11. For example, a prophecy that concerns God's universal rule in history (like Daniel 7) embraces the detail of visions like chapters 8 and 11 with their focus on a particular period in history. Similarly, the Antichrist suggested by the vision here in chapter 7 embraces all antichrists through history, including an individual like Antiochus IV Epiphanes, the focus of the detailed prophecies in chapters 8 and 11.

Working on the text

The structure of the chapter is as follows:

(1) Setting of Daniel's vision (v. 1)

(2) Vision of the four beasts, ten horns and a little horn (vv. 2-8)

(3) Vision of the heavenly throne room, Ancient of Days and coronation of the Son of Man as King over God's Everlasting Kingdom (vv. 9-14)

(4) Interpretation of the vision (vv. 15-27) – further divided into:

  i) *Overview (vv. 17-18)*

  ii) *Fourth beast, ten horns, little horn and God's everlasting Kingdom (vv. 19-27)*

(5) Daniel's reaction to what he has seen (v. 28)

There is evidence here of a chiastic structure, which draws attention to verses 9-14 as the focal point of the chapter (Fig. 4).

Fig. 4 Chiastic structure of Daniel 7

>   **a** (v. 1)
>   **b** (vv. 2-8)
>   **c** (vv. 9-14)
>   **b** (vv. 15-27)
>   **a** (v. 28)

(1) Setting of Daniel's vision (v. 1)
[See comments above on the dating of the vision.]

The phrase at the end of verse 1 – 'He wrote down the substance of his dream' – makes the point that what God revealed to Daniel is God's written revelation in Scripture. What God reveals through His Prophets is a message for the people of God and for all humanity.

*(2) Vision of the four beasts, ten horns
    and a little horn (vv. 2-8)*

The vision opens with a turbulent and violent scene as four great beasts emerge from a stormy sea (vv. 2-3). The language is rich and evocative, drawing from earlier Scripture and possibly also echoing religious mythological elements from the culture of the time. These beasts, like the four-part statue in chapter 2, are representative of human power.

A number of details are worthy of note. The reference to the 'four winds of heaven' (v. 2) is suggestive of comprehensiveness. These beasts represent the full extent of human power throughout history (similar to the four-part statue in Ch. 2). The phrase also echoes the opening of Genesis where the Spirit of God hovers (literally swoops like an eagle) over the waters (Gen. 1:2). God the Creator is at work in the processes of history. This does not mean that God is complicit in / directs evil in the world; simply that even the fallen and disordered world is under His control. Nothing is outside or beyond His overarching sovereignty. A similar point is made, for example, in Revelation 6 when the four horsemen of the apocalypse are permitted to reign in the earth under God's sovereign control (Rev. 6:1-8). God, the Creator, is always working out His purposes, and even when human power is riding high, God is in control. The place from which human power originates is the 'great sea' (v. 2). This is probably a geographical reference to the Mediterranean. Power will shift away from the old empires of the East and move to the new powers of Greece and Rome (see further discussion on the interpretation of the vision below). More importantly, however, the sea throughout Scripture is used to convey the fallen and disordered world. So, for example, the sea is used to refer to the raging power of the nations:

> 'Oh, the raging of many nations –
> > they rage like the raging sea!
> Oh, the uproar of the peoples –
> > they roar like the roaring of great
> > > waters!'   *(Isa. 17:12)*

The sea is the primeval deep, the haunt of evil (see e.g. Ps. 74:12-14; Job 41:31; Rev. 13:1). The Devil is active in history, attempting to thwart God's purposes. This is a particular focus of the final vision in chapters 10–12 (particularly Ch. 10) when the veil is drawn aside and we are given a glimpse of the cosmic conflict being waged behind the scenes of human history.

The four beasts are striking in their appearance. The first beast, verse 4, is 'like a lion', powerful, dangerous and menacing. This beast has human features: 'it stood on two feet like a man, and the heart of a man was given to it' (v. 4). It has human features, but is in-human, distorted humanity, the shattered image of God. The second beast '…looked like a bear. It was raised up on one of its sides, and it had three ribs in its mouth between its teeth…' (v. 5). A dreadful sight, half beast and half man, fallen human power. The third beast is '…like a leopard… This beast had four heads and it was given authority to rule' (v. 6). Again, man and beast. Notice also, this beast is 'given authority to rule'. All authority to rule in this world is God-given, even fallen human power is under the overarching sovereignty of God. Seen together, these beasts teach us about the ambiguous nature of human power. They are clearly destructive and menacing – the power of the lion, the ferocity of the bear and the rapacious speed of the eagle and leopard. But human power is also impressive and fascinating: 'the heart of a man was given to it' (v. 4). This is echoed throughout the book, where we observe, on the one hand, the undoubted significance and cultural achievements of the Babylonian kingdom, while on the other hand, flagrant human sin.

The fourth beast, described in verses 7-8, is of a different order and magnitude. The marked distinction from the first three beasts is indicated by the longer and formal introduction in verse 7: 'After that, in my vision at night I looked…' (compared, for example, to verse 6: 'After that, I looked…') The longer introduction in verse 7 mirrors the introduction to the vision as a whole in verse 2. The fourth beast corresponds to no known animal, drawing on features of all the other beasts. It is utterly destructive, symbolic of the worst of human power and totalitarianism, shorn of all culture, civilisation and humanity. The iron teeth suggest militarism, and the frightening violence of the beast is further emphasised by words such as 'crushed', 'devoured' and 'trampled'.

Another feature of this fourth beast (that makes it different from the other beasts) is that it had ten horns (v. 7). The ten horns represent enormous power (see also Zech. 1:18-21), yet the climax of the vision is the little horn which comes up among the horns and uproots three of them (v. 8). The description of this little horn is sinister.

It 'had eyes like the eyes of a man and a mouth that spoke boastfully' (v. 8).

(3) *Vision of the heavenly throne room, Ancient of Days and coronation of the Son of Man as King over God's Everlasting Kingdom (vv. 9-14)*

Theologically this is the centre and focal point of the chapter (the centre of the chiastic structure). The scene changes abruptly to the heavenly throne room. The phrase 'thrones were set in place' (v. 9a) is not to be taken chronologically as if this was the next event after the emergence of the beasts; rather this is a parallel reality. In other words, while the nations rage, God rules. An immediate contrast is apparent; light, majesty, calmness and authority replace the violent imagery of verses 1-8. In contrast to the activity of the beasts and horns which is fallen and disordered, here there is order – linguistically (it is poetry), visually (light as opposed to dark) and theologically (God is attended and worshipped rather than opposed).

The focus is on the Ancient of Days taking His seat on His throne in the heavenly court, familiar from such passages as 1 Kings 22 and Job 1 and 2. The title for God, 'Ancient of Days', suggests that His reign, unlike the beasts and horns, is not limited by time. In the Psalms, God is frequently spoken of in such eternal terms:

> 'But you, O God, are my king from of
>   old…' *(Ps. 74:12)*

> 'Before the mountains were born
>   or you brought forth the earth and
>   the world,
>   from everlasting to everlasting you
>   are God.' *(Ps. 90:2)*

The stability of the throne is suggested by the words 'set in place' (v. 9a). White clothing and hair (v. 9b) suggest purity (e.g. Ps. 51:7; Isa. 1:18). The majesty, sovereignty and authority of God are conveyed by the thousands upon thousands who attended Him (v. 10b).

Fire (vv. 9b-10a) is a common biblical symbol of the presence of God, e.g. the flaming sword at the gates of Eden (Gen. 3:24), the burning bush (Exod. 3:2) and Sinai (Exod. 19:18). God's continuous controlling presence in history is symbolised by the stream of fire which flows from the throne (v. 10a). Fire, of course, is also a sign of the presence of God in judgement, which is precisely what we see:

> 'The court was seated,
> and the books were opened.' (v. 10c)

The vision of the heavenly throne room, which has been in poetry, now reverts to prose (vv. 11-12). The boastful words of the little horn are silenced as the fourth beast is destroyed (v. 11). It is not altogether clear why the other beasts have their time prolonged (v. 12), but the text makes it quite clear that God is in control of their destiny. We might also legitimately infer from this that judgement is discriminating, and that because of its evil nature, the fourth beast deserves sterner punishment.

The focus shifts again to a figure coming with the clouds of heaven (v. 13). Here we have echoes of earlier Old Testament revelation. God appears in a cloud (Exod. 19:9; 34:5; Num. 11:25) and in Psalm 104:3 makes the clouds His chariot. The figure does not arise from the sea, nor is He a beast, but is described as 'one like a son of man'. The inference, therefore, is that He is both divine and human.

Two issues are important: first, who is the Son of Man; and, second, what event is being described?

The Son of Man is Jesus, King of God's Everlasting Kingdom. This is clear from the use of the term in the New Testament, particularly in the Gospels, where Jesus often uses the title for Himself, for example, the key verse in Mark's Gospel: 'For even the Son of Man did not come to be served, but to serve, and to give his life as a ransom for many' (Mark 10:45). Matthew and Mark, in their passion narratives, specifically echo Daniel 7:13 in speaking of the Son of Man seated at God's right hand and coming on the clouds of heaven (Matt. 24:30; Mark 14:62). Strikingly, Luke, at the end of the Olivet Discourse, links it with coming judgement: 'Be always on the watch, and pray that you may be able to escape all that is about to happen, and that you may be able to stand before the Son of Man' (Luke 21:36). The term is also used throughout John's Gospel (e.g. John 6:27, 53; 12:23, 34). Beyond the Gospels, the usage of the title is equally clear. In Acts 7, Stephen, suffering at the hands of the beast which oppresses the saints sees heaven opened and the Son of Man standing at the right hand of God (Acts 7:56). And John, on the island of Patmos, has a glorious vision of someone 'like a son of man' (Rev. 1:13) standing in rule and authority over the Church and towering over human history.

If the Son of Man here in Daniel 7 is Jesus, what event is being described? The text clearly indicates that the Son of Man is entering heaven rather than coming from it: 'He approached the Ancient of Days and was led into his presence' (v. 13b). This is the ascension of Jesus, therefore, rather than His second coming. This interpretation is given further weight when we see what happens next:

'He was given authority, glory and sovereign power; all peoples, nations and men of every language worshipped him. His dominion is an everlasting dominion that will not pass away, and his kingdom is one that will never be destroyed.' (v. 14). This describes the coronation of the Son of Man (Jesus) as King of God's Everlasting Kingdom. He is given dominion, a clear echo of Genesis 1:26, indicating that He has come to restore humanity's lost dominion over creation. Just as the fallen creation has produced the four beasts which reign for a limited time, so the rule of the Son of Man in a new restored creation will be eternal. All of this parallels the rock and the mountain in chapter 2 (the rock is Jesus, the mountain God's everlasting Kingdom).

If the description of the Son of Man here in Daniel 7 is of Jesus entering heaven to be crowned as King of God's Everlasting Kingdom, what do we make of the Gospel passages that speak of the Son of Man coming on the clouds of heaven in judgement (i.e. coming from heaven rather than entering it)? Similarly, Revelation 1 speaks about the Son of Man coming from heaven in judgement (Rev. 1:7-20). Is this a contradiction? No. There is an inauguration and a consummation, a now and a not yet dimension to the everlasting Kingdom of God. With Jesus' first coming (the events of His incarnation, death, resurrection, ascension and coronation) the everlasting Kingdom of God was established and the clock is ticking to the day when the Lord Jesus will come again to bring in the New Creation. Thus, the ascension and coronation of the Son of Man mean that the great saving events which will culminate in His second coming are irresistibly on course and the Kingdom He is given is eternal. His enthronement

as He approaches the Ancient of Days is a sign that
nothing can prevent the coming of the Kingdom. Creation
will be renewed because the Son of Man, the second Adam,
will undo the disastrous consequences of the first Adam's
failure.

The reference to 'all peoples, nations and men of every
language worshipped him' (v. 14) is a commentary on what
will happen at Jesus' second coming (Phil. 2:9-11), but
in the context of the book of Daniel there is an intended
contrast with the events of chapter 3 when 'peoples, nations
and men of every language' are commanded to worship
Nebuchadnezzar's golden image (3:4-5). What a contrast
between worshipping a lifeless statue and worshipping the
Man who will judge the world.

This central section of what is the central chapter in
the book of Daniel expresses wonderful truths. It reminds
us of God's universal sovereign rule. It points to the very
heart of God's purposes for the world and humanity – to
establish His everlasting Kingdom. It points to the Lord
Jesus as King of God's everlasting Kingdom, one of the
clearest prophecies in the Old Testament, written five
centuries before the events described took place.

(4) Interpretation of the vision (vv. 15-27)

This vision, like Nebuchadnezzar's dream in the parallel
chapter 2, needs to be interpreted. Notice first, though,
the effect the vision had on Daniel – he was 'troubled in
spirit' and 'disturbed' by what he had seen (v. 15). This
is a natural response to the frightening picture of the
beasts, notwithstanding God's sovereignty and judgement.
Likewise, Abraham was subject to 'thick and dreadful
darkness' (Gen. 15:12) because of the time in Egypt which

God's people would undergo even though there is a bright future beyond it. And so Daniel asks 'one of those standing there' (i.e. one of the heavenly court) for an interpretation (v. 16). There are two parts to the interpretation: an overview (vv. 17-18) and a detailed explanation concerning the fourth beast, ten horns, little horn and God's everlasting Kingdom (vv. 19-27).

i) Overview (vv. 17-18)

The interpretation is brief and focuses on the earth and on humanity. The four beasts are four kingdoms that will rise from the earth (v. 17). The fact that these kingdoms rise from the earth rather than from the sea (v. 3) is not a contradiction; the author's intention here is simply to emphasise their earthly origin. We must beware of rigidity and lack of imagination in interpreting apocalyptic imagery. The point being made is the same – this is fallen human power.

Which kingdoms do the beasts represent? Given the strong parallels between chapters 2 and 7, and based on the interpretation of the four-part statue in chapter 2, it is reasonable to infer that the four kingdoms are, respectively, Babylon (625–539 B.C.), Medo-Persia (539–331 B.C.), Greece (331–63 B.C.) and Rome (63 B.C.–A.D. 476). There are details in the description of the beasts that accord with such an interpretation, for example the lion representing Babylon. The beasts reveal the nature of human power. They are destructive and frightening. And the kingdoms they represent – Babylon, Medo-Persia, Greece and Rome – in their turn conquered the world with violence and conquest. While such specific interpretation is appropriate, a general interpretation to all human kingdoms throughout history is equally valid. The nature and characteristics of human power represented by the beasts are perennially valid. A general interpretation is strongly suggested by the description of the fourth beast (see discussion below).

In verse 18, the focus shifts from the beasts to God's everlasting Kingdom. Whereas in verse 14 it is the Son of Man who is given the Kingdom, here in verse 18 the promise is to the 'saints of the Most High' who will 'receive the kingdom and will possess it for ever – yes, for ever and ever.' Again, this is not a contradiction, simply another facet of the everlasting Kingdom of God. The triumph of the Son of Man is first-fruits of a Kingdom where His followers will one day live and reign with Him (in the New Creation).

ii) Fourth beast, ten horns, little horn and God's Everlasting Kingdom (vv. 19-27)

The second part of the interpretation is much longer (vv. 19-27) and concentrates on the identity of the fourth beast with the horns. Daniel does not doubt that God is in control, or that He will finally overthrow evil, but he is alarmed and dismayed at the power of the opposition represented by the fourth beast. That alarm is conveyed by his desire to know more about the beast and horns (vv. 19-20).

Before we get to the interpretation proper in verses 23-27 (signalled by the words 'He gave me this explanation'), verses 19-22 recap the earlier description of the fourth beast and horns and judgement of the little horn by the Ancient of Days (vv. 7-12). We are reminded that the fourth beast is different from the other beasts, unparalleled in its destructive power – fallen human power at its very worst (v. 19). Likewise, the ten horns and sinister little horn which was more imposing than the other horns, crushed three of them, and spoke boastfully (v. 20). The little horn wages war against the saints (the people of God) and defeats them (v. 21), until the Ancient of Days comes in judgement. God pronounces judgement in favour of the saints (His people), who inherit the Kingdom (v. 22).

Verses 23 to 27 explain what this means. While the fourth beast is described as a fourth kingdom that will appear on the earth (v. 23a), the interpretation (mirroring the description) focuses on the difference between this fourth kingdom and the other kingdoms. It is different because of its ferocious intention to dominate the whole earth and destroy everything in its path (v. 23b). This suggests a general interpretation to all human kingdoms and power. While beasts represent kingdoms, horns represent kings or individuals (v. 24a). The focus of the text is not so much on the ten kings who come from this fourth kingdom as the king who is different from the earlier ones and who subdues three of them (v. 24b). Verse 25 describes what this king does. He speaks blasphemously against God and persecutes the people of God (v. 25a). This individual king's power, however, and the length of this period of persecution, are governed by God's overarching sovereignty (v. 25b). This echoes the point made in the opening verses of the book. In spite of what it looks like, or feels like, God is in control. Notice the details of the text: 'The saints will be handed over to him for a time, times and half a time' (v. 25b). In apocalyptic language this means a defined period of time, determined by God. Evil and oppression of God's people are real and devastating, but are limited and defined by God. God's judgement will come (v. 26). God's people will inherit the everlasting Kingdom of God (v. 27a) and all rulers will worship and obey God (v. 27b).

Who is this individual represented by the little horn? Given the big-picture focus of this vision in its sweep of world history from the Exile right through to the New Creation when God's people (the saints) will inherit God's everlasting Kingdom, we take the little horn to be the Antichrist at the end of history. This is the man of lawlessness Paul speaks about in 2 Thessalonians 2:1-10. How does this square with the fact that the detailed description in the text of the activities of the little horn is similar to chapters 8 and 11 which focus on the persecution under Antiochus in the second century B.C., for example, the reference in verse 25 to changing 'the set times and the law'. Antiochus changed the Jewish calendar and Jewish Law. The expression 'a time, times and half a time' (v. 25b) may also have a specific meaning. Antiochus desecrated the Temple in 167 B.C. and the period from then until its rededication, following the victories of Judas Maccabaeus in 164 B.C., was approximately three and a half years – 'a time, times and half a time' could refer to such a period. This does not give us an interpretive problem if we understand that the big picture encompasses the detail. And not simply that the big-picture of history encompasses a detailed period in history, also that the big picture and the detailed prophecies are expressed in a common apocalyptic language of beasts, horns and numbers. Fig. 5 summarises.

Fig. 5 Interpretation of vision

Vision	Interpretation
Four beasts	
Lion	Babylonian kingdom
Bear	Medo-Persian kingdom
Leopard	Greek kingdom
Fourth beast	All human kingdoms/power
Ten horns	Individuals (antichrists)
Little horn	The Antichrist
Ancient of Days	God on the throne
Coronation of son of man as King of God's everlasting Kingdom	The Lord Jesus is King of God's everlasting Kingdom

(5) *Daniel's reaction to what he has seen (v. 28)*
We have already observed the effect the vision had on Daniel (v. 15). That point is reiterated here. While final victory is assured, Daniel is deeply affected by the sober reality of the difficult and turbulent present. The phrase, 'the end of the matter', may allude to Daniel's understanding that the end of history had been revealed to him. No wonder he was overwhelmed!

From text to message

(1) Get the message clear

i) Big idea
God rules and is building an everlasting Kingdom.

(ii) Key questions
Preaching or teaching on this passage should answer the following questions:

- What is human power like?

- In contrast to human power, what is God's power like?

- What is God's everlasting Kingdom?

- Has God's everlasting Kingdom come?

- What does the future hold for God's people?

- What will happen to those who oppose God and His people?

- How should humanity respond to the fact of God's rule?

(2) Engage the hearer

i) Point of contact
A good point of contact would be the coronation of a monarch at the beginning of their reign (e.g. the coronation of Queen Elizabeth II in 1953). Alternatively, you might describe the inauguration of a President at the beginning of their period of office, if that would be more appropriate to your context. These points of contact get us to the heart of the passage and the coronation of the Son of Man as King of God's everlasting Kingdom.

Another option would be to begin the sermon or talk reading something that vividly conveys the frightening nature of the beasts. An excellent example would be the description of the hound of the Baskervilles in Arthur Conan Doyle's classic: 'There was a thin, crisp, continuous patter from somewhere in the heart of the crawling bank. The cloud was within fifty yards of where we lay, and we glared at it, all three, uncertain what horror was about to break from the heart of it…A hound it was, an enormous coal-black hound, but not such a hound as mortal eyes have ever seen. Fire burst from its open mouth, its eyes glowed with a smouldering glare, its muzzle and hackles and dewlap were outlined in flickering flame. Never in the delirious dream of a disordered brain could anything more savage, more appalling, more hellish be conceived than that dark form and savage face which broke upon us out of the wall of fog.'

ii) Dominant pictures / Illustrations
This is big-picture stuff, conveying God's universal rule. A helpful picture to have in our minds is the earth seen from space.

Another dominant picture is that of contrasts, in particular the contrast between human and divine power.

Also, when preaching or teaching on prophecy written in apocalyptic language, it is important to acknowledge and convey in your teaching the powerful sensory impact of what is described in the visions. Daniel's own reaction (vv. 15, 28) is a gauge of this impact.

(3) Work on application

- The obvious similarities between the prophetic visions should not obscure the important

differences. While we should never be concerned
with repeating an important message, equally we
should be attentive to the differences and reflect
that in our teaching. With chapter 7, it is important
to keep the 'big picture' in view: human power, the
Antichrist, God on His throne, the Son of Man, the
everlasting Kingdom, the inheritance of the saints.

- Beasts and horns represent human power in a
  fallen and disordered world – human kingdoms
  and individuals. While general and specific
  interpretations are appropriate you should
  err toward the general. There will be plenty
  of scope for detail in chapters 8 and 11. The
  important points to convey concern the timeless
  characteristics of human power: war and strife
  as nations and individuals battle for supremacy,
  opposition to God and His people, and the
  transient nature of human power (super-powers
  and powerful individuals come and go).

- These characteristics should be illustrated both
  from history and from the world today. This will
  help people appreciate their timeless nature. In
  terms of opposition to God and His people you
  need to think carefully about applications relevant
  to your context, but also be aware of what is
  happening around the world.

- God's universal rule is seen supremely in His
  building an everlasting Kingdom under the rule
  of His all-powerful King. In applying the passage
  it is important to note that what is prophesied in
  Daniel (the coronation of God's King) has already

happened. The Son of Man, the Lord Jesus, has come, establishing God's everlasting Kingdom.

- In this regard, it is important to convey the now and not yet dimension to the Kingdom of God. With Jesus' first coming, the Kingdom is established and the power of evil in the world conquered, but until Jesus returns, opposition and strife will continue. The age of proclamation will be the age of opposition. When Jesus returns He will establish a New Creation, where His people will live and reign with Him for eternity. This is the inheritance of the saints.

- God's judgement on those who oppose Him and His people is seen throughout history. But that judgement is merely a pointer to the full and final judgement that will occur at the end of history when Jesus returns.

- While the message and application of the chapter are predominantly for Christians, it is also relevant to unbelievers. Chapter 7 concludes the Aramaic section, with its universal applicability, both to believers and unbelievers. The pattern and progress of world history are set. With the first coming of Jesus, God has inaugurated His everlasting Kingdom which will be fully and finally established with His return at the end of history. All people will be raised on that day. Those who have submitted to the rule of God's King in this life will receive the glorious inheritance of this Kingdom, but those who have not submitted to His rule will be judged for eternity.

Outline for a sermon or talk

The suggested outline tries to convey the big-picture perspective of the chapter. In terms of specific verses, for each point, you will need to refer both to the description of the vision in the first half of the chapter and the interpretation that follows.

An outline is included in the next chapter that takes Daniel 7 and 8 together.

Title: God's universal rule
Text: Daniel 7

Structure:

(1) The fallen and disordered world

    i) Characteristics of human power

    ii) Opposition to God and His people

(2) The sovereignty of God

    i) The nature of God

    ii) God's everlasting Kingdom and King

(3) A glorious inheritance and a certain judgement

    i) Inheritance of the saints

    ii) Judgement on those who oppose God and His people

Bible study on Daniel 7

A Bible study is included in the next chapter that takes Daniel 7 and 8 together.

Read Daniel 7

(1) Introduce the issues

   i) From a first reading of the chapter, what do you think is the key message for believers?

  ii) From a first reading of the chapter, what do you think is the key message for unbelievers?

 iii) What are some of the features of Apocalyptic Literature that you notice from this chapter? What impression does this kind of literature make on you?

(2) *Study the passage*

   i) When did Daniel receive this vision and what's the significance of the timing (vv. 1-2a)?

  ii) What do the four beasts represent (vv. 2b-10; 15-27)?

 iii) What do the horns, and in particular, the little horn represent (vv. 2b-8; 19-27)? What does the little horn do (vv. 8b, 11, 20b-21, 25)?

 iv) Verses 9-14 are at the centre of the vision. How are these verses given prominence in the text?

  v) Who are the 'Ancient of Days' (vv. 9-10) and the 'one like a son of man' (vv. 13-14, 27)?

 vi) What's the setting of verses 9-14 and what's going on (see esp. vv13-14)?

 vii) What happens to the little horn (vv. 11-12, 22, 26)?

viii) What is promised to the people of God (vv. 18, 22, 27)?

 ix) What do you make of Daniel's reaction to the vision (v. 28)?

(3) *Apply the passage*

   i) What God reveals is that He will build an everlasting Kingdom under the rule of His all-powerful King. From our perspective as Christians to what extent has this promise been fulfilled?

  ii) What are the main lessons we can draw from this chapter in terms of the:

     (a) opposition / pressure we face as Christians / the Church;

     (b) our confidence in God;

     (c) our present and future deliverance?

 iii) Given that the book of Daniel was written in the 6th century B.C., what does this chapter teach us about the authority and inspiration of Scripture (think of Daniel's reaction in verse 28)?

(4) *Pray it through*

9

TRUSTING GOD IN
STRESSFUL TIMES
(DANIEL 8)

Setting in context

(1) Dating

This second vision is dated as 'the third year of King Belshazzar's reign' (v. 1), just two years after the first vision (Ch. 7). The date is 550 B.C.

(2) Context – structure of book

Fig. 1 in the precious chapter details the four visions recorded in the second half of the book. Each vision is precisely dated, allowing us to relate the visions to particular times and events described in the narrative chapters 1–6.

The prophetic material in Daniel, including prophetic material like chapter 2 in the first half of the book, can be divided into prophecy that takes a big-picture, wide-angled view of the future, and prophecy that focuses on the detail. Chapters 8 and 11 are the detailed prophecies focusing on a particular period in the second century B.C. Fig. 1 summarises the relationship between the big picture and detailed prophecies.

Fig. 1 *Relationship between big-picture and detailed prophecies*

Ch. 2	Ch. 7	Ch. 8	Ch. 11	Interpretation
Four-part statue	*Four beasts*			
Head of gold	Lion			
Chest and arms of silver	Bear	Ram		
Belly and thighs of bronze	Leopard	Goat	Kings of South and North	Greek kingdom *(331–63 B.C.)*
Legs of iron, feet of iron and clay	Fourth beast			

The focus of the detailed prophecies in chapters 8 and 11 is the intense period of persecution God's people suffered under Antiochus IV Epiphanes who reigned from 175 to 164 B.C. Fig. 2 summarises the historical detail of the prophetic vision in Daniel 8 and the corresponding vision in chapter 11.

Fig. 2   Correspondence between Daniel 8 and 11

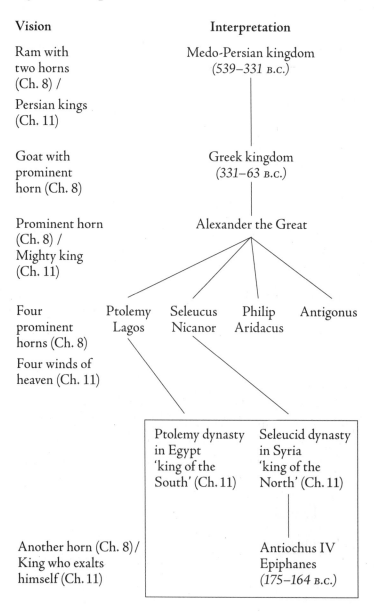

Vision

Interpretation

Ram with two horns (Ch. 8) /

Persian kings (Ch. 11)

Medo-Persian kingdom
(*539–331* B.C.)

Goat with prominent horn (Ch. 8)

Greek kingdom
(*331–63* B.C.)

Prominent horn (Ch. 8) / Mighty king (Ch. 11)

Alexander the Great

Four prominent horns (Ch. 8)

Four winds of heaven (Ch. 11)

Ptolemy Lagos   Seleucus Nicanor   Philip Aridacus   Antigonus

Ptolemy dynasty in Egypt 'king of the South' (Ch. 11)

Seleucid dynasty in Syria 'king of the North' (Ch. 11)

Another horn (Ch. 8) / King who exalts himself (Ch. 11)

Antiochus IV Epiphanes
(*175–164* B.C.)

With reference to Fig. 2, the Medo-Persian kingdom, conquerors of Babylon, was overthrown by Alexander the Great, first king of the Greek kingdom. Following Alexander's death, power was seized by four of his generals and the kingdom divided into four. The names of these generals are Ptolemy Lagos, Seleucus Nicanor, Philip Aridacus and Antigonus. Two emerged as dominant, Ptolemy and Seleucus and their respective dynasties who vied for power over the next hundred years – the Ptolemy dynasty in Egypt (referred to in Ch. 11 as the 'king of the South') and the Seleucid dynasty in Syria (referred to in Ch. 11 as the 'king of the North'). Attention focuses on the Seleucid dynasty and especially on one particular king, Antiochus IV Epiphanes. Antiochus was not a major player in world history, but very significant in the history of the people of God. The vision recorded in chapter 11 covers the same material as the vision here in chapter 8 but includes a lot of additional detail on the power struggle between the 'king of the South' and 'king of the North' (the Ptolemy and Seleucid dynasties), before focusing like chapter 8 on the Seleucid king, Antiochus IV Epiphanes.

From the beginning of chapter 8 the writing returns to Hebrew (from Ch. 2:4 through to the end of Ch. 7 the book is written in Aramaic). While the Aramaic section deals with matters of universal significance, the Hebrew sections focus on material of particular relevance to the people of God. The detailed prophecies in chapters 8 and 11 concerning the future of the people of God are striking examples of this.

(3) Context – message of book

The message of Daniel is that God rules, is building an everlasting Kingdom, and calls people to live in light of that *fact*. While Daniel 2 and 7 with their panoramic survey of world history concern God's overarching or universal rule, here in chapter 8 (and again in Ch. 11), the spotlight is on a particular period of history, reminding us that God is as much in control of the detail. That is a very important message. God is sovereign over all of history, but is also sovereign over every detailed period. Nothing is outside His control.

Moreover, the focus here (and again in Ch. 11), on a time of persecution for the people of God, is a powerful reminder that through such times God is with His people and that these periods of persecution will last only for a time. This is a timeless message of encouragement for God's people, now as then, to trust Him. In this regard, the connection between the prophetic visions and the narrative chapters in the first part of the book, is striking. Daniel received this vision early in Belshazzar's reign. Belshazzar ruled from 552–539 B.C., the bleakest period for God's people during the Exile. The incident recorded in chapter 5, when Belshazzar in his blasphemous arrogance desecrates the temple vessels, foreshadows Antiochus' blasphemy and desecration of the temple. Moreover, the fate of Belshazzar foreshadows Antiochus' fate. The 'writing on the wall' signalled not only the death of Belshazzar but the fall of the Babylonian kingdom. And in spite of the intensity of the persecution and his apparent dominance, Antiochus perished as the people of God and the temple were liberated by Judas Maccabaeus in 164 B.C. In spite of what it looks like, or feels like, God is in control. This note was first sounded in the opening verses of the book (Ch. 1:1-2), and has been a consistent refrain throughout. God gives and removes power in accordance with His sovereign will.

Whereas the big-picture prophecies like Daniel 7 embrace the detailed prophecies like Daniel 8 and 11, the reverse is also true. The detail points to the big picture. The persecution of God's people in a particular period of history points to the persecution of God's people throughout history. The character and actions of an antichrist like Antiochus point to all antichrists throughout history and *the* Antichrist at the end of history. This relationship between the detail and the big picture is expressed in similar apocalyptic language in the different visions.

Working on the text

The structure of the chapter is as follows:

(1) Setting of Daniel's vision (vv. 1-2)

(2) Vision of ram, goat, prominent horn, four horns and another horn (vv. 3-14)

(3) Messenger from heaven (vv. 15-19)

(4) Interpretation of the vision (vv. 20-26)

(5) Daniel's reaction to what he has seen (v. 27)

(1) Setting of Daniel's vision (vv. 1-2)

[See comments above on the dating of the vision in Belshazzar's reign.]

Chapter 7 ended with Daniel perplexed and confused (7:28) needing further explanation and reassurance. The connection in the text (8:1) between this vision and the earlier vision, indicates that this further revelation (together with what follows in the rest of the book), is in response to that need.

The setting of the vision is the Ulai canal in Susa, the 'citadel' or 'capital' of Persia. The Ulai canal was a prominent feature in the city. This is an appropriate setting for a vision that begins with the Medo-Persian kingdom, and the dominance of Persia within that kingdom.

(2) Vision of ram, goat, prominent horn, four horns and another horn (vv. 3-14)

The scene is intensely dramatic and unfolds swiftly. It begins with a ram with two horns, one of which was longer than the others (v. 3). The once all-powerful ram (v. 4) is destroyed by a goat with a prominent horn that comes from the west (vv. 5-7). The details of the text powerfully convey the all-encompassing and rapid conquests of the goat with its prominent horn. But at the height of its power, the large horn is broken off and in its place four horns appear which 'grew up towards the four winds of heaven' (v. 8). This phrase also occurred in chapter 7 (7:2) and is suggestive not only of comprehensiveness, but of God's control and direction of all human powers and principalities.

From one of these four horns comes another horn which starts small but grows in power (v. 9). The detailed references in verses 9-12 indicate that this individual (in apocalyptic language horns represent individuals) is intent on opposing God and destroying God's people: his conquest extends to the 'Beautiful Land'; he throws down the starry host and tramples on them; he sets himself up to be as great as the commander of the army of the Lord; he abolishes the daily sacrifice and desecrates the temple. Verse 12 summarises his apparent dominance – the people of God suffer, he prospers and truth is thrown to the ground.

The conversation between two 'holy ones' (angels) in verse 13 is concerned with how long the persecution will last. They are aware of the suffering of God's people and are concerned for them. The question as to how long receives a specific answer – '2,300 evenings and mornings; then the sanctuary will be reconsecrated' (v. 14). This is a reassuring word. Persecution will come, but God will also bring it to an end.

[We will return to the significance of these details in the section on the interpretation of the vision.]

(3) Messenger from heaven (vv. 15-19)

Daniel's desire to understand the vision is rewarded by a messenger from heaven, the angel Gabriel (vv. 15-16). The 'man's voice' (v. 16) summoning Gabriel to explain the meaning of the vision to Daniel is probably God Himself. Even Gabriel, the archangel, is a messenger whose authority lies in the divine origin of the message. Daniel's reaction to seeing Gabriel (v. 17) is initially one of fear as he falls to the ground prostrate (v. 17a). He then falls into a deep sleep (v. 18), reminiscent of Abraham before he too hears a word from the Lord (Gen. 15:12). And like Abraham, Daniel is given a revelation about the future, a revelation that will both be reassuring, reminding him that God is in control, but also sobering in light of the reality of suffering to come. The vision concerns 'the time of the end' (vv. 17b, 19) and 'what will happen later in the time of wrath' (v. 19). This latter phrase usually refers to the judgement of God on the disobedient (e.g. Isa. 10: 5-11; Zech. 1:12). A number of layers of meaning are suggested. The first is to the specific events prophesied in the vision – the Medo-Persian and Greek kingdoms through to the time of Antiochus. But beyond these specific events, it is appropriate to understand these phrases as referring to all manifestations of human power which oppose God and His people. They also point forward to the end of all things – the final judgement when Jesus returns and His Kingdom comes in its fullness. Again, this is an illustration of the specific prophecies pointing to the general pattern of human history.

Yet there is more than revelation here; there is the encouraging touch which enables Daniel to stand up and face what is to come (v. 18). We see something similar in chapter 10 (10:10) when Daniel receives his final vision. This blend of sober realism about the present and the future, and the fact that God gives us the grace to stand firm, is a timeless truth about the way God deals with His people. In 1 Peter, for example, a letter written to Christians suffering because of their distinctive witness, the encouragement is to stand fast in the true grace of God (1 Pet. 5:12).

(4) Interpretation of the vision (vv. 20-26)

The vision needs to be interpreted. The detail is striking and we are left in no doubt as to the meaning. The period in history is the Medo-Persian and Greek kingdoms (vv. 20-21). In chapter 2 (the four-part statue), these kingdoms were symbolised by the chest and arms of silver and the belly and thighs of bronze (2:32, 39). In chapter 7, they were symbolised by the bear and the leopard (7:5-7). Here they are represented by the ram and goat, two other symbols of power associated with these kingdoms (as in Ezek. 34:17). The ram with its two horns symbolises 'the kings of Media and Persia' (v. 20). The longer of the two horns (vv. 3-4) almost certainly represents the dominance of Persia in the Medo-Persian kingdom and, in particular, the rapid

conquests of Cyrus as he pushed into Babylon and Asia
Minor. He 'became great' (v. 4b), literally 'did great things',
is a description often used of God (e.g. 1 Sam. 12:24;
Ps. 126:2-3). But when the expression is used of humans
it tends to suggest overbearing arrogance (e.g. Ps. 35:26).
The final manifestation of this 'spirit' is found in Revelation
13:4 – 'Who is like the beast? Who can make war against
him?' This is human power, seemingly unstoppable, and
yet God is in control. All human power is given and taken
by God.

Just at this moment of unchallenged power the ram is
destroyed by a new opponent, a goat with a prominent horn
(v. 5). The interpretation indicates that this is the Greek
kingdom and its first king (v. 21) – Alexander the Great. The
description of him 'crossing the whole earth without touch-
ing the ground' (v. 5b) refers to Alexander's spectacularly
swift conquest, arguably unparalleled in history. In 334 B.C.
at the River Granicus, Alexander defeated a Persian army
holding a strong position. In the following year he faced
Darius III and won by brilliant cavalry tactics. In 331 B.C
he won a decisive victory at Gaugemala. Verses 6 and 7
describe the fall of the Medo-Persian kingdom, unable to
resist Alexander's power.

Yet Alexander's rule was short-lived and he died in
Babylon aged only thirty-two. With Alexander's death,
signified by the large horn that is broken off, power was
seized by four generals, each ruling over a different part
of the kingdom. These are the four prominent horns that
replaced the large horn (vv. 8, 22): Ptolemy Lagos, Seleucus
Nicanor, Philip Aridacus and Antigonus. Ptolemy and
Seleucus emerged as dominant and their respective dynasties vied for power over the next hundred years – the

Ptolemy dynasty in Egypt (referred to in Ch. 11 as the 'king of the South') and the Seleucid dynasty in Syria (referred to in Ch. 11 as the 'king of the North').

This hugely significant period in world history is described in only six verses (vv. 3-8), with the interpretation (vv. 20-22) even shorter. It serves as background context to the 'significant' events described in verses 9-14 and interpreted in verses 23-25, the period of persecution under Antiochus IV Epiphanes from 167–164 b.c. From the perspective of world history, Antiochus is a minor player compared to Alexander the Great. Yet because he attacks God and God's people, from a divine perspective he is a significant figure.

Antiochus emerges from the Seleucid dynasty at a time of increasing wickedness (v. 23a). He is described as 'a fierce-looking king, a master of intrigue' (v. 23b). The Hebrew is literally 'a king of bold face', a phrase also used of the dark lady of Proverbs 7.13 who is the deadly enemy of godly wisdom. We know from history that Antiochus' rise to power was through deception and manipulation (e.g. 2 Macc. 4:7-29 describes his success in manipulating high priestly circles). The phrase 'but not by his own power' (v. 24a) referring to the reason for his strength and domination, points to the demonic forces of evil in history opposing God and His people (powerfully conveyed through the description of the beasts in the vision in Daniel 7). Yet behind that (in the sense of where ultimate power and control lies) is a reference to the fact that all human power is 'given' and under the control of God. That is a consistent and powerful message of the book of Daniel. All human power, whether Nebuchadnezzar, Belshazzar, Cyrus, Alexander the Great or Antiochus, and all who have come before them and follow them, is given and taken by God. God rules.

Like all tyrants in history, for a time Antiochus seemed unstoppable: 'He will cause astounding devastation and will succeed in whatever he does' (v. 24b). This reaches its height when he focuses his attack against God and His people (vv. 24c-25). The 'Beautiful Land' (v. 9) is the land where God's glory dwells and, in particular, the Temple, the visible sign of Yahweh's presence. The taking away of the daily sacrifice from the Lord and the desecration of the sanctuary (v. 11) refer to the suppression of the whole range of sacrifices and thus the disruption of the daily worship of God's people. The throwing of truth to the ground (v. 12) probably refers to the destruction of Torah scrolls. 1 Maccabees 1 tells of Antiochus who stole the Temple treasures (1 Macc. 1:20-24*ff*), forbade the worship of Yahweh (vv. 44*ff*) and built a pagan altar over the altar of burnt offering (v. 54*ff*).

In attacking God's people and Temple he is attacking God Himself. The 'Prince of princes' (v. 25), referred to earlier as 'the commander of the army of the Lord' (v. 11) is possibly the Lord Himself or an angel, whether Gabriel (v. 15) or Michael who is referred to in a later vision as the chief or great prince (10:13, 21; 12:1). Antiochus' supreme blasphemy (reminiscent of Nebuchadnezzar) is to be as great as God (v. 11). That is also conveyed in verse 10, Antiochus' desire to reach the host of heaven and throw down some of the starry host.

God's rule and His protection and preservation of His people are seen in the destruction of Antiochus (v. 25). Antiochus died in mysterious circumstances sometime in November / December 164 B.C. while returning from Persia.

1 Maccabees 6:9 speaks of a 'deep grief' which continually gripped him; 2 Maccabees 9 of an agonising internal pain and the 'end of his life by a most pitiable fate, among the mountains in a strange land'. We have a striking parallel in the death of Herod in Acts 12:23. Allied to that, the temple was liberated by Judas Maccabaeus in 164 B.C. Antiochus may have died of some disease, and Judas Maccabaeus may have liberated the temple, but the agent of Antiochus' death and God's people's deliverance, is God. That is clear from the phrase at the end of verse 25: 'Yet he will be destroyed, but not by human power.' We have seen this again and again throughout Daniel. For example, Belshazzar and his Babylonian kingdom may have fallen to Darius / Cyrus and the Medo-Persian kingdom but God is behind it (5:25-28).

The statement in verse 26 as to the truth of the vision of the evenings and the mornings is a reference back to verses 13-14. In verse 13 the conversation between the 'holy ones' (angels) concerns how long the persecution will last. The answer is 2,300 evenings and mornings before the sanctuary is re-consecrated (v. 14). It seems reasonable to take this as the period from Antiochus' desecration of the Temple in 167 B.C. to its liberation by Judas Maccabaeus in 164 B.C. How does this tie in with the numerate references in the other visions? In chapter 7 there is a reference to 'time, times and half a time' when the holy people (God's people) are delivered into the hands of the Antichrist (7:25). The final section in chapter 12 which focuses on the future of God's people until the time of the end, makes references to 'time, times and half a time' (12:7) and to 1,290 and 1,335 days (12:11). To precisely quantify and compare these numerate references is to miss the point. In apocalyptic language, they signify a fixed period of time (determined by God), whether a short time or a long time. And so in a detailed prophecy like chapter 8 this kind of language can be taken as referring to a short period of time (e.g. the persecution under Antiochus which lasted three and a half years), whereas in the big-picture prophecies like chapter 7 and the closing verses in the book in chapter 12, it can be taken as referring to a much longer period of time (e.g. the period between the time of Daniel and the time of the end or the period of intense distress that will happen before the end). In all cases, whether long or short, it is a fixed period of time, determined by God. This answer from the 'holy ones' (angels), therefore, is profoundly reassuring. Periods of intense persecution will come, but God's sovereign rule means He will bring them to an end. And the whole of human history, which is characterised by the persecution of God's people, will come to an end and God's people will inherit the everlasting Kingdom of God in all its fullness.

The assurance in verse 26 of the reliability of revelation is also given in 10:1 and 11:2. The instruction to 'seal up the vision' (v. 26) simply means that the full significance of what is prophesied lies in the future. From Daniel's time nearly four centuries were to pass before the time of Antiochus when all this happened.

(5) Daniel's reaction to what he has seen (v. 27)

Any idea that the message of this chapter is irrelevant to ordinary living is dispelled by this final verse where Daniel (as in 7:28 and 4:19) finds this revelation overwhelming and exhausting. Seeing into the divine counsel involves sharing something of the divine sorrow at human wickedness and also compassion for the suffering of God's people. The word 'appalled' is also used for the abominable desolation in verse

13 (see also 9:27 and 12:11). Daniel has seen something of evil as God sees it and is deeply affected.

Yet in spite of this he gets up and goes about the king's business which, as we have seen, could hardly have been enjoyable under Belshazzar. Yet for Daniel this is seen in the wider context of the business of the King of Kings. One further detail – Daniel says he did not understand the vision. This does not mean he had no understanding, only that its full significance was hidden. Daniel will ask God for further understanding (10:12) but full understanding belongs to God alone.

From text to message

(1) Get the message clear

i) Big idea
God rules in the details of history. God's people will face stressful times but God will bring these times to an end.

ii) Key questions
Preaching or teaching on this passage should answer the following questions:

- What is human power like?
- How is God's universal rule worked out in the details of history?
- Why do God's people face stressful times / intense periods of persecution?
- What is the nature of that persecution?
- How is God's rule evident in these stressful times?
- What do God's people need to know during such times?

- What will happen to those who oppose God and
  His people?

- What does a vision like this tell us about the
  inspiration of God's Word?

(2) Engage the hearer

i) Point of contact

Following Hudson-Taylor's pioneering work in China, and
the great encouragement of a breakthrough for the gospel
in China, in 1951-52 the CIM missionaries were expelled.
This opposition to God, His people and the gospel was
devastating to many at the time. Yet God was in control and
brought great blessing through the raising up of indigenous
Chinese believers. And the CIM missionaries, expelled
from China, went into South-East Asia. In the toughest,
most stressful times, God is in control. Significant set-
backs and opposition last for a time but God brings them
to an end and His Kingdom advances.

ii) Dominant pictures / illustrations

Drawing a contrast with the big-picture vision in chapter
7 might be helpful. In chapter 7 we're looking at the earth
from space, whereas here in chapter 8 we're zooming in on a
particular place at a particular time in history. On a similar
theme, you could draw a contrast between the timeline in
chapter 7 (from the Babylonian kingdom to the return of
Jesus at the end of history when the everlasting Kingdom of
God will come in its full and final form) and the three and
a half years in the second century B.C. when God's people
were persecuted under Antiochus IV Epiphanes.

Another dominant picture is the ultimate futility and
transience of human power. The mighty superpower of

Medo-Persia, and its overthrow by the Greek kingdom under Alexander the Great, is dealt with in just a few verses. Their power was given and taken by God. Much more attention is given to this obscure king in the second century B.C., Antiochus. Insignificant in world history, perhaps, but very significant in the history of the people of God. Likewise, his power was given and taken by God. And through it all, God builds His everlasting Kingdom.

(3) Work on application

- Sometimes visions like Daniel 8 and 11 are seen as detailed, obscure, difficult to understand and perhaps of less relevance than the big-picture stuff in chapters 2 and 7. It is certainly true that Daniel 8 and 11 are the least taught chapters in the book. They might be difficult at first, but once you get into them they have a very important message.

- Having studied chapter 7 which takes a big-picture view of history (God's universal rule) it is important to emphasize, by contrast, the detailed focus of this vision and the fact that God is in control of the details of history as well as the big sweep. This is a very encouraging and steadying truth for Christians to grasp.

- This vision has a particular focus on a stressful time for God's people. It is true that God's people will experience opposition and suffer all of the time, but there are times when this is particularly intense. You can illustrate this from history, whether globally or nationally (whatever your context). It might also be appropriate to illustrate this in relation to a particular period in a church's life. And also, with appropriate caveats and caution, it can be applied to situations today (including our own situations and experience) where God's people are facing stressful times.

- Another way to build this kind of application is by relating the vision to Daniel's circumstances at the time he receives this vision, i.e. early in Belshazzar's reign. Daniel receives the visions in chapters 7 and 8 at the bleakest time for him in the Exile. One application of this would be the encouragement these prophetic visions are to Christians living in the West today feeling increasingly like exiles in the world (1 Pet. 1:1).

- Another line of application is the hostility directed against God and His people. This is a timeless truth and is invariably used by God to advance the gospel. This is a helpful line of application to draw a link to Christ. The pattern for His life is suffering for the advance of the gospel. And that is the pattern He commends for all who will follow Him.

- It is important not to minimize the intensity of hostility / persecution God's people faced then, and face still in parts of the world. The kind of persecution described in these visions lifts our eyes from our own circumstances to the persecuted Church in different parts of the world. Equally, we shouldn't think the kind of opposition we experience in the West is not real opposition. It is nothing like other parts of the world, but it is real nonetheless and, perhaps, increasing in intensity.

- Very helpfully the text of this vision asks 'how long?' The answer to that is that God has fixed a defined time. It will come to an end. This needs to be applied carefully and pastorally. The vision tells us what we are to know. There are things that we would like to know but can't know.

- In relating a passage like this to Christ, it is important to make clear that the Devil (the prince of the world who is behind all human power opposed to God and His people) has been defeated at the cross. Although he has been defeated spiritual warfare will continue until Jesus returns and God's people will continue to be opposed.

- God's judgement on those who oppose Him and His people is seen throughout history. This is a pointer to the full and final judgement that will come at the end of history when Jesus returns.

- What are we to make of the detailed predictive prophecy (God's detailed control of events) in terms of human free will and choice? At one level God's sovereignty is absolute and He does control all. But we need to be careful not to conflate too simplistically God's sovereignty and human free-will. In life we make choices all the time, but God is working out His purposes in all things and through all things.

- A striking feature of Daniel's record of these visions is his personal reaction to what he sees. He is deeply

affected by the revelation. We saw something
similar in chapter 7 and will see it again, much
more fully, in the introduction to the final vision in
chapter 10. It is helpful to consider how we react
to what is revealed in God's Word. Like Daniel, at
times there is an appropriateness to being deeply
affected, humbled and fearful at what we read.

- The visions in Daniel, and perhaps the detailed
  visions in particular, give an astonishing perspective
  on the inspiration of God's Word. We are reading
  a detailed prophetic description of events hundreds
  of years before they happened. The most powerful
  application of this is that what is prophesied in the
  Word of God, and is still yet to happen, will happen.

- While the message and application of the chapter
  is predominantly for Christians (this prophecy is
  in Hebrew and of particular relevance to God's
  people), it is clearly relevant for unbelievers. Those
  who oppose God and His people will be judged.
  God's judgements in history are a sign of His final
  judgement at the end of history. And in the last
  analysis all those who rejected God's rule, whether
  antagonistically or with passive indifference, will be
  judged for all eternity.

Outline for a sermon or talk

The first outline is on Daniel 8.

In preaching or teaching this chapter, rather than working through the text systematically, it is probably better
under each point to embrace both the description of the

vision in the first half of the chapter and the interpretation that follows.

The visual explanation in Figs. 1 and 2 at the beginning of this chapter might be helpful to use at the start of a sermon or talk. Getting our bearings in a chapter like this is important. Most people will be unaware of the historical details.

A second outline takes Daniel 7 and 8 together (this might be appropriate for a shorter series on the book).

Outline 1

*Title: **Trusting God in stressful times***
*Text: **Daniel 8***

Structure:

(1) God's people will experience stressful times

(2) God rules over these stressful times

    i) God will bring them to an end

    ii) God's judgement in history is a sign of His final judgement

    iii) God will build His Kingdom

    iv) God will deliver His people

(3) How God's people should react

    i) Trusting God in stressful times

    ii) Humbled before the sovereignty of God

The sub-points above may or may not be used in the outline. They are included here simply to help with the flow of logical thought.

Outline 2 (Dan. 7 and 8 together)

Title: *God's comprehensive rule*
Text: *Daniel 7-8*

Structure:

(1) **God's rule over all history**

(2) **God's rule in the details of history**

(3) **Our reaction to God's rule**

Bible study on Daniel 8

Read chapter 8

(1) Introduce the issues

   i) The vision in Daniel 8 focuses on God's rule in a
particular period of history when God's people
faced intense persecution. From a first reading of
the chapter, what do you think is the key message
for God's people?

   ii) What are some of the features of apocalyptic
language that you notice from this chapter? What
impression does this kind of language make on
you?

(2) Study the passage

   i) When did Daniel receive the vision and what's the
significance of the timing (vv. 1-2)?

   ii) The vision concerns 'the time of the end' (vv. 17b,
19) and 'what will happen later in the time of
wrath' (v. 19). What do these phrases mean? Are
both specific and general meanings intended?

   iii) Looking at the detail, taking the explanation
    (vv. 3-14) and interpretation (vv. 20-26) together,
    who / what do the following represent (you may
    also wish to refer to the introductory notes on
    context at the beginning of the chapter):

     (a) ram (vv. 3-4, 20);

     (b) goat with a prominent horn (vv. 5-7, 21);

     (c) four horns (vv. 8, 22);

     (d) another horn (vv. 9-12, 23-25)?

   iv) What is the meaning of the conversation between
    the 'holy ones' (the angels) in verses 13-14 and 26?
    In particular, what does the reference to '2,300
    evenings and mornings' (v. 14) mean?

   v) What are we to understand by Daniel's reaction
    to seeing the angel Gabriel (vv. 15-18) and his
    reaction after the vision is explained (v. 27)? And
    what are we to understand by the 'touch' from
    Gabriel (v. 18)?

(3) *Apply the passage*

   i) What is human power like? Are the
    manifestations of human power we see here
    timeless in their application?

   ii) How is God's rule worked out in the details of
    history? How important is it that God rules over
    the detail as well as the big picture?

   iii) When God's people face stressful times / intense
    periods of persecution, what are the key messages
    of this vision that we need to remember?

iv) What is the relevance of this detailed vision to the times / circumstances in which we are living today?

v) As believers what is our reaction to this vision? Can we identify with Daniel's reaction?

vi) What confidence does this vision give us in the inspiration and reliability of God's Word?

(4) Pray it through

Bible study on Daniel 7 and 8

Read chapters 7 and 8

(1) Introduce the issues

i) From a first reading of the chapters what do you think the key messages are? How do the messages of these two chapters differ / complement one another?

ii) What are some of the features of apocalyptic language that you notice from this chapter? What impression does this kind of language make on you?

(2) Study the passage

i) When did Daniel receive these visions and what is the significance of the timing (7:1-2a; 8:1-2)?

ii) What is the meaning of the vision in chapter 7?

iii) What is the meaning of the vision in chapter 8?

(3) Apply the passage

i) What is human power like? Are the manifestations of human power we see here timeless in their application?

ii) The vision in chapter 7 powerfully conveys God's universal rule over all history, whereas the vision in chapter 8 focuses on God's rule in a particular period of history. In other words, God's rules over the big picture and the details. Why are both important?

iii) What are the significance of these visions for us?

iv) As believers what is our reaction to these visions? Can we identify with Daniel's reaction?

v) What confidence do these visions give us in the inspiration and reliability of God's Word?

(4) *Pray it through*

10
PRAYING IN LIGHT
OF GOD'S RULE
(DANIEL 9)

Setting in context

(1) Dating
Daniel's prayer and vision are precisely dated. It is 539 B.C., the first year of Darius (v. 1).

(2) Context – structure of book
The precise dating helps us position Daniel 9 in the structure of the book. The year 539 B.C. is significant. The events of chapter 5 (Belshazzar's feast) are right at the end of the Babylonian kingdom, 539 B.C. The chapter ends with the fall of the Babylonian kingdom to the Medo-Persian kingdom under Darius the Mede / Cyrus the Persian (5:30-31). (We take Darius and Cyrus to be the same person.) Chapter 6 (Daniel and the lions' den) is in the first year of Darius / Cyrus, again 539 B.C. The decree to end the Exile was also in 539 B.C. (2 Chron. 36:22-23; Ezra 1:1-4; Isa. 45:1). Given the content of Daniel's prayer (he prays for the Exile to end), it must have preceded the decree.

Daniel's prayer is included in the section of the book that records the prophetic visions Daniel received during the Exile (Chs. 7–12). One reason is that in answer to his prayer, Daniel receives a prophetic vision, hence the logic of including it in this section of the book. Fig. 1 in the chapter dealing with Daniel 7 details the four prophetic visions Daniel received. These visions can be divided into prophecy that takes a big-picture wide-angled view of the future and prophecy that focuses on the detail. Chapters 2, 7, 9 and 12 are the big-picture prophecies, with chapters 8 and 11 focusing on a detailed period in the second century B.C.

Chapter 9 is in the Hebrew section of the book (1:1-2:3; 8:1-12:13) dealing with matters of particular relevance to God's people. The Aramaic section (2:4–7:28) is of universal significance.

Finally in terms of structure, Daniel 9 gives us another literary genre. The book of Daniel contains a rich variety of literary genres, in the main narrative and prophecy expressed in apocalyptic language. There are also a number of examples of poetry (e.g. 7:9-10). And here in Daniel 9 we have one of the great prayers of the Bible. It is legitimate to consider prayer as a distinct biblical literary genre.

(3) Context – message of book

The message of Daniel is that *God rules, is building an everlasting Kingdom, and calls people to live in light of that fact*. Whether it's over the big sweep of history (Ch. 7) or in the details (Ch. 8), God rules and is building His Kingdom. Daniel 9 teaches us how to pray in light of God's rule.

Daniel 9 is also placed immediately before the final vision (Chs. 10–12). The final vision begins with a lengthy introduction about prayer and spiritual warfare. And so while chapter 10 structurally belongs with chapters 11 and 12, there is also an intended thematic connection in the author's mind with chapter 9. In light of this, for a shorter series that nonetheless takes you right through the book, we suggest taking Daniel 9 and 10 together as a single study (a sermon or talk outline and a Bible study is included in the next chapter along these lines). Through prayer we engage in spiritual warfare and the outworking of God's purposes as He builds His everlasting Kingdom. (We focus on this in more detail in the next chapter.)

The connection between prayer and spiritual warfare as God builds His Kingdom is an important theme. Daniel's prayer also reveals two other important connections / relationships. The first is the relationship between prayer and the Word of God. Daniel prays according to the Word of God. It is in reading Scripture that he is moved to pray and the content of his prayer is saturated in Scripture. The second important relationship (and connected to the first) is between prayer and covenant. Daniel's prayer is grounded in God's covenant relationship with His people. [See comments in *'Getting our Bearings in Daniel'* (section on the *'Message of Daniel'*); also in the Introductory Study in Daniel 1:1-2.] One other important observation about Daniel's prayer; it is both personal and corporate. At one level, it is Daniel, the Lord's servant (9:17) praying to his God ('I prayed to the Lord *my* God…' (v. 4)). In that sense it is personal. Yet as we read the prayer it is clear that Daniel is praying on behalf of God's people: 'The Lord *our* God…' (vv. 9, 13, 15). Indeed, the petitions in the prayer are almost entirely expressed in the plural – *'we* have sinned…*we* have been wicked…*we* have turned away…' (v. 5) – a pattern that runs through the prayer. This corporate orientation reflects the covenant theme.

The vision of seventy weeks ('sevens') recorded here in answer to Daniel's prayer (9:20-27) encompasses the period from the end of the Exile to the coming of Jesus to inaugurate God's everlasting Kingdom. At the heart of this vision is a clear prophecy about the sacrificial death of Jesus and its significance. Like the other visions in Daniel there are complexities in interpreting some of the details, but the main lines are clear. Daniel's prayer and answer are wonderfully encouraging, humbling and sobering.

Working on the text

The structure of the chapter is as follows:

(1)   Setting, context and basis of Daniel's prayer (vv. 1-3)

(2)   Content of Daniel's prayer (vv. 4-19)

(3)   Answer to Daniel's prayer – vision of the seventy weeks ('sevens') (vv. 20-27)

(1) Setting, context and basis of Daniel's prayer (vv. 1-3)
[See comment above on dating the vision]

Daniel prays according to the Word of God. He is reading the Scriptures (v. 2a). This reference to the Scriptures suggests some kind of recognised canon (also evident from the prayer). The particular Scripture Daniel is reading is Jeremiah 25:8-14 which speaks of the nation serving the king of Babylon for seventy years (see also Jer. 29:10). Daniel prays after the fall of Babylon (9:1). What are we to make of the period of seventy years? If we take the beginning of the Exile to be 605 B.C. (1:1) and the date of chapter 9 to be 539 B.C., sixty-six years have passed. This doesn't present an interpretative problem. The seventy years in Jeremiah is a round number. Moreover, 'seventy years' has a theological significance, described as a Sabbath rest for the land (2 Chron. 36:21). The point is clear. As Daniel reads in Jeremiah that after seventy years the rule of Babylon and the Exile will end, so he is moved to pray. He prays according to the Word of God. That is the basis of his praying.

Moreover, the manner of his prayer is striking, verse 3: 'So I turned to the Lord God and pleaded with him in prayer and petition, in fasting, and in sackcloth and ashes.' Daniel's demeanour conveys powerfully his seriousness and discipline in prayer. Here is a man of deep faith. We have seen this right through Daniel's life, from a very young man in chapter 1 (1:8) to an old man in his eighties (6:10). We will see something similar in chapter 10 which refers to a three-week intense period of prayer before an answer was given (10:2).

(2) Content of Daniel's prayer (vv. 4-19)

In the introductory verses (1-3) we saw how Daniel prays according to the Word of God. As we turn to the content of the actual prayer, it is saturated in Scripture, in particular language that expresses God's words of covenant with His people. Verse 4b: 'Lord, the great and awesome God, who keeps his covenant of love with those who love him and keep his commandments...' Daniel is praying to Yahweh, the covenant God, who is committed to His people by promises that He cannot and will not break. This gets right to the heart of what covenant is. It is a covenant of love. God remains faithful and the covenant is not set aside because of the disobedience of the people. And yet for the covenant blessings to be enjoyed, the response of God's people matters. They are to 'love him and keep his commandments' (v. 4). Covenant commitment is not half-hearted or lip-service. God expects from His people serious, practical obedience.

There is a clear logic / movement in Daniel's prayer. He begins with confession of sin (vv. 4-6). Confessing the sin of God's people leads Daniel to acknowledge the fairness (justice) of God's judgement in giving them into exile (vv. 7-14). In a spirit of repentance Daniel then appeals to God's mercy. Remembering with gratitude God's covenant faithfulness and past mercies, Daniel appeals once again for God's merciful intervention (vv. 15-16). Finally, Daniel is moved to appeal to God to restore Jerusalem and the temple for the sake of the glory of His own name (vv. 17-18).

Confession of sin (vv. 4-6)

The key-note in the first part of the prayer (vv. 4-6) is confession: 'I prayed to the Lord my God (Yahweh, the covenant God) and *confessed*:' (v. 4a). Daniel prays confessing the sin of God's people. The disobedience of God's people has been comprehensive, so the confession of sin is comprehensive. This is no vague feeling or expression of guilt, and in verse 5 Daniel uses a number of specific phrases to show how this disobedience had affected every part of their lives: 'we have sinned' reveals the fundamental problem; 'done wrong' implies a godless and self-centred approach to living; 'we have been wicked and rebelled' implies guilt, evil and rebellion against a sovereign ruler which deserves punishment; 'we have turned away from your commands and laws' suggests determined disobedience, even apostasy. The key to it all is verse 6: 'We have not listened to your servants the prophets, who spoke in your name...' (v. 6a) By not listening to the Word of God through the prophets the people of God had not listened to God. This has affected all of God's people: '…our kings, our princes and our ancestors, and to all the people of the land' (v. 6b). The people of God are without excuse, without hope, except for the mercy and grace of God.

Fairness of God's judgement (vv. 7-14)

Confessing the sin of God's people leads Daniel to acknowledge the fairness (justice) of God's judgement (vv. 7-14). God is righteous (v. 7). God's righteousness is His total integrity and consistency. A clear understanding of the fact that God is righteous, explains both the fairness (justice) of God's judgement against His disobedient people and also leads them to repentance and restoration. We know exactly where we are with God. God's anger against His people is just, never petty nor vindictive. When we come to realise that, it then leads to repentance and restoration. These themes are expressed powerfully in the Psalms, for example in psalm 89, a psalm of the Davidic covenant:

> 'If his sons forsake my law
> > and do not follow my statutes,
> if they violate my decrees
> > and fail to keep my commands,
> I will punish their sin with the rod,
> > their iniquity with flogging;
> but I will not take my love from him,
> > nor will I ever betray my faithfulness.
> I will not violate my covenant,
> > or alter what my lips have uttered.
> Once for all, I have sworn by my
> > holiness – …'
> > > > (Ps. 89:30-35)

It is important to note the scope of Daniel's prayer: '...the people of Judah and the inhabitants of Jerusalem and all Israel, both near and far, in all the countries where you have scattered us because of our unfaithfulness to you' (v. 7). Daniel embraces the two Exiles – the fall of the southern kingdom Judah to Babylon and the earlier fall of the northern kingdom to Assyria. Verse 8 is a repetition of verse 6b – all of God's people are affected.

While the focus in this section of the prayer is on the fairness (justice) of God's judgement as a reflection of His righteous character, in verse 9 Daniel alludes briefly to God's love and mercy (he will return to this more fully in verses 15-16). Verse 9: 'The Lord our God is merciful and forgiving, even though we have rebelled against him; we have not obeyed the Lord our God or kept the laws he gave us through his servants the prophets. All Israel has transgressed your law and turned away, refusing to obey you.' The word 'merciful' (Hebrew *rahamin*) (v. 9) is an intimate word, expressive of God's covenant family love. For example, Jeremiah 31:20 –

> 'Is not Ephraim my dear son,
>   the child in whom I delight?
> Though I often speak against him,
>   I still remember him.
> Therefore my heart yearns for him;
>   I have great compassion (*rahamin*) for him,'
>   declares the Lord.

God is not only merciful towards His people; He actively pursues our good.

In verse 10 Daniel returns to the theme of God's just judgement on his people. Verses 10-11a are a repletion of verse 6 – disobedience of God by not listening to the Word of God through the prophets and how this has affected all God's people. To illustrate this in more depth Daniel focuses on Moses, the great Prophet. The only hope for God's people is to turn back in obedience to the words of Moses, which are the words of God. The reference in verse 11b to 'the curses and sworn judgements written in the Law of Moses, the servant of God' are to the covenant curses set out in Leviticus 26:14-45 and Deuteronomy 28:15-68. God's covenant with His people, set out in the writings of His servant Moses, was expressed in terms of blessings for obedience and curses for disobedience. For example, Deuteronomy 28 begins: 'If you fully obey the Lord your God and carefully follow all his commands that I give you today, the Lord your God will set you high above all the nations on earth. All these blessings will come on you and accompany you if you obey the Lord your God…' (Deut. 28:1-14 elaborates on these blessings.) The second half of the chapter begins: 'However, if you do not obey the Lord your God and do not carefully follow all his commands and decrees I am giving you today, all these curses will come on you and overtake you…' (Deut. 28:15-68 elaborates on these curses.)

Because of the disobedience of God's people, these covenant curses have been fulfilled. Unique privilege has led to unique punishment: 'Under the whole heaven nothing has ever been done like what has been done to Jerusalem' (v. 12b). There is probably a deliberate echo here of Deuteronomy 4:32 – 'ask from one end of the heavens to the other. Has anything so great as this ever happened, or has anything like it ever been heard of?' The events of the Exile (like God's people being taken into slavery in Egypt before the Exodus) were devastating for God's people – deportation, captivity, the destruction of the city and the temple. The word 'disaster' is used in verse 13. The most significant point, however, is that God is the architect of the Exile. God delivered His people into exile because of their covenant disobedience. That point was made right at the start of the book (1:1-2). Verses 13-14 are repetition, emphasising the justice of God's actions in sending His people into exile. It was because of their sin and refusal to give attention to the truth of God's Word (9:13). There is also a suggestion in verse 13 that even after this disaster has come upon God's people they are slow to turn to God in confession and repentance. The book of Daniel teaches us that then (and now) there are few, like Daniel, who recognise the reasons for the state and plight of God's people, the righteousness and justice of God, and the urgent need for corporate confession of sin and repentance. Verse 14 parallels verse 7 and brackets this section – the reason God has done this is because He is 'righteous in everything he does'.

Appeal to God's mercy (vv. 15-16)
Having confessed the sin of God's people acknowledging the rightness of God's judgement, Daniel now prays in a spirit of repentance appealing to God's mercy (vv. 15-16). The righteous God who punishes His people because of their covenant infidelity is also the merciful God who will forgive and restore blessing to His people if they turn to Him in repentance and faith. Daniel remembers with gratitude God's covenant faithfulness and past mercies, appealing once again for His merciful intervention. His focus is on the deliverance from slavery in Egypt (the Exodus). God intervened with 'a mighty hand' (v. 15a) and glorified His name in delivering His people (v. 15b). Verse 16 is important. The fact that God is righteous is

the reason for the Exile (vv. 7, 14). And the fact that God is righteous is the reason Daniel petitions God to end the Exile and restore the reputation of God's people. If there is genuine repentance and obedience God will hear and act. Turning *away* His anger and wrath from His people is as much in keeping with His righteous acts as turning His anger and wrath *against* His people. The God of the covenant is as faithful to His promises of covenant blessing as to His promises of covenant curses.

Appeal to God's glory (vv. 17-19)

The final movement in Daniel's prayer is to appeal to God's zeal for the glory of His own name (vv. 17-19). Daniel appeals to God to restore Jerusalem and the temple for the sake of the glory of God's own name. There have been hints of this earlier in the prayer. For example, in verse 15 where the events of the Exodus 'made for yourself a name that endures to this day'. And in verse 16, Daniel refers to '*your* city', '*your* holy hill', '*your* people' and the reputation of the city and people of God (and by implication, God Himself) to the surrounding nations. What was implicit is now explicit in verses 17-19. 'For your sake, Lord, look with favour on your desolate sanctuary.' (v. 17b) 'Give ear, our God, and hear; open your eyes and see the desolation of the city that bears your Name.' (v. 18a) 'Lord, listen! Lord, forgive! Lord, hear and act! For your sake, my God, do not delay, because your city and your people bear your Name.' (v. 19)

As we reflect on the content of Daniel's prayer it is important to appreciate his affections. By affections we mean his earnestness, sincerity and emotion expressed in the language he uses in the prayer. In the way he prays we see a humble man of God. These are not words to impress but simple and sincere words to express the anatomy of a heart deeply conscious of sin and repentance with a passionate desire for the restoration of the glory of God's name.

(3) Answer to Daniel's prayer – vision of the seventy weeks ('sevens') (vv. 20-27)

In answer to Daniel's prayer the angel Gabriel comes to him with a vision (vv. 20-27). The actual vision is recorded in verses 24-27. The preface in verses 20-23 gives a number of insights as to the nature and purpose of prayer. We will see a similar pattern in the final vision in chapters 10–12, where chapter 10 is an introduction / preface (the theme is prayer and spiritual warfare) before the content of the vision in chapters 11 and 12. Here in chapter 9, Daniel is still praying when the angel Gabriel came to him (v. 21). We are told that Gabriel is the man Daniel had seen in the earlier vision (the reference is to 8:13). Gabriel then tells Daniel that as soon as he began to pray an answer was given (v. 23). Likewise in chapter 10 (the final vision in the book) we are told that Daniel's prayer was heard as soon as he began to pray (10:12). While we can take this as a principle – that prayer borne of a sincere, humble heart is heard immediately – we cannot state as a principle *when* the answer to prayer is given. Here in chapter 9 the answer is given immediately, but in chapter 10 there is a delay of three weeks before the answer is given (10:12-14). God hears our prayers immediately but answers them in accordance with His will and time.

Two other points of note. Daniel is given 'insight and understanding' (v. 22). We see something very similar in chapter 10 where Daniel prays in order to gain understanding (10:12). And the content of the visions in answer to his prayers are precisely that – knowledge and understanding of God's purposes. This suggests a connection between prayer and knowledge of God's purposes. A believer who is prayerful is wise and knowledgeable. A church that is prayerful is wise and knowledgeable. The second point to note is that Daniel is given this insight and understanding because he is 'highly esteemed' (v. 23). Again there are similar references in chapter 10 (10:11, 19). Referring to Daniel as 'highly esteemed' is an indication as to the kind of man Daniel was – a righteous man. This suggests a connection between the state of mind and heart of the person who prays and the effectiveness of their prayers. So, for example, we read in James: 'The prayer of a righteous person is powerful and effective.' (James 5:16)

Turning to the vision itself (vv. 24-27) it is usually referred to as the vision of the seventy weeks or 'sevens'. The numbers seven / seventy are of rich theological significance, symbolising concepts like Creation, completeness, perfection and rest. Clearly in Daniel's mind as he prayed was the end of the Babylonian Exile and the restoration of God's people, the city of Jerusalem and the temple. While this vision clearly speaks of these events, it looks beyond that 'exodus' and restoration to the ultimate and final Exodus and restoration. The return of the exiles from Babylon and the rebuilding of Jerusalem and the temple must have seemed to Daniel like a mountain peak after all these years in exile, but as he ascends that first mountain peak in the vision he sees down the centuries to a mightier peak by far.

Before getting into the timeline and the detail, verse 24 is a summary statement of all that will be achieved within the period the vision covers: 'Seventy "sevens" are decreed for your people and your holy city to finish transgression, to put an end to sin, to atone for wickedness, to bring in everlasting righteousness, to seal up vision and prophecy and to anoint the Most Holy Place.' Reading this verse through the lens of the New Testament, this is clearly a reference to the cross of Christ. Indeed, we would struggle to find a more succinct and comprehensive statement anywhere in Scripture about what the death of Jesus achieves. Jesus' death will be the once and for all sacrifice for sin: 'finish transgression', 'put an end to sin', 'atone for wickedness'. It will be the final word. It will bring about the ultimate Exodus and restoration. It will bring in the everlasting Kingdom of God. The reference to the 'Most Holy Place' is no longer to the Ark of the Covenant in the temple, but the true ark, the Lord Jesus, who became flesh and made His dwelling among us (John 1:14).

Turning now to the timeline and the detail.

Verse 24, as we have seen, covers the entire period of seventy 'sevens'.

Verse 25 covers the first sixty-nine 'sevens'. Again, it's helpful to set the verse out in full: 'Know and understand this: from the time the word goes out to restore and rebuild Jerusalem until the Anointed One, the ruler, comes, there will be seven "sevens", and sixty-two "sevens". It will be rebuilt with streets and a trench but in times of trouble.' The sixty-nine 'sevens' are divided into two periods: one of seven 'sevens' and one of sixty-two 'sevens'.

The period of seven 'sevens' we take to be the period from Cyrus' decree to the rebuilding of the temple and city of Jerusalem. The 'word...to restore and rebuild Jerusalem' is almost certainly Cyrus' decree in 539 B.C. to end the Exile. The temple restoration was completed in 516 B.C. with the walls and city rebuilt in 445 B.C. and rededicated in 444 B.C. The books of Ezra and Nehemiah are a record of this period. The reference in Daniel's vision to rebuilding 'in times of trouble' is amplified in Ezra and Nehemiah with the many setbacks / opposition to rebuilding. But in the end it was done. That's the first period, the seven 'sevens'.

This is followed by the sixty-two 'sevens', the period from the completion of Jerusalem to the coming of the Anointed One, the ruler. The Anointed One, the ruler, is the Lord Jesus. There are echoes here of the earlier visions in chapter 2 and, especially chapter 7. In chapter 7 the Lord Jesus, referred to as 'one like a son of man' is crowned as King of God's everlasting Kingdom. Whereas in chapter 7 the focus was on the coronation of the King, here in chapter 9 the focus is on the King's cross / the death of the King.

This brings us to verses 26 and 27. Here the focus is on the final or seventieth 'seven'. Both verses 26 and 27 describe separately this final 'seven'. In other words, the verses are parallel rather than chronological. We will take each in turn.

First, verse 26: 'After the sixty-two "sevens", the Anointed One will be put to death and will have nothing. The people of the ruler who will come will destroy the city and the sanctuary. The end will come like a flood: war will continue until the end and desolations have been decreed.' The first part of the verse is clearly a reference to the death of Jesus. Texts like Isaiah 53:8 come to mind: 'for he was cut off from the land of the living...' What do we make of the rest of verse 26? The middle of the verse implies that God's people will destroy the city and the sanctuary. How can this be? We take this to be a reference to the destruction of the city and the temple in A.D. 70 by Titus Flavius Vespasianus. It was the Romans who destroyed the city and the temple but the underlying cause of destruction was the Jews' rejection of the Messiah (hence blame is attributed to them). The final part of the verse is probably a reference to the period between the coming of Christ and His return at the end of time. This will be the focus of the latter part of the final vision (11:26-12:13). The end times will be times of distress for the people of God with an intensifying period of distress just before the end (the time of the Antichrist). But God rules and the end will come, the Lord Jesus will return and the Kingdom of God will come in all its fullness.

Finally, verse 27: 'He will confirm a covenant with many for one "seven". In the middle of the "seven" he will put an end to sacrifice and offering. And at the temple he will set up an abomination that causes desolation, until the end that is decreed is poured out on him.' The first part of the verse is again clearly referring to the Lord Jesus, His once and for all sacrifice for sin and the everlasting covenant sealed at Calvary. What do we make of the second part of the verse? Clearly the 'he' cannot be the Lord Jesus. He does not set up an abomination that causes desolation; and nor does He meet His end in judgement. If we take verses 26 and 27 as parallel rather than chronological (a device common in apocalyptic writing), then we can see this as corresponding to the activities of 'the people of the ruler'. Sacrifices in the Jerusalem temple obviously ceased with its destruction in A.D. 70. The 'abomination that causes desolation' is probably the destruction of the temple by Titus; the 'wing of the temple' can mean 'edge' or 'extremity' and could be the whole siege of Jerusalem working up to this climactic moment. Alternatively (or in addition to this interpretation) the second half of the verse could be referring to the period of the Antichrist before the end of history. We suggest this as a plausible interpretation of 12:11.

Fig. 1 summarises the vision of the seventy weeks ('sevens').

Fig. 1 Vision of seventy weeks ('sevens')

Cyrus' decree to end the Exile (539 B.C.)

Period of seven 'sevens'

Temple and Jerusalem restored (444 B.C.)

Period of sixty-two 'sevens'

Final 'seven'   Coming of Jesus / death of Jesus
(Ultimate Exodus and restoration)

> Destruction of the temple and Jerusalem in A.D. 70

> Time of the Antichrist

> End of history

While we cannot be certain about some of the details, the main lines of the vision are clear. Daniel prayed that the Exile would come to an end. It did. And yet he was shown a far greater Exodus that brought a far greater Exile to an end. It would take the death of the Anointed One, the Lord Jesus. Yet even when the Lord Jesus has come, and the everlasting Kingdom of God has broken in, there will be a long period of continued distress until the end comes and the Lord Jesus returns bringing His Kingdom in all its fullness.

From text to message

(1) Get the message clear

i) Big idea

Praying in light of God's rule. Praying according to the Word of God that reflects God's covenant with His people.

(ii) Key questions

Preaching or teaching on this passage should answer the following questions:

- What does it mean to pray in light of God's rule?

- What does it mean to pray according to the Word of God?

- What is the nature of God's covenant with His people today?

- What should we expect of God when we pray?

- What do we learn from Daniel's attitude and demeanour in prayer?

(2) Engage the hearer

i) Point of contact

A good point of contact would be to read an account of earnest biblical prayer that has preceded a time of revival in the Church.

Or, as we come nearer to the end of the book, it might be helpful to given an overview / summary of Daniel as a man of God and prayer. You could begin with Daniel as a teenager in chapter 1 through to an old man at the end of the Exile (Chs. 5, 6, 9, 10-12). This might be a helpful way of rooting the chapter into people's day to day prayer life.

ii) Dominant pictures / Illustrations

In relation to the comment above, a dominant picture is the seriousness / earnestness of Daniel as a man of prayer. His outward demeanour expresses the state of his heart. More-over, the affections he reveals in the language and expression he uses are striking.

Daniel's prayer is at the heart of the section dealing with the prophetic visions in Daniel. The dominant picture

of these visions is that God rules and is building an everlasting Kingdom. That is happening in the context of
spiritual warfare.

In relation to the vision Daniel receives as the answer
to his prayer, a helpful picture is of climbing a mountain.
When we reach what we think is the summit, we realise it is
just one peak with much larger peaks ahead.

It would be helpful to illustrate the nature of God's covenant with His people. Common illustrations are a contrac-
tual agreement or a marriage.

(3) Work on application

- Daniel's demeanour, manner and the words /
  language he uses in prayer merit careful application.
  Matthew 6:5-8 is very helpful, where the emphasis
  is on praying in secret to be seen and heard by God
  alone (rather than praying to be seen by others) and
  praying with simple words to express what is in our
  hearts rather than words to impress others.

- Praying according to the Word of God means,
  amongst other things, praying according to how
  the Bible teaches us to pray. Jesus' teaching on
  prayer (e.g. Matt. 6:9-15) is very helpful, in many
  senses a New Testament application of the content
  of Daniel's prayer. The opening petitions are
  particularly relevant: 'hallowed be your name', 'your
  kingdom come', 'your will be done, on earth as it is in
  heaven' (Matt. 6:9-10). These petitions mean praying
  for the honour of God's name / God's glory, the
  growth of God's everlasting Kingdom and the return
  of Jesus so that God's Kingdom will come in all its
  fullness. Another fruitful way of applying Daniel's

prayer might be through the lens of some of the prayers in the New Testament letters. For example, Paul's prayer for the Philippians is for knowledge and depth of insight so that they might discern what is best (Phil. 1:9-11). This has strong resonances with Daniel's reason for praying in chapters 9 and 10.

- Daniel's prayer is grounded in God's covenant with His people. As Christians, as the Church, what is the covenant relationship we have with God? Through faith in Jesus as our Saviour and Lord we enter into an everlasting covenant sealed in Jesus' blood. While there are many differences with the covenant framework in Daniel's prayer, the essential principles are the same. God expects us to live distinctively in light of His rule. If we reject His Word and disobey Him we cannot expect Him to ignore that. The letters to the churches in Revelation 1–3 make that clear. In the New Covenant God still punishes and disciplines His people.

- In this regard, what does it mean for us to confess the sins of God's people? Or what does it mean for us to pray for a desolate Church? We begin by acknowledging our own sin, but corporate confession of sin is also important. We can bear the sins of others as we pray – our local church or the Church on a bigger canvas. It is helpful to remember that Daniel's confession of sin is specific.

- What does it mean for us to acknowledge the fairness (justness) of God's judgement? Certainly in the West it is not hard for us to see the consequences of our loss of distinctiveness and clarity as God's people. Is the Church in the West under God's judgement? Rather than speculating on whether or not it is, we should pray with a deep spirit of repentance acknowledging the spiritual poverty of the times in which we live.

- What does it mean for us to pray with thanksgiving recalling God's merciful intervention in the past, appealing once again to His mercy? We can recall in prayer how God has intervened again and again through the Bible to restore and revive His work. We can recall in prayer instances in Church history. Equally, we might recall circumstances in our local church context or individual lives.

- What does it mean to pray, appealing to God's zeal for the glory of His own name? In this part of his prayer (9:17-19) Daniel is at his most direct and bold in the language he uses. It reveals a heart consumed with a passionate desire for God's glory. This cannot be manufactured. It is a God-given burden that longs for the glory of God to return to His Church.

- In terms of answer to prayer, we can expect our prayers to be heard immediately, but when and how God answers is for Him to determine.

- In terms of the vision of seventy weeks ('sevens') we are living in the period after the vision or in the period of the final 'seven' (depending on our interpretation). Either way, we are waiting for the return of Jesus with a certainty that He will come. The times in which we are living, waiting for His return, are stressful times.

Outline for a sermon or talk

The suggested outline follows the structure of the prayer and then the answer. The logical movements in Daniel's prayer suggest this approach.

An outline is included in the next chapter that takes Daniel 9 and 10 together.

Title: Praying in light of God's rule
Text: Daniel 9

Structure:

(1) *Covenant praying according to the Word of God (vv. 1-3)*

(2) *Praying for restoration (vv. 4-19)*

   i) *Confession of sin (vv. 4-6)*

   ii) *Fairness of God's judgement (vv. 7-14)*

   iii) *Appeal to God's mercy (vv. 15-16)*

   iv) *Appeal to God's glory (vv. 17-19)*

(3) *God's answer (vv. 20-27)*

   i) *The vision of the seventy weeks ('sevens')*

   ii) *What are we praying for today?*

Bible study on Daniel 9

A Bible study is included in the next chapter that takes Daniel 9 and 10 together.

Read Daniel 9

(1) Introduce the issues

   i) This is one of the great prayers of the Bible. In terms of first impressions, what are some of the striking features of Daniel's prayer?

   ii) What is the significance of including Daniel's prayer in the section of the book containing the prophetic visions (Chs. 7–12)?

   iii) Daniel's prayer is thoroughly biblical and grounded in covenant theology. Again, in terms of first impressions, how is that evident in his prayer?

   iv) There is a clear logic / movement in Daniel's prayer. What is that pattern?

(2) Study the passage

   i) What is the significance of the timing of Daniel's prayer (9:1) in the context of the book as a whole (think in particular of Chs. 5 and 6 and Cyrus' decree to end the Exile)?

   ii) Daniel prays according to the Word of God (v. 2). What is the content / significance of the Scripture passage he has been reading (Jer. 25:8-14; also Jer. 29:10)?

   iii) What is conveyed about Daniel's attitude / seriousness in the way that he prays (vv. 2-3)?

   iv) The prayer is both personal and corporate. How is that conveyed in the text of the prayer?

   v) Daniel's prayer is grounded in God's covenant with His people (v. 4b). What is the nature of that covenant?

vi) Daniel begins with confession of sin (vv. 4-6). What is the content / scope of that confession?

vii) Next, Daniel expresses in his prayer the fairness of God's judgement (vv. 7-14). Why is God's judgement on His people fair?

viii) On what grounds does Daniel appeal to God's mercy (vv. 15-16)?

ix) Daniel concludes his prayer by boldly appealing to God's own glory (vv. 17-19)? What does this tell us about Daniel's understanding about who God is?

x) When is Daniel's prayer heard (v. 23)? Can we take that as a general principle? What about the timing of God's answer to our prayers?

xi) What is the meaning of the vision of seventy weeks ('sevens') (vv. 24-27)? (We suggest you work carefully through the detailed explanation in the notes.)

xii) What do we learn from this vision about the cross (vv. 24, 26, 27)?

(3) *Apply the passage*

i) What can we learn and apply to our prayer life from Daniel as an example?

ii) What does it mean for us to pray according to the Word of God?

iii) What is the nature of God's covenant with us and what does it mean for us to pray in light of this covenant?

iv) In light of Daniel's prayer, what should we be praying for the Church in our day? More specifically:

   (a) What does it mean for us to pray, confessing the sins of God's people?

   (b) What does it mean for us to pray, acknowledging the fairness (justice) of God's judgement?

   (c) What does it mean for us to pray with thanksgiving recalling God's merciful interventions in the past?

   (d) What does it mean for us to pray, appealing to God's zeal for the glory of His own name?

v) What answer are we looking for / can we expect from God?

vi) What confidence does this vision give us in the inspiration and reliability of God's Word?

vii) In summary, what does it mean to pray in light of God's rule?

(4) *Pray it through*

II

PRAYER AND SPIRITUAL WARFARE
(DANIEL 10:1–11:1)

Setting in context

(1) Dating

This final vision in the book is dated as the 'third year of Cyrus king of Persia' (v. 1). The date is 536 B.C. Daniel receives the vision after Cyrus' decree in 539 B.C. to end the Exile (2 Chron. 36:22-23; Ezra 1:1-4; Isa. 45:1).

(2) Context – structure of book

Fig. 1 in the chapter dealing with Daniel 7 details the four visions recorded in the second half of the book. Each vision is precisely dated, allowing us to relate the visions to particular times and events in the Exile. Daniel chapters 10–12 record a single vision. Fig. 1 explains the structure.

Fig. 1 Final vision in Daniel 10–12

Vision	Description
Ch. 10:1–11:1	Prayer and spiritual warfare
Ch. 11:2-45	God's rule through history
Ch. 12	God's rule in the end

Chapter 10 is an extended introduction before the vision is explained from verse 2 of chapter 11. The vision in chapter 11 focuses on the same detailed period of history as the vision in chapter 8 – the persecution under Antiochus in the second century B.C. In chapter 12 the lens widens to look forward to the end of history and the security of God's people till then.

This final vision (like the visions in Chs. 8 and 9) is in Hebrew, dealing with matters of particular relevance to the people of God. The Aramaic section (2:4–7:28) concerns matters of universal significance.

(3) Context – message of book
The message of Daniel is that *God rules, is building an everlasting Kingdom, and calls people to live in light of that fact.* This final vision is a fitting conclusion to the message of the book.

It begins in chapter 10 with a 'behind the scenes' look at the spiritual warfare going on through history. This introductory material also gives us a fascinating insight into the relationship between prayer and spiritual warfare.

The content of the vision in chapter 11 is very detailed. Such detailed focus on a particular period of history shows that God is in control as much in the detail as in the big picture. It also shows God's concern for His people, His preservation of them and the advance of His Kingdom through tough times. As we shall see (in particular towards the end of Ch. 11) the detailed prophecy points to the bigger picture. The focus on Antiochus as an antichrist is suggestive of a repeated pattern throughout history, where individuals and powers will oppose God and His people (many antichrists). It also points forward to *the* Antichrist at the end of history.

Into chapter 12, the final part of the final vision (and the last words of the book), the perspective shifts. What we have is a long lens looking down through the centuries to the end of history. God rules through history (Ch. 11) but also over the end of history (Ch. 12). The end will happen when He determines. All people will be resurrected and judged. And we are to live in light of that fact.

While it is important to remember that chapters 10–12 record a single vision, there is so much content and rich detail that we will take each chapter in turn as a separate study.

Working on the text

The structure of the chapter is as follows:

(1) The timing, content and context of the vision (vv. 1-3)

(2) Daniel sees the Son of Man and is overwhelmed (vv. 4-9)

(3) Daniel receives reassurance and a revelation about prayer and spiritual warfare (vv. 10-14)

(4) Daniel is overwhelmed and receives further reassurance (10:15–11:1)

We take verse 1 of chapter 11 along with chapter 10.

(1) The timing, content, and context of the vision (vv. 1-3)
Daniel receives this vision in the third year of Cyrus (v. 1). The Exile is over and the first group of exiles had returned to the land following Cyrus' decree a few years earlier. Daniel is still in Babylon (v. 4). The reference in verse 1 to 'Daniel (who was called Belteshazzar)' suggests a deliberate link with chapter 1. Belteshazzar was the Babylonian name given

to Daniel seventy years earlier (1:7). The opening chapter, describing the beginning of the Exile and Daniel's early years in Babylon, also functions as a Prologue to the book as a whole. It ends with a statement that Daniel 'remained there (in Babylon) until the first year of king Cyrus' (1:21). In other words, God kept Daniel right through the Exile to its end. It is now the third year of Cyrus (10:1). Daniel is an old man, perhaps withdrawn from active service. Daniel's faithfulness and perseverance, and more particularly, God's preservation of Daniel and the outworking of His purposes are underlined. After the traumatic events of the Exile what did the future hold for God's people? The experience of the first group of returning exiles had been discouraging (Ezra 4). Was that a sign of things to come?

It is at this significant time Daniel receives this revelation or vision which is true (authoritative) and which concerns a great war or conflict (v. 1). This word translated 'great war' or 'conflict' is used, for example, in Isaiah 40:2 of the Exile itself – 'her (i.e. Zion's) warfare or conflict is over'. A more general meaning is probably intended here – that the progress of history is spiritual warfare as God builds His everlasting Kingdom in a hostile, godless world.

The reference in verse 2 to a three week period of mourning and fasting is suggestive of an intense period of prayer Daniel has been engaged in *before he receives this vision*. Again, there are echoes of chapter 1. Daniel's decision not to take the royal food and wine (1:8) was indicative of his serious commitment to and allegiance to God. And in chapter 9, Daniel's abstinence and demeanour (9:3) reflect the seriousness and earnestness of his praying. What has Daniel been praying about here in chapter 10? We are told in verse 12 – to gain understanding and to humble himself before God. In light of the visions Daniel had already received concerning the future (Chs. 7, 8 and 9) he wants to understand more. He wants to understand more about the future of God's people and God's purposes. The answer to prayer he receives is further confirmation this is what he has been praying for. The answer concerns 'what will happen to your people in the future…a time yet to come' (v. 14). It is striking that Daniel's prayer for understanding is accompanied by a desire to humble himself before God. We saw this in the manner of Daniel's praying in chapter 9. Understanding is given because of his humble dependence on God.

(2) Daniel sees the Son of Man and is overwhelmed (vv. 4-9)

The precise date – the twenty-fourth day of the first month (v. 4a) – emphasises that Daniel receives the vision after the three-week period of prayer. Moreover, it is a simple factual statement. There is nothing vague about when Daniel received this vision. The date is precise and so is the location. Daniel was standing on the bank of the great river, the Tigris (v. 4b). Daniel sees a heavenly messenger (vv. 5-6). The messenger is dressed in linen, a priestly garment, but more especially associated with the Day of Atonement (Lev. 16:4). It was also the dress of the angelic visitor in Ezekiel 9:2. The belt of gold is a sign of royalty. The eyes of fire and powerful voice suggest a presence of overwhelming majesty. Lightning in Scripture is characteristic of a theophany, an appearance of God (e.g. Exod. 19:16; 20:18; Ezek. 1:13-14; Ps. 18:12). Who is this heavenly messenger? In the earlier visions in chapters 8 and 9 the messenger is the angel Gabriel (8:13; 9:21), but here in chapter 10 it is the Lord Jesus. How can we be sure? The description in verses 5 and 6 is very similar to the description of the Son of Man in Revelation 1:12-15. Moreover, the description of the Son of Man in Daniel 7 gives further weight to this interpretation. So here we have a pre-incarnate appearance of the Lord Jesus.

Daniel, like Paul on the road to Damascus, is the only one who sees the vision, and those with Daniel, like those with Paul (Acts 9:3ff), are terrified but do not understand what is happening (v. 7). Left alone, the effect on Daniel of what he has seen is significant (v. 8). It leaves him completely powerless, drained of health and energy. As the messenger begins to speak Daniel falls into a deep sleep, his face to the ground (v. 9).

(3) Daniel receives reassurance and a revelation about prayer and spiritual warfare (vv. 10-14)

Reassurance comes in two ways. First there is a personal encouragement for Daniel (vv. 10-11) and then further revelation (vv. 12-14).

The personal encouragement is physical as well as verbal. The touch (v. 10a) comes first and conveys warmth and affection. Yet even that sets Daniel trembling (v. 10b). The words 'Daniel, you are highly esteemed' (v. 11a) reinforce the encouragement of the touch. The Lord Jesus has been sent to speak to Daniel and he is able to stand up, although still feeling weak (v. 11b).

Reassurance also comes through further revelation (vv. 12-14). These verses take us to the heart of the mystery of prayer. Three things to note:

First, Daniel is told that as soon as he began to pray for understanding his prayers were heard (v. 12). The delay in

Daniel being given the answer is not because his prayer was not heard. It was heard immediately.

Second, Daniel is told the reason for the delay. Verse 13: 'But the prince of the Persian kingdom resisted me twenty-one days. Then Michael, one of the chief princes, came to help me, because I was detained there with the king of Persia…' The delay is because the Lord is engaged in a spiritual battle. On the Lord's side is Michael (the angel Michael), and they are engaged in a battle against the 'prince of the Persian kingdom'. Looking forward to verses 20-21 and the first verse of chapter 11, the description is similar: 'Do you know why I have come to you? Soon I will return to fight against the prince of Persia, and when I go, the prince of Greece will come; but first I will tell you what is written in the Book of Truth. (No-one supports me against them (that is against the 'prince of Persia' and the 'prince of Greece') except Michael, your prince. And in the first year of Darius the Mede, I took my stand to support and protect him.)' Who is the 'prince of the Persian kingdom' and the 'prince of Greece'? In the visions in Daniel, a contrast is drawn repeatedly between human kingdoms, where rule is exercised without reference to God, and God's everlasting Kingdom where God's people submit to the rule of God's King. The detailed visions in chapters 8 and 11 focus on a particular period of history, the Medo-Persian (539–331 B.C.) and Greek (331–63 B.C.) kingdoms. These are the kingdoms that followed the Babylonian dynasty. The 'prince of the Persian kingdom' and the 'prince of Greece' are ways of describing, in apocalyptic language, the evil forces that characterized these superpowers. Their intent is to dominate the world, to conquer all before them, to rule without reference to God and persecute the people of God.

This is the specific interpretation intended (to Medo-Persia and Greece) but, as we have seen, apocalyptic language also suggests a general interpretation to all manifestations of fallen human power through history. Behind it all is the Devil, referred to as the prince or ruler of this world (John 12:31, 14:30, 16:11; Eph. 2:2). The reason for the delay, therefore, is spiritual warfare. This revelation Daniel receives not only explains why there has been a delay in the answer to his prayer, but makes the more general point that behind the scenes of human history there is spiritual warfare. That was true in Daniel's day. It is true still. Even though the Devil has been defeated at the cross, spiritual warfare will continue until Jesus returns. It is what the apostle Paul refers to in Ephesians 6: 'Finally, be strong in the Lord and in his mighty power. Put on the full armour of God, so that you can take your stand against the Devil's schemes. For our struggle is not against flesh and blood, but against the rulers, against the authorities, against the powers of this dark world, and against the spiritual forces of evil in the heavenly realms.' (Eph. 6:10-12)

The third thing we learn from these verses is the connection between prayer and spiritual warfare. At one level, simply to appreciate the fact of spiritual warfare impresses on us the need to depend on God in prayer. Daniel's dominant reaction in this chapter is fear at what he sees. These are matters way beyond our ability and bring us to our knees in humble dependence on God. Prayer also engages us in this spiritual warfare. We cannot understand fully what this engagement or participation means, or exactly how God uses the prayers of His people in the outworking of His purposes. The fact is He does. How He does is largely a mystery beyond our comprehension.

(4) Daniel is overwhelmed and receives further reassurance (10:15–11:1)

We have already seen in verses 8 and 9 Daniel's reaction to what he sees and the reassurance and further revelation he is given (vv. 10-14). That same cycle is repeated here. Daniel's reaction is to be humbled and left speechless (v. 15). He receives another touch from the Lord, this time on the lips enabling him to speak (v. 16a). This is reminiscent of how God touched Isaiah's lips with fire from the altar (Isa. 6:7), a cleansing touch which led to Isaiah proclaiming a message. Yet again Daniel expresses his extreme weakness (vv. 16b-17) and receives a third strengthening touch (v. 18). Like Elijah in a similar situation (1 Kings 19:5-8) he is given help to continue. The strengthening touch is accompanied by words of encouragement: 'Do not be afraid, you who are highly esteemed,' he said. 'Peace! Be strong now; be strong.' (v. 19a). Daniel is strengthened and asks the Lord to speak (v. 19b). The Lord indicates that He will soon return to the battle ground of spiritual warfare but first (v. 21) will tell Daniel what is written in the 'Book of Truth'. We have already been told what is written in this book – 'what will happen to your people in the future, for the vision concerns a time yet to come' (v. 14). The point is that the future is already determined and controlled by God. The promises concerning God's everlasting Kingdom repeated through Daniel will happen. Humanly speaking it looks and feels impossible. But what God promises will happen. The inevitable progress of human history is the triumph of good over evil, the coronation of the Son of Man as King of God's everlasting Kingdom and His return in triumphant glory. These events were determined and set in God's 'Book of Truth' in the ages of time. God has committed Himself to bring them to pass.

Verse 1 of chapter 11 is probably better taken as the ending of chapter 10. The first year of Darius / Cyrus (539 B.C.) is the year that marked the end of the Exile (9:1). It was Cyrus who decreed the end of the Exile but behind the scenes it is the outworking of spiritual warfare. Verse 21 of chapter 10 and verse 1 of chapter 11 convey the reality of the toughness of this warfare. It might look and feel like God is on the back foot, yet God reigns and is building His Kingdom. The mighty superpowers of the Medo-Persian and Greek kingdoms have come and gone, but God's everlasting Kingdom is marching on.

From text to message

(1) Get the message clear

i) Big idea

God rules and is building an everlasting Kingdom. That is happening through spiritual warfare.

ii) Key questions

Preaching or teaching on this passage should answer the following questions:

- Who is spiritual warfare between?

- What do we learn about the Lord Jesus in terms of spiritual warfare?

- What do we learn about the role of angels in spiritual warfare?

- In terms of this spiritual warfare and its outcome, what happened at the cross?

- What is the relationship between prayer and spiritual warfare?

- What do we learn about our attitude in prayer and the focus and content of our prayers?

- What do we learn about the Lord Jesus' care for us?

(2) Engage the hearer

i) Point of contact

C. S. Lewis' enchanting book *The Lion, the Witch and the Wardrobe* remains as fresh and charming as when it was first published over sixty years ago. Perhaps no small part of its fascination is the connection of the everyday world to the land of Narnia by means of an ordinary wardrobe. Both Narnia and the wardrobe are real, but Narnia is a deeper country and what happens there profoundly and decisively affects what happens in the visible world on this side of the wardrobe. In this final section of Daniel, once again, the visible world (in this case the banks of the Tigris) opens into a deeper country and the events on earth are seen as echoes of events in the unseen world. Our eyes need to be opened to this world, which is not less real, the realm of spiritual warfare.

ii) Dominant pictures / illustrations

The relationship between what we see on the surface and what is happening behind the scenes is a dominant picture. This can be illustrated in a number of ways. For example, as we go about our business in the modern world, there are all sorts of people and agencies who are working in the background to protect us. In politics, there are politicians we see, but behind them in the background the machinery of state and the civil service where, in many ways, the real power lies. In sport, we see famous victories on the pitch or the race track, but the real battle is fought on the training ground or in the gym. Another helpful illustration might be a theatre. We see the drama unfolding on the stage, but behind the scenes there are all sorts of people at work, changing the scenery, controlling the lights and sound. And, of course there is the Director, the most important person who remains unseen.

When preaching or teaching on prophecy written in apocalyptic language, it is important to acknowledge and convey in your teaching the powerful sensory impact of what is described in the visions. The description here is very dramatic.

As dramatic as the description of spiritual warfare is, the way Daniel is reassured, both physically and verbally, is very moving. Appropriate illustrations of this might be a parent reassuring a child, or maybe an army General reassuring a soldier.

Daniel's demeanour, attitude and seriousness in prayer are striking. He functions in Scripture as a model believer, a picture or illustration of what we should be like.

(3) Work on application

- The reality of spiritual warfare is the dominant application of this chapter. It is important to explain clearly the spiritual battle that is going on behind the scenes in human history and who the chief protagonists are: on one side the Lord and His angels and on the other side, the Devil and his angels. The nature of the battle is the advance of God's purposes (the building of His everlasting Kingdom) against the forces of evil. Ephesians

6:10-12 is a helpful New Testament text that summarises the message of Daniel 10.

- We argue that the heavenly messenger in this vision is the Son of Man, the Lord Jesus. The almost identical description of the Lord Jesus in Revelation 1 is decisive in this interpretation. The closing book of the Bible is Christ's revelation to the Church, much of which is concerned with the reality and nature of spiritual warfare. The connection between a book like Daniel and Revelation is important. While the decisive victory in the spiritual battle was won at the cross (the Devil has been defeated), spiritual warfare will continue until the time of the end when the Lord Jesus returns. Indeed, as we shall see in chapters 11 and 12, it will intensify before the Lord Jesus returns.

- The relationship between prayer and spiritual warfare / the outworking of God's purposes is an important application. Simply to appreciate the fact of spiritual warfare impresses on us the need to depend on God in prayer. But prayer also engages us in this spiritual warfare. While we cannot understand fully what this engagement or participation means, or exactly how God uses our prayers, the fact is He does. This brings a seriousness and urgency to our prayer lives.

- Daniel's motivation to pray is to gain understanding and to humble himself before God (v. 12). The Bible teaches us a number of reasons why we should pray, but Daniel's desire for understanding and to humble himself before God should certainly be among them. Given we have God's full and final revelation in His Word, what does this mean for us? Simply that we will understand God's Word. Do we pray with a serious desire for that? And do we pray simply in order to humble ourselves before God.

- Daniel's manner in prayer is striking. We saw this in the prayer in chapter 9, his outward demeanour reflecting the seriousness of his mind and heart. And again here, this three-week period of mourning and waiting on the Lord (vv. 2-3). These are not prescriptive practices that we must follow, but there is a great deal we can learn in terms of attitude of mind and heart.

- Daniel's reaction to what he sees in this vision is striking. He is profoundly affected by it, frightened by what he sees. Understanding the reality of spiritual warfare is frightening and Daniel's reaction is real, authentic. In preaching or teaching this passage we should expect people to react in this way. Indeed, we want to encourage people to react in this way – it is what the text impresses on us.

- Daniel's real reaction is met by real encouragement from the Lord. We need to remember that the touch of the Lord Jesus was not physical in the sense of it actually happening. The touch was in the vision, no less real, but spiritual. We too can receive that touch as the Holy Spirit reassures us, strengthens us, ministers to us. The Lord Jesus also spoke to Daniel and then in the content of the vision in chapters 11 and 12 that follow gave him the understanding he prayed for. If, like Daniel, we are serious, earnest and humble before God, the words of encouragement he is given and takes to heart, we need to hear and take to heart as given to us. In this dramatic and frightening vision about spiritual warfare there is a sweetness and intimacy about how the Lord Jesus comes to Daniel personally and encourages him. He will do the same for us.

Outline for a sermon or talk

The first outline is on Daniel 10.

It is important to convey that chapter 10 is the introduction to the final vision that covers chapters 10–12. Setting chapter 10 in this context adds power and relevance to the talk.

Given the cyclical nature of the revelation in the chapter a thematic approach rather than a systematic approach is better, in other words the different points in the sermon or talk would draw on verses from across the chapter.

A second outline takes Daniel 9 and 10 together (this might be appropriate for a shorter series on the book).

Outline 1

Title: Prayer and spiritual warfare
Text: Daniel 10.1–11.1

Structure:

(1) The final vision (Chs. 10–12)

(2) Reality of spiritual warfare

  i) *Nature of the conflict*

  ii) *The outcome of the battle*

iii) *The end of the battle*

(3) **Prayer and spiritual warfare**

   i) *Daniel's praying*

   ii) *The Lord's encouragement and answer*

   iii) *Participation in spiritual warfare*

The sub-points above may or may not be used in the outline. They are included here simply to help with the flow of logical thought.

Outline 2 (Daniel 9 and 10 together)

Title: Praying in light of God's rule
Text: Daniel 9–10

Structure:

(1) **Daniel's prayer and answer (Ch. 9)**

(2) **Prayer and spiritual warfare (Ch. 10)**

(3) **Daniel's example in prayer**

Bible study on Daniel 10:1–11:1

Read chapter 10:1–11:1

(1) Introduce the issues

   i) In Daniel 10, we're taken 'behind the scenes' and given a sight of the spiritual warfare that is going on throughout history. What first impressions does this chapter leave you with?

   ii) The chapter gives us an insight into the relationship between prayer and spiritual warfare as God builds His everlasting Kingdom. How do you think prayer engages us with that conflict as God builds His Kingdom?

(2) *Study the passage*

   i) Remembering that Daniel 10 is an Introduction / Preface to the final vision in the book (Chs. 10–12), when did Daniel receive this vision and what's the significance of the timing (10:1)?

   ii) The text suggests that Daniel has been engaged in an intense period of prayer before he receives the vision (vv. 2-3). What does this tell us about Daniel's attitude / seriousness in prayer?

   iii) What are the two reasons Daniel is praying and how do they relate to one another (v. 12)?

   iv) When is Daniel's prayer heard (v. 12)? Can we take that as a general principle? What about the timing of God's answers to our prayers?

   v) The answer to prayer Daniel is given concerns 'a great war' or conflict (v. 1) and 'what will happen to your people in the future…a time yet to come' (v. 14). This will be the focus of the vision recorded in chapters 11–12. What do these phrases mean?

   vi) Who is the heavenly messenger that comes to Daniel and what accounts for Daniel's reaction (vv. 4-9)?

   vii) What reassurance is Daniel given and what is revealed to him about prayer and spiritual warfare (vv. 10-14)?

   viii) How does Daniel react and what further reassurance is he given (10:15-11:1)?

(3) *Apply the passage*

   i) Daniel prays for understanding and to humble himself before God (v. 12). He also prays with an evident seriousness (vv. 2-3)? What can we learn and apply to our prayer life from Daniel as an example?

  ii) Daniel was deeply affected by what he saw – both seeing the heavenly messenger and the reality of spiritual warfare. What effect does God's revelation in His Word about Jesus, spiritual warfare and the outworking of His purposes have on us?

 iii) What do we learn from this chapter about the reality of spiritual warfare? Living this side of the cross, when God's everlasting Kingdom has come, is there still spiritual warfare (Eph. 6:10-12)?

 iv) What is the relationship between prayer and spiritual warfare?

  v) What encouragement can we take as believers from this chapter?

(4) *Pray it through*

Bible study on Daniel 9 and 10

Read chapters 9 and 10:1–11:1

(1) *Introduce the issues*

Chapters 9 and 10 powerfully convey the seriousness and significance of prayer. From reading these two chapters what are some of the things we can learn about the way Daniel prayed?

(2) *Study the passage*

   i) What is the significance of the timing of Daniel's prayer (9:1) in the context of the book as a whole (think in particular of Chs. 5 and 6 and Cyrus' decree to end the Exile)?

  ii) Daniel prays in accordance with the Word of God and God's covenant with His people. How is this evident in his prayer?

 iii) What is the logic / movement in Daniel's prayer?

    (a) What is the scope of his confession of sin (9:4-6)?

    (b) How does he express in prayer the fairness of God's judgement (9:7-14)?

    (c) On what grounds does Daniel appeal to God's mercy (9:15-16)?

    (d) Why does Daniel appeal to God's own glory (9:17-19)?

 (iv) What is the meaning of the vision of seventy weeks ('sevens') (9:24-27)? (We suggest you work carefully through the detailed explanation in the notes.)

  (v) In Daniel 10, we're taken 'behind the scenes' and given a sight of the spiritual warfare that is going on throughout history. What do we learn?

 (vi) Who is the heavenly messenger that comes to Daniel and what accounts for Daniel's reaction (10:4-9)?

(vii) What reassurance is Daniel given and what is revealed to him about prayer and spiritual warfare (vv. 10-14)?

(viii) How does Daniel react and what further
reassurance is he given (10:15-11:1)?

(3) *Apply the passage*

  i) What can we learn and apply to our prayer life
  from Daniel as an example?

  ii) What does it mean for us to pray according to
  the Word of God and in light of God's covenant
  (Ch. 9)?

  iii) In light of Daniel's prayer in chapter 9, what
  should we be praying for the Church in our day?
  What answer are we looking for / can we expect
  from God?

  iv) What do we learn from Daniel 10 about the
  reality of spiritual warfare? Living this side of the
  cross, when God's everlasting Kingdom has come,
  is there still spiritual warfare (Eph. 6:10-12)?

  v) What is the relationship between prayer and
  spiritual warfare?

  vi) What encouragement can we take as believers
  from Daniel 10?

(4) *Pray it through*

12

GOD'S RULE THROUGH HISTORY
(DANIEL 11:2-45)

Setting in context

(1) Dating

This is part of the final vision in the book, dated as the 'third year of Cyrus king of Persia' (10:1). The date is 536 B.C., after Cyrus' decree to end the Exile.

(2) Context – structure of book

Daniel chapters 10–12 record a single vision. Fig. 1 explains the structure:

Fig. 1 Final vision in Daniel 10–12

Vision	Description
Ch. 10:1–11:1	Prayer and spiritual warfare
Ch. 11:2-45	God's rule through history
Ch. 12	God's rule in the end

Chapter 10 is an extended introduction before the vision is explained from verse 2 of chapter 11. The vision described in chapter 11 focuses on a particular period in history – the persecution under Antiochus IV Epiphanes in the second century B.C. This is the same period as the vision in chapter

8. In chapter 12 the lens widens to look forward to the end of history and the security of God's people till then

Fig. 2   Correspondence between Daniel 8 and 11

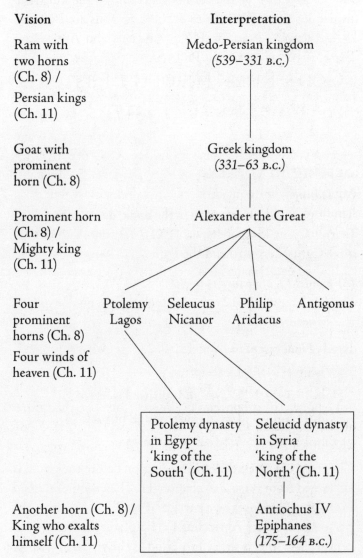

Vision	Interpretation
Ram with two horns (Ch. 8) / Persian kings (Ch. 11)	Medo-Persian kingdom *(539–331 B.C.)*
Goat with prominent horn (Ch. 8)	Greek kingdom *(331–63 B.C.)*
Prominent horn (Ch. 8) / Mighty king (Ch. 11)	Alexander the Great
Four prominent horns (Ch. 8) Four winds of heaven (Ch. 11)	Ptolemy Lagos Seleucus Nicanor Philip Aridacus Antigonus
Another horn (Ch. 8) / King who exalts himself (Ch. 11)	Ptolemy dynasty in Egypt 'king of the South' (Ch. 11) Seleucid dynasty in Syria 'king of the North' (Ch. 11) — Antiochus IV Epiphanes *(175–164 B.C.)*

With reference to Fig. 2, the Medo-Persian kingdom, conquerors of Babylon, was overthrown by Alexander the Great, first king of the Greek kingdom. Following Alexander's death, power was seized by four of his generals and the kingdom divided into four. The names of these generals are Ptolemy Lagos, Seleucus Nicanor, Philip Aridacus and Antigonus. Two emerged as dominant, Ptolemy and Seleucus, and their respective dynasties vied for power over the next hundred years – the Ptolemy dynasty in Egypt (referred to here in Ch. 11 as the 'king of the South') and the Seleucid dynasty in Syria (referred to as the 'king of the North'). Attention focuses on the Seleucid dynasty (the 'king of the North') and one particular king, Antiochus IV Epiphanes (175–164 B.C.). Antiochus is not a major player in world history, but very significant in the history of the people of God.

While the vision here in chapter 11 covers the same period / material as the earlier vision in chapter 8, a lot of additional detail material is included on the power struggle between the 'king of the South' (Ptolemy dynasty) and the 'king of the North' (Seleucid dynasty) before focusing like chapter 8 on the Seleucid king, Antiochus. This additional detail reveals a great deal about the nature of human power and ambition.

From 1:1-2:3 and 8:1 to the end of the book, is written in Hebrew. The prophecies in Hebrew focus on the future of the people of God. The Aramaic section (2:4–7:28) which includes prophetic material (Chs. 2 and 7) concerns matters of universal significance

(3) Context – *message of book*
The message of Daniel is that *God rules, is building an everlasting Kingdom, and calls people to live in light of that*

fact. This final vision (Chs. 10–12) is a fitting conclusion to the message of the book.

It begins in chapter 10 with a 'behind the scenes' look at the spiritual warfare going on through history. Chapter 10 also gives a fascinating insight into the relationship between prayer and spiritual warfare.

Daniel had prayed for understanding about the future (10:12). The content of the revelation recorded in chapters 11–12 explains that future. Chapter 11 begins at a rapid pace, covering hundreds of years in just a few verses, before the vision focuses on the battle for power between the 'king of the South' and 'king of the North', and then on one particular king, Antiochus IV Epiphanes. At the heart of the vision is a three and a half year period during Antiochus' reign when he systematically persecuted God's people. The focus on such a narrow period shows God's rule through the details of history as well as His rule over all of history. In other words, God's rule is not just evident on the big-picture canvas of history but in the detail. It is one thing to know where history is headed. It is another to know God is in control through history to that end. Big-picture visions like Daniel 7 are inspiring and encouraging but the detailed visions are equally important. They carry pastoral weight, simply because our experience is in the detail not the big picture. This detailed prophetic material is especially important to God's people when they are experiencing persecution. God's concern for His people, His promise to be with them and build His Kingdom, is a vital message of encouragement.

In the latter part of the chapter (11:36-45), while the focus is still on Antiochus, the language is suggestive of an application to all antichrists through history and points forward to *the* Antichrist at the end of history.

This shift in perspective towards the end of chapter 11 is a bridge into the final part of the vision in chapter 12, where the focus is on the end of history. Taking the content of the vision as a whole, God rules through history (Ch. 11) and God rules over the end of history (Ch. 12).

Working on the text

The structure of the chapter is as follows:

(1) Vision of the successive kingdoms of Medo-Persia and Greece (vv. 2-4)

(2) Vision of the battle for power between the 'king of the South' and the 'king of the North' (vv. 5-20)

(3) Vision of a particular king who will persecute God's people (vv. 21-35)

(4) Further revelation about this king who exalts himself (vv. 36-45)

There is no division in chapter 11 between explanation and interpretation, whereas the parallel vision in chapter 8 has a clear structural division between explanation (8:3-14) and interpretation (8:15-26). Why is this? Simply because the vision in chapter 11 is further understanding of what was revealed in the earlier vision. The explanation and (in particular) *interpretation* of that earlier vision is assumed.

(1) Vision of the successive kingdoms of Medo-Persia and Greece (vv. 2-4)
The particular period of history being referred to here is the Medo-Persian kingdom and its successor, the Greek

kingdom. In the period 539–331 B.C. the Persian Empire was the superpower in the ancient world, succeeded by the Greek Empire (331–63 B.C.). Verse 2 refers to successive kings in the Persian kingdom. Verse 3 refers to the appearance of a 'mighty king', Alexander the Great, the first ruler of the Greek kingdom. Alexander conquered all before him, but died as a young man at the height of his power. He was succeeded by four of his generals – Ptolemy Lagos, Seleucus Nicanor, Philip Aridacus and Antigonus – and his kingdom was divided into four (v. 4). Two of these generals, Ptolemy and Seleucus, emerged as dominant and their respective dynasties vied for power over the next hundred years – the Ptolemy dynasty in Egypt (the 'king of the South') and the Seleucid dynasty in Syria (the 'king of the North').

The verb 'given' at the end of verse 4 is significant. Power is given and taken away by God. This is something we have seen repeatedly through Daniel. The fact that human power is given is also expressed in the contrast between the phrases 'rule with great power and do as he pleases' (v. 3) and 'his empire will be broken up' (v. 4). The great powers of human history will come and go. God rules over it all.

(2) Vision of the battle for power between the 'king of the South' and the 'king of the North' (vv. 5-20)

This section of the vision is a detailed explanation of the power struggle between the 'king of the South' and the 'king of the North'. We mustn't be confused by the reference to the 'king of the South / North' (i.e. singular) as opposed to 'kings of South / North' (i.e. plural). The 'king of the South' is the generic name for the Ptolemy dynasty and therefore refers to a succession of kings. Likewise, the 'king of the North' refers to a succession of kings in the Seleucid dynasty. God's people find themselves wedged between two hostile powers, both of which threaten their existence. The account is detailed yet selective, 'telescoping' historical events, with the emphasis on ambition, power and control. It is important to assimilate at least some of the detail. It is in the detail we see different aspects of human power and ambition.

The 'king of the South' in verse 5 is Ptolemy I. Ptolemy's commander, who becomes stronger than Ptolemy, ruling his own kingdom with great power, is Seleucus I ('king of the North'). After a number of years, 'apparent' harmony between the two powers is achieved through marriage alliance, a bargaining chip in the game of power politics (v. 6). The kings referred to in verse 6 are different from verse 5. The focus is now on Ptolemy II and Antiochus II (in the Seleucid dynasty). The date is around 250 B.C. Ptolemy's daughter Berenice married Antiochus II, who divorced his wife Laodice to marry her. Harmony, however, is short-lived – betrayal and intrigue dominate.

In verses 7-13 we read of the continued tension and power struggle between the two dynasties. Often this spills over into military conflict and bloodshed. Over the period described in verses 7-13 the balance of power shifts towards the 'king of the North' (Seleucid dynasty).

Verses 14-20 detail further humiliations inflicted on the 'king of the South' and another marriage alliance (v. 17). However, this attempt by Antiochus III ('king of the North') to cement his power comes unstuck. He arranged for his daughter Cleopatra to be married to Ptolemy V. However, she became fiercely loyal to her husband and in fact succeeded him as regent and encouraged an alliance with the rising power of Rome. This led to a downward

trend in Antiochus III's fortunes (v. 18) when he attacked
the 'coastlands' (a group of cities in Asia Minor and
some of the Greek islands). He was abruptly halted by a
'commander', the Roman Lucius Cornelius Scipio who
defeated him at Magnesia near Smyrna. Antiochus III's end
was inglorious (v. 19) and he was briefly succeeded (v. 20)
by Seleucus IV who faced crippling financial problems,
the result of his predecessor's failed military campaigns.
The 'tax collector' referred to in verse 20 was Seleucus IV's
chancellor Heliodorus who tried to rifle the temple treasury
in Jerusalem (2 Macc. 3) and who was later involved in the
murder of Seleucus IV.

These verses highlight the two human passions – ambition and love – which, perhaps more than any others, have
determined the course of history. Repeated phrases like
'become strong' (v. 5) and 'do as he pleases' (v. 16) highlight
human ambition and a desire for power. The motivation
behind the 'arranged' marriage alliances (vv. 6, 17) is political
advancement, but in the latter example the power of human
love frustrates the plans of Antiochus III.

Another feature of these verses is the mention of the
'Beautiful Land' (v. 16), echoing 8:9 and anticipating 11:41.
The 'Beautiful Land' is the land where God's glory dwells
and, in particular, the Temple, the visible sign of Yahweh's
presence. It is significant that it is at this point, when
Antiochus III establishes himself in the 'Beautiful Land',
with (to all appearances) the power to destroy it (v. 16) that
his power begins to weaken. It is from this point we can
chart his demise. This is another reminder of God's rule.
Humanly speaking the power struggle between the 'king of
the South' and 'king of the North' determines the course
of events, but God is behind it all.

(3) *Vision of a particular king who will persecute God's people (vv. 21-35)*

Attention now turns to Antiochus IV Epiphanes. He is the 'contemptible person' (v. 21), the embodiment of the evil which exalts itself above the God of heaven. We have already seen in chapter 8 why Antiochus, largely ignored by history, is given so much emphasis in these visions compared, for example, to Alexander the Great. The reason is Antiochus' significance in the history of God's people and his determined attempt to destroy them.

These verses are not so much concerned with giving a history of Antiochus' reign, although many significant details are included, as with the overall impact of his policies and strategies. He made and broke alliances as it suited him (vv. 22, 24) and his government was wholly corrupt. He interfered with spiritual matters – 'a prince of the covenant will be destroyed' (v. 22). This may refer to the High Priest Onias III who was deposed and murdered in 171 B.C.

In these verses that describe Antiochus' ambition and arrogance there are two important phrases. The first is in verse 21: '[Antiochus] has not been *given* the honour of royalty'. At one level, simply an historical statement that he was not the rightful heir, but as we have seen throughout the book of Daniel, the word 'given' is of theological significance. All human power and authority is given and taken by God. The second important phrase is in verse 24 – 'but only for a time' – a reminder that human power is given for a time determined by God.

From verse 25 Antiochus' military exploits are described. His thirst for power leads him to attempt to conquer Egypt. His first invasion of Egypt took place in 170 B.C., and through a combination of military expertise and internal political intrigue at the Egyptian court, Antiochus won a victory. A world of deceit and devious practices is suggested by verse 27. And yet neither military force nor political scheming can thwart the rule of God.

Verses 29-30 describe Antiochus' second invasion of Egypt in 168 B.C. A new player comes on the scene – 'the ships of the western coastlands' (v. 30). This is a reference to Rome. This incident is described in 1 Maccabees 1:29 and also by the Roman historian Livy. Livy tells of how Antiochus, besieging Alexandria, was confronted by the Roman consul Gaius Popillius Laenas who demanded that he withdraw from Egypt. When Antiochus hesitated, the consul drew a circle around him in the sand and insisted Antiochus give an answer before he left the circle. Furious and humiliated Antiochus had to withdraw from Egypt.

Antiochus turns his fury against God's people: 'Then he will turn back and vent his fury against the holy covenant' (v. 30). The language is very similar to the description of the Dragon in Revelation 12. Antiochus unleashes his anger on Jerusalem. The city walls were torn down (reminiscent of the Exile) and a strong citadel built. A more detailed account of these events can be found in 1 Maccabees. A series of events culminate in the desecration of the Temple in 167 B.C. (see also 8:11). This begins the period of approximately three and a half years when the city of God and the Temple are under severe attack and persecution. The suspension of daily sacrifices, the heartbeat of the community's life of faith, was the prelude to 'the abomination that causes desolation' (v. 21), when an altar, or possibly an image of Zeus, was set up on the altar of burnt offering (reminiscent of Belshazzar's blasphemous actions in the feast described in Ch. 5).

Verses 32-35 speak of some seduced by Antiochus' flattery and others who stoutly resist him. Two phrases are used to describe the faithful who stand firm: 'the people who know their God' (v. 32) and 'those who are wise' (v. 33). These phrases resonate with a theme that has run through the book. As the book begins, Daniel and his friends exemplify those who know their God and are wise (1:17). Moreover, the source of their wisdom is underlined – it is God-given. At the end of the book, reference is made to the wise who 'will shine like the brightness of the heavens, and those who lead many to righteousness, like the stars for ever and ever' (12:3). And in 12:10, 'those who are wise will understand'. The unity of the book and its message is underlined. Through the Exile, Daniel and his friends had consistently shown these qualities in all kinds of situations. For example, Daniel had repeatedly emphasised to Nebuchadnezzar how God alone reveals truth, which ultimately led Nebuchadnezzar to saving faith (Ch. 4). The incidents in chapters 3 and 6 contrast the foolishness of human wisdom with the wisdom of God's servants. The wise are persecuted but, in the end, vindicated by God.

Verse 34 says that the wise 'will receive a little help'. This is a reference to the resistance movement under Judas Maccabaeus who routed the Syrian armies in 164 B.C., which led to the purification and rededication of the temple, an event celebrated in the Hanukkah festival. The phrase 'a little help' seems odd. It is not meant as a disparaging comment. What Judas Maccabaeus did was significant, but ultimately it was God's sovereign rule that secured His people (hence the comment). Yet God uses means to achieve His ends. He uses those who oppose Him and He uses those who are for Him. We see this, for example, in the Acts of the Apostles, where on different occasions Roman officials protect Paul and the other apostles. The text in Daniel 11 refers to 'many who are not sincere will join them' (v. 34). This probably refers to those who joined the Maccabaean resistance once they saw the tide was turning – a pragmatic rather than a principled decision. The meaning of 'stumble' (v. 35) is disputed. Some take it as meaning they will die and others that they will fall away. In either case the meaning of the rest of the verse is unaltered. The time of trouble is to be one of testing and refining, not of destruction. The references to 'the time of the end' and 'the appointed time' (v. 35) refer both to the end of this particular time of crisis for God's people and to the end of all things.

While this passage is specific to the time of Antiochus it is a timeless word to all those who resist the wisdom of the world and follow the wisdom from God. During the time of Antiochus, and many other times in history, there will not be miraculous divine intervention to save from sword and flame, captivity and plunder. Yet as the book of Daniel has consistently emphasised, this will only be for a time and is not the final reality. God rules.

(4) Further revelation about this king who exalts himself (vv. 36-45)

The increasing focus on the appointed time and the time of the end brings us to the last section of this chapter. While the focus is still on Antiochus, the language is suggestive of an application to all antichrists through history and points forward to *the* Antichrist at the end of history.

The emphasis here is on his presumption and arrogance. His blasphemous claims to be God echo the language of Isaiah 14:12-15 of the king of Babylon who wanted to ascend to heaven and raise his throne 'above the stars of God' (also the prince of Tyre in Ezekiel 28:2 – 'I am a god and sit on the throne of a god.') Fundamentally, it echoes the language of Genesis 3:5 where the serpent says 'you will be like God'. Behind all these passages is the conviction that human pride echoes demonic pride and that this spirit of antichrist manifests itself throughout history. Again, in spite of Antiochus' pretensions he is simply acting under permission until 'what has been determined must take place' (v. 36).

Verses 37-39 expand on Antiochus' disregard of family traditions in worship. Again, there are echoes of Belshazzar and his disregard of his heritage. The 'one desired by women' (v. 37) is often taken to refer to Tammuz, a handsome god who died and rose again, referred to in Ezekiel 8.14 – 'women weeping for Tammuz'. The reference to the 'god of fortresses' (v. 38) is probably pointing out that he worshipped the god of militarism, the terrifying fourth beast with iron teeth which crushed, trampled underfoot and devoured (7:7, 19). Swollen with arrogance, he focuses all his wealth on military conquests.

Verse 39 has details which are not entirely clear and are difficult to fit in to what is known of Antiochus' campaigns. The difficulty in pinning down exactly what is being referred to is consistent with the interpretation that from verses 40-45 we appear to be moving away from the figure of Antiochus himself to the final embodiment of evil, the last of the many antichrists – *the* Antichrist.

In verses 40-45 'the time of the end' and 'the Beautiful Land' remind us of what is at stake. This is part of the great battle which has raged since Gen. 3:15. The fact that old enemies like Edom, Moab and Ammon are mentioned as well as Egypt is a deliberate reminder of those nations which had continually affected the destiny of Israel. Verse 44 echoes the words used about Sennacherib in Isaiah 37:7. The final battle will be in the 'Beautiful Land' where evil will finally be destroyed.

From text to message

As we move from text to message, it is clear that there are many similarities with the vision in chapter 8 (and hence the message we preach or teach). As a general principle we should not be wary of repetition. God in His inspired wisdom and revelation has given us two very similar visions. He must know we need this stuff twice. That said, there are differences between the two visions that we need to bring out. Three, in particular, can be identified:

First, the second vision is much more detailed. The additional material focuses, in the main, on the power struggle between the 'king of the South' (Ptolemy dynasty) and 'king of the North' (Seleucid dynasty) before focusing like chapter 8 on the Seleucid king Antiochus. This additional material reveals a great deal about the nature of human power and ambition.

Second, the vision in chapter 11 focuses on how, as God's people, we are to live through stressful times. A distinction is drawn between the faithful who stand firm (the 'wise') and those who compromise / are seduced.

Third, the vision in chapter 11:36-45, shifts perspective from focusing on Antiochus as an antichrist to all antichrists throughout history and, in particular, *the* Antichrist at the end of history. This, in turn, flows into chapter 12 where the focus is on the end of history, including a period of distress / the time of the Antichrist and the great division at the last between those who have submitted to God's rule (the 'wise') and those who have not.

(1) Get the message clear

i) Big idea

God rules through history, including stressful times. God will bring these times to an end and expects His people to trust Him and live distinctively through these times.

ii) Key questions

Preaching or teaching on this passage should answer the following questions:

- What is human power like?

- What are some of the particular features or characteristics of human power?

- How is God's universal rule worked out in the details of history?

- Why do God's people face stressful times / intense periods of persecution?

- What is the nature of that persecution?

- How is God's rule evident in these stressful times?

- What do God's people need to know during such times?

- What does God expect of His people during such times?

- What will happen to those who oppose God and His people?

- Is this a pattern we see repeated through history (i.e. many antichrists)?

- Who is *the* Antichrist and what is associated with the time of *the* Antichrist?

- What does a vision like this tell us about the inspiration of God's Word?

(2) Engage the hearer

i) Point of contact

As a point of contact for this passage, we suggest a short but detailed overview of the particular period of history that is the focus of this chapter. For one thing it will help get people into the kind of material in the chapter. It will also raise the important question right at the start of the sermon / talk: What is the relevance of this for us today? Something along the following lines.

The Babylonian kingdom ruled the Ancient World from 625–539 B.C. The conquerors of Babylon were the Medo-Persian kingdom (539–331 B.C.). In time they were conquered by the Greek kingdom (331–63 B.C.) and their first king, Alexander the Great. Alexander dominated the Ancient World, conquering all before him but died as a young man at the height of his power. He was succeeded by four of his generals – Ptolemy Lagos, Seleucus Nicanor, Philip Aridacus and Antigonus – and his kingdom was divided into four (v. 4). Two of these generals, Ptolemy and Seleucus emerged as dominant and their respective dynasties vied for power over the next hundred years – the Ptolemy dynasty in Egypt (the 'king of the South') and the Seleucid dynasty in Syria (the 'king of the North'). In the first quarter of the second century B.C. the Seleucid dynasty had emerged as dominant and in their succession of kings, Antiochus IV Epiphanes came to the throne in 175 B.C. He ruled until 164 B.C. He hardly features in the annals of world history, yet in the annals of biblical history he is a major player. In a three and a half year period from 167–164 B.C. he systematically persecuted God's people and nearly destroyed them until a resistance movement under Judas Maccabaeus routed Antiochus and his Syrian army in 164 B.C. and God's people were liberated. What is the relevance of this ancient history for us here today? That's the key question this vision asks us to consider.

ii) Dominant pictures / illustrations
A dominant picture is the nature and characteristics of human power. Ambition, greed, brutality, love, lust, intrigue, corruption all figure in this vision. These are evident in the period of history described in the vision; but they are evident throughout human history.

Another dominant picture is the detail. This is not a broad brush canvas that gives an 'impression' of God's rule; it is a detailed line drawing that shows God's rule in the intricate details.

Daniel is a powerful illustration of how God expects His people to live distinctively through stressful times. The rationale for living distinctively is that God rules. As we near the end of the book it might be helpful to illustrate this from Daniel's life through the Exile (Daniel received this vision as an old man after the end of the Exile).

(3) *Work on application*
In setting out the applications, we include first the relevant applications that were suggested for the vision in chapter 8. This is followed by some applications that reflect the new material in this vision.

- Sometimes visions like Daniel 8 and 11 are seen as detailed, obscure, difficult to understand and perhaps of less relevance than the big-picture stuff in chapters 2 and 7. It is certainly true that Daniel 8 and 11 are the least taught chapters in the book. They might be difficult at first, but once you get into them they have a very important message.

- Having studied chapter 7 which takes a big-picture view of history (God's universal rule) it is important to emphasize, by contrast, the detailed focus of this vision and the fact that God is in control of the details of history as well as the big sweep. This a very encouraging and steadying truth for Christians to grasp.

- This vision has a particular focus on a stressful time for God's people. It is true that God's people will experience opposition and suffer all of the time, but there are times when this is particularly intense. You can illustrate this from history, whether globally or nationally (whatever your context). It might also be appropriate to illustrate this in relation to a particular period in a church's life. And also, with appropriate caveats and caution, it can be applied to situations today (including in our own situations and experience) where God's people are facing stressful times.

- Another line of application is the hostility directed against God and His people. This is a timeless truth and is invariably used by God to advance the gospel. This is a helpful line of application to draw a link to Christ. The pattern for His life is suffering for the advance of the gospel. And that is the pattern He commends for all who will follow Him.

- It is important not to minimize the intensity of hostility / persecution God's people faced then, and face still in parts of the world. The kind of persecution described in these visions lifts our eyes from our own circumstances to the persecuted Church in different parts of the world. Equally, we shouldn't think the kind of opposition we experience in the West is not real opposition. It is nothing like other parts of the world, but it is real nonetheless and, perhaps, increasing in intensity.

- In relating a passage like this to Christ, it is important to make clear that the Devil (the prince of the world who is behind all human power opposed to God and His people) has been defeated at the cross. Although he has been defeated spiritual warfare will continue until Jesus returns and God's people will continue to be opposed.

- God's judgement on those who oppose Him and His people is seen throughout history. This is a pointer to the full and final judgement that will come at the end of history when Jesus returns.

- What are we to make of the detailed predictive prophecy (God's detailed control of events) in terms of human free will and choice? At one level God's sovereignty is absolute and He does control all. But we need to be careful not to conflate too simplistically God's sovereignty and human free-will. In life we make choices all the time, but God is working out His purposes in all things and through all things.

- The visions in Daniel, and perhaps the detailed visions in particular, give an astonishing perspective on the inspiration of God's Word. We are reading a detailed prophetic description of events hundreds of years before they happened. The most powerful application of this is that what is prophesied in the Word of God, and is still yet to happen, will happen.

- While the message and application of the chapter is predominantly for Christians (this prophecy is in Hebrew and of particular relevance to God's people), it is clearly relevant for unbelievers. Those who oppose God and His people will be judged. God's judgements in history are a sign of His final judgement at the end of history. And in the last analysis all those who rejected God's rule, whether antagonistically or with passive indifference, will be judged for all eternity.

Additional lines of application:

- Based on the detailed description in the vision of the nature of human power it is important to bring this out, explaining and illustrating from the text and also with contemporary applications.

- With the detailed nature of the prophecy there might be a risk that we get bogged down in the detail, but in many ways that's the point. God's universal rule, His control over the big-picture sweep of history, is an important principle and message for God's people. His control through different periods of history is an important principle

and message for God's people. And His control of
the details in these detailed periods of history a
further principle and encouraging message for God's
people. This is the realm in which we experience
life, the detail of the detail. To know that God is in
control of everything is very important.

- The message of the book of Daniel is that God
  rules, is building an everlasting Kingdom, and
  expects His people to live in light of that fact. That
  includes how we are to live as His people during
  stressful times. This is drawn out powerfully in the
  vision in the description of the 'wise'. Others will
  compromise or are seduced. It will be helpful to
  illustrate from the text of the vision, from Daniel's
  life through the Exile and also with contemporary
  examples of what it looks like for God's people to
  live distinctively in stressful times.

- Antiochus is an example of an individual in
  history who opposed God and His people.
  His aggression towards God and His people is
  unusual in its severity perhaps (hence the record
  in Scripture) but by no means unique. He stands
  for all antichrists through history who have
  opposed God and His people. You can illustrate
  that from different periods in history. Antiochus
  also points to / prefigures *the* Antichrist at the
  end of history. And the time of stress experienced
  by God's people at the hands of Antiochus points
  to the time of significant distress that will be
  experienced by God's people at the hands of *the*
  Antichrist before the time of the end. This is

developed more fully in the closing part of the
vision in chapter 12.

Outline for a sermon or talk

It is important to convey that chapter 11:2-45 is part of
the final vision that covers chapters 10–12. Setting chapter
11:2-45 in this context adds power and relevance to the talk.

In Daniel 11:2-45 the explanation and interpretation of
the vision are integrated through the chapter. Therefore,
we suggest an outline that follows the logic of the vision
systematically.

An outline is included in the next chapter that takes
Daniel 11 and 12 together.

Title: *God's rule through history*
Text: *Daniel 11:2-45*

Structure:

(1) The final vision (Chs. 10–12)

(2) The nature of human power (11:2-20)

    i) *The big players (vv. 2-4)*

    ii) *The battle for power (vv. 5-20)*

(3) God's rule in stressful times (11:21-35)

    i) *God will bring them to an end*

    ii) *God will build His Kingdom*

    iii) *God calls His people to live distinctively*

(4) A pointer to the time of the end (11:36-45)

The sub-points above may or may not be used in the
outline. They are included here simply to help with the flow
of logical thought.

Bible study on Daniel 11:2-45

Read chapter 11:2-45

(1) *Introduce the issues*

   i) From a first reading of the chapter, what do you think is the key message for God's people?

   ii) The content of the visions in chapters 8 and 11 are similar, focusing on a detailed period of persecution for God's people. What do we make of the fact that material in God's inspired Word is repeated? What does chapter 11 add to the vision in chapter 8?

   iii) What are some of the features of apocalyptic language that you notice from this chapter? What impression does this kind of language make on you?

   iv) The material in this chapter is extremely detailed. What does this detailed prophetic material reveal about the inspiration of God's Word?

(2) *Study the passage*

   i) The vision focuses on the successive kingdoms of Medo-Persia and Greece (vv. 2-4). What is the meaning of the details in these verses?

   ii) What is the significance of the word 'given' in verse 4 and how has this been a consistent point through the book?

   iii) Verses 5-20 are a detailed account of the battle for power between the 'king of the South' and 'king of the North'. What are some of the characteristics of human power and ambition revealed in these verses?

iv) Verses 21-35 focus on Antiochus IV Epiphanes and his persecution of God's people. What do we learn in these verses that adds to what we learned of Antiochus in chapter 8? (For example, the new material in 11:32-35 describes how different groups reacted to the persecution, a reminder perhaps of how different people reacted at the beginning of the Exile (1:6).)

v) Verses 36-45 give more information about the persecution under Antiochus, but also point beyond Antiochus, and this particular period of persecution in the second century B.C., to all antichrists through history and to *the* Antichrist at the end of history and the period of intense distress associated with the Antichrist. How does the text of the vision suggest these different interpretations / horizons?

(3) *Apply the passage*

i) What is human power like? Are the manifestations of human power we see here timeless in their application?

ii) How is God's rule worked out in the details of history? How important is it that God rules over the detail as well as the big picture?

iii) When God's people face stressful times / intense periods of persecution, what are the key messages of this vision that we need to remember?

iv) What is the relevance of this detailed vision to the times / circumstances in which we are living today?

v) What confidence does this vision give us in the inspiration and reliability of God's Word?

(4) *Pray it through*

13

God's Rule in the End
(Daniel 12)

Setting in context

(1) Dating
This is part of the final vision in the book, dated as the 'third year of Cyrus king of Persia' (10:1). The date is 536 B.C., after Cyrus' decree to end the Exile.

(2) Context – structure of book
Daniel chapters 10–12 record a single vision. Fig. 1 explains the structure:

Fig. 1 Final vision in Daniel 10–12

Vision	Description
Ch. 10:1–11:1	Prayer and spiritual warfare
Ch. 11:2-45	God's rule through history
Ch. 12	God's rule in the end

Chapter 10 is an extended introduction before the vision is explained from verse 2 of chapter 11. The vision described in chapter 11 focuses on a particular period in history – the persecution under Antiochus IV Epiphanes in the second

century B.C. In chapter 12 the lens widens to look forward
to the end of history and the security of God's people till
then.

From 1:1–2:3 and 8:1 to the end of the book, is written
in Hebrew. The prophecies in Hebrew focus on the future
of the people of God. The Aramaic section (2:4–7:28),
which includes prophetic material (Chs. 2 and 7), concerns
matters of universal significance

(3) Context – message of book

The message of Daniel is that *God rules, is building an everlasting Kingdom, and calls people to live in light of that fact.*
This final vision (Chs. 10–12) is a fitting conclusion to the
message of the book.

It begins in chapter 10 with a 'behind the scenes' look
at the spiritual warfare going on through history. Chapter
10 also gives a fascinating insight into the relationship
between prayer and spiritual warfare. Daniel had prayed
for understanding about the future (10:12).

The content of the vision in chapters 11–12 explains
that future. The part of the vision recorded in chapter 11
focuses on a narrow period in history, the persecution of
God's people under Antiochus in the second century B.C.
The key message is that God rules through the details of
history. In the latter part of the chapter (11:36-45), while
the focus is still on Antiochus, the language is suggestive of
an application to all antichrists through history and points
forward to *the* Antichrist at the end of history.

This shift in perspective towards the end of chapter 11
is a bridge into the final part of the vision here in chapter
12, where the focus is on the end of history. Chapter 12
contains wonderful and rich material, and like chapters 10

and 11 we devote a separate study to the chapter. That said, it is important to keep the progression and scope of the whole vision in view – God rules through history (Ch. 11) and God rules over the end of history (Ch. 12).

Working on the text

The structure of the chapter is as follows:

(1) God's rule of the end of history (vv. 1-4)

(2) Living in light of God's rule, then ruling with God for eternity (vv. 5-13)

(1) God's rule of the end of history (vv. 1-4)

These verses are packed with important details, each phrase loaded with theological significance. We will deal with each phrase in turn.

The opening phrase in verse 1 – 'At that time...' – ties this section to the preceding vision, in particular the concluding verses of chapter 11 (11:36-45). In chapter 11 the bulk of the vision (11:2-35) focused on the detail of the second-century persecution under Antiochus, but in the concluding verses the perspective shifted to the end of history and the time of *the* Antichrist. It is this time of the end that is the *main* focus in 12:1-4. We use the word '*main*' intentionally. As we have come to see, the prophetic material in Daniel takes a big-picture or detailed focus. That said, the big picture embraces the detail and the detail points to the big picture. And so while the main focus in 12:1-4 is the time of the end and God's rule of the end of history, the language has a relevance and meaning to God's rule in the details of history.

Verse 1 continues: 'At that time Michael, the great prince who protects your people, will arise.' The word translated 'arise' or 'stand over' (12:1), as well as having a general meaning of protecting, has a specific legal meaning of opposing an accuser in court. In this case the accuser is Satan and the court is the heavenly court. The angel Michael has already appeared in the introduction to the vision (10:13, 21). Chapter 10 took us 'behind the scenes' to see the spiritual warfare going on through history. The Lord Jesus, who is the central figure in the vision in chapter 10, is assisted in His spiritual warfare by the angel Michael. In Revelation 12:7ff Michael leads his angels against the Dragon and his angels. In 1 Thessalonians 4:16 the coming of the Lord is heralded by 'the voice of the archangel' (Michael). Angels are referred to on a number of occasions in the visions in Daniel, for example, in chapter 8 the angel Gabriel strengthens and encourages Daniel (8:15-19). God's angels are part of His government of the universe, the 'mighty ones who do his bidding, who obey his word' (Ps. 103:20).

The text continues: 'There will be a time of distress such as has not happened from the beginning of nations until then' (v. 1). The expression 'time of distress' occurs several times in the Old Testament. For example, Jeremiah 30:7 uses the phrase to refer to the coming Exile. Here in Daniel 12 it is referring to the time of the end, suggestive of a final intensifying of evil before the Lord's return. Jesus' teaching in the Gospels (e.g. Mark 13) speaks of oppression and persecution as the experience of God's people in every generation (Mark 13:5-13), but in the period before He returns it will intensify (Mark 13:14-27). This period of intensifying distress at the end is associated with the time of *the* Antichrist at the end of history, the man of lawlessness Paul speaks about in 2 Thessalonians 2:1-10. This is a major focus of the big-picture prophecy in Daniel 7. And the focus of the detailed prophecies in Daniel 8 and 12 on an antichrist in history (and antichrists through history) point forward to *the* Antichrist at the end of history.

Verse 1 concludes: 'But at that time your people – everyone whose name is found written in the book – will be delivered.' '[At] that time' we take to mean the Lord's return, but what is the book that is referred to? In the introduction to the vision in chapter 10, the reference to the 'Book of Truth' (10:21) is to God's pre-determined plan for history. The progress of human history is determined and controlled by God. The book referred to here in 12:1 is the record of the names of God's people. God knows who His people are through history and their names are recorded in His book. This is a rich biblical theme, for example in the Psalms (e.g. Ps. 69:28; 139:16). In Malachi, the faithful in the post-exilic community are said to be recorded in a 'scroll of remembrance' (Mal. 3:16). The clearest New Testament reference is in Revelation 20:11-15, where judgement is determined by whether or not people's names are found in the 'book of life'. In Daniel there are examples of God's miraculous deliverance of His people (Chs. 3 and 6). But that is the exception, not the norm. Through the centuries many have died for their faith. Their names are recorded in the book of life. And countless millions of faithful believers have reached the end of their lives before the time of the end when the Lord returns, and their names are recorded in the book of life. At the time of the end they will all be delivered.

Verse 2 develops this theme but shifts the perspective to describe the resurrection of *all humanity*: 'Multitudes who sleep in the dust of the earth will awake: some to everlasting life; others to shame and everlasting contempt.'

These verses are referring to the general resurrection at the end, where all humanity (both believers and unbelievers) will be raised and judged. It is helpful to pause and take note of where we are reading this. This is Old Testament prophecy in the sixth century speaking of the time of the end, resurrection, eternal life and eternal punishment. It is astonishing and humbling as we reflect on the divine inspiration of God's Word, written many centuries before the events described happened.

All humanity will be raised, but there will be a great division. God's people, those whose names are recorded in the book of life, will be raised to everlasting life. Those who have rejected God will be raised to shame and everlasting contempt. These themes are amplified in the New Testament in the Gospels and Epistles. The clear teaching of the Bible is that all will be raised – believers to an eternity with the Lord in a New Creation; unbelievers to an eternity in hell experiencing the wrath of God.

Verse 3: 'Those who are wise will shine like the brightness of the heavens, and those who lead many to righteouness, like the stars for ever and ever.' This verse has a dual meaning. The primary meaning is the eternal destiny of the believer – 'to shine like the brightness of the heavens...like the stars for ever and ever'. This is sugges-tive of the fulfilment of God's purpose for humanity in Creation. Believers will live for eternity as a radiant fulfilment of that purpose. Matthew 13:43 echoes this: 'Then the righteous will shine like the sun in the kingdom of their Father'. While the primary meaning of this verse is the eternal destiny of the believer, there is also an application as to how believers should live now in light of that eternity. In chapter 11 the faithful who stand firm against persecution are described as 'those who are wise' (11:33). Throughout the book we have seen Daniel and his friends exemplify godly wisdom in all sorts of situations. Their actions and distinctive witness have led many to righteousness, most obviously Nebuchadnezzar. Yet beyond that, the record of their godly lives recorded in the book of Daniel has been used powerfully by God down the centuries to lead many more to righteousness. This is an encouragement to God's people in every generation to live wisely in light of God's rule and, through their witness, lead many to righteousness.

Finally in this section, verse 4: 'But you, Daniel, roll up and seal the words of the scroll until the time of the end. Many will go here and there to increase knowledge'. 'Sealing the words' or 'sealing the scroll' is an indication to Daniel that the content of this long vision has come to an end (there is a similar reference in 8:26). Daniel prayed for understanding concerning the future (10:12) and the content of the revelation in chapters 11 and 12 has explained that future. Daniel has seen remarkable things. He has been shown a time in the future when God's people will suffer intense persecution. Yet God will preserve His people and build His Kingdom. Beyond that, he has seen down the long years of history to the time of the end when the Kingdom of God will come in its fullness. The word 'seal' embraces completeness, authenticity and finality. Yet verse 4 is not simply an indication to Daniel that the content of the vision is complete; it is an instruction to write down the vision, along with the other visions, and the account of the Exile in the book we know as Daniel. What a wonderful book it is, central to the unfolding drama of salvation and the unity and coherence of the

Bible. The reference at the end of verse 4 to the many who 'will go here and there to increase knowledge' is a sober comment that many will search in vain for wisdom and knowledge. This is probably intended to recall the stark contrast between human wisdom and divine wisdom in the early chapters of the book. In chapter 2, for example, the failure of the wise men of Babylon to describe and interpret Nebuchadnezzar's dream is contrasted with the powerful demonstration that God alone reveals truth. Moreover, Daniel and his friends consistently stand apart from the wise men of Babylon since they have been given wisdom from God.

(2) Living in light of God's rule, then ruling with God for eternity (vv. 5-13)

This final section is still part of the vision in chapters 10–12, but functions a bit like an Epilogue to the vision and, indeed, the book as a whole. Back in chapter 10, the extended introduction to the vision, Daniel is standing on the bank of the Tigris when he sees a heavenly messenger, a man clothed in linen (vv. 4-6). The heavenly messenger is the Son of Man, the Lord Jesus. It is the Lord Jesus who goes on to reveal to Daniel what will happen in the future. Here in 12:5 we are back on the bank of the river. Daniel is there along with the man clothed in linen who is 'above the waters of the river' (v. 6) symbolizing his status and authority. Two new characters are introduced (two angels). We are not told the identity of the angels, although they may be Michael and Gabriel who have figured in the visions (see comments above on verse 1). What follows is a dialogue between the two angels, the Lord Jesus and Daniel. Fig. 2 summarises:

Fig. 2 Structure of 12:5-13

Verse 6:	Question from one of the angels to the Lord Jesus
Verse 7:	Answer from the Lord Jesus
Verse 8:	Question from Daniel to the Lord Jesus
Verses 9-13:	Answer from the Lord Jesus

We will work through the text following the structure of the dialogue.

Question from one of the angels to the Lord Jesus (v. 6)
Verse 6: 'One of them said to the man clothed in linen, who was above the waters of the river, "How long will it be before these astonishing things are fulfilled?"'

We recall a similar question in the vision recorded in chapter 8, where two 'holy ones' (angels) want to know how long the prophesied persecution will last (8:13). Here in chapter 12 the angel wants to know how long it will be before the time of the end. Remember that Daniel receives this vision in 536 B.C. How long will it be before the Lord Jesus comes at the end of history – not His first coming (prophesied in Daniel 2 and 9:20-27), not His coronation as God's King (7:13-14) but His return at the end of time? That's the big question, but embraced within that are other important questions. For example, how long will the time of distress be when the people of God are delivered into the hands of the Antichrist and experience suffering?

Answer from the Lord Jesus (v. 7)
The answer comes from the Lord Jesus. Verse 7: 'The man clothed in linen, who was above the waters of the river, lifted his right hand and his left hand towards heaven, and

I heard him swear by him who lives for ever, saying, "It will be for a time, times and half a time. When the power of the holy people has been finally broken, all these things will be completed."'

The answer given is of great importance. It was normal practice to raise one hand when swearing an oath (e.g. Gen. 14:22; Exod. 6:8; Ezek. 20:5), but to raise two hands suggests something unusually significant. Perhaps the most striking parallel is Deuteronomy 32:40 – 'I lift my hand to heaven and solemnly swear: as surely as I live for ever…' These words were spoken by the Lord Himself at the end of the Exodus journey just before the people entered the Promised Land. Now it is the end of the Exile and the question concerns the time of the end, when God's people will receive their inheritance and enter *the* Promised Land, the New Creation. One cannot exaggerate the importance of the question and the importance of the answer that will be given. Like the Lord in Deuteronomy, the Lord Jesus here in Daniel 12 '[swears] by him who lives for ever'. This picks up on a key theme in the book. Human kings and kingdoms rise and fall, but the eternal God (the 'Ancient of Days' (7:9-10)) is building His everlasting Kingdom under the rule of His all-powerful King who will reign forever. This is a guarantee that what is said here is true and will be fulfilled.

Then comes the answer: 'It will be for a time, times and half a time.' This phrase is used in Daniel 7 to refer to the time God's people are delivered into the hands of the Antichrist. While a similar interpretation is appropriate here (the reference in 12:7b – 'When the power of the holy people has been finally broken, all these things will be completed' – giving further weight to this interpretation), the primary interpretation must be to the time between the giving of this prophecy and the end of history. How is a dual interpretation possible? In apocalyptic language, these numerate references signify a fixed period of time (determined by God), whether a short or long period of time. In other words, the time between the giving of this prophecy and the end of history has been determined and set by God. It is unalterable. It will happen. This gives reassurance to God's people, who wait for, who long for that day. Moreover, it is of profound reassurance that the 'time of distress' will be brought to an end. God is in control. God rules in all things. Evil seems to triumph, yet deliverance will come.

While these 'big-picture' interpretations seem appropriate for the material here in chapter 12, we need to remember that the general embraces the detail. For example, the persecution under Antiochus lasted approximately three and a half years and the phrase 'a time, times and half a time' could refer to such a period. As we read the prophetic material in a book like Daniel both general and specific interpretations are suggested by the apocalyptic language.

Question from Daniel to the Lord Jesus (v. 8)

Daniel responds in verse 8 with his own question. 'I heard, but I did not understand. So I asked, "My lord, what will the outcome of all this be?"' (Daniel is addressing the Lord Jesus.)

Verse 8 marks a slight shift in emphasis in the text from the future of God's people to the future of Daniel himself. A great deal has been revealed to Daniel. At the start of the Exile (the events of Ch. 1) Daniel was given

extraordinary insight and understanding and the ability
to interpret dreams and vision. A few years into the Exile
(Ch. 2) he was given understanding of the vision of the
statue, rock and mountain. Human kingdoms will come
and go but God will establish an everlasting Kingdom.
God's everlasting Kingdom will be built on the rock
that is Jesus Christ. Later in Nebuchadnezzar's reign,
Daniel was given understanding of what would happen
in Nebuchadnezzar's life, events that led to his conversion
(Ch. 4). At the beginning of Belshazzar's reign (the bleakest
time for Daniel during the Exile) he was given a vision that
powerfully conveys God's universal rule (Ch. 7). A few
years later he received a further vision that prophesied a
specific time long into the future when God's people would
suffer intense persecution (Ch. 8). Yet God will vindicate
them and build His Kingdom. God is sovereign over the big
picture of history but also in the detail of history. Right at
the end of the Exile, Daniel was given understanding of the
writing on the wall – God's judgement on Belshazzar and
the end of the Babylonian kingdom (Ch. 5). That same year
after his miraculous deliverance from the lions' den (Ch. 6),
inspired by the Word of God, he prayed for the end of the
Exile (Ch. 9). In answer to that prayer, Daniel received an
astonishing vision (Ch. 9) that not only confirmed the end
of the Exile, but looked beyond to the rebuilding of the
walls and temple in Jerusalem, then beyond to a further
horizon, the coming of Jesus who will die a sacrificial
death. And then a few years after the Exile has ended,
Daniel received this final vision (Chs. 10–12) which has an
immediacy (Ch. 10), a long range view of a period in the
future when God's people would face persecution (Ch. 11),
and beyond to the very end of history (Ch. 12). Daniel is

uniquely privileged ('highly esteemed' (10:11, 19)) in the revelation given to him (and to us through him).

All this has affected Daniel profoundly. It humbled him before Almighty God. We have seen this reaction again and again (e.g. 7:15, 28; 8:27; 10:8-9, 16-17). Daniel was humbled by the revelation and understanding given to him, but it has also encouraged him to want to know more. For example, the final vision in chapters 10–12 was given to him because he expressly prayed for understanding about what will happen to God's people in the future (10:14). And once again here he wants to know more. He does not understand what he has seen and heard and wants further explanation.

Answer from the Lord Jesus (vv. 9-13)

The Lord Jesus answers Daniel personally in response to his question. Verses 9-13: 'He replied, "Go your way, Daniel, because the words are rolled up and sealed until the time of the end. Many will be purified, made spotless and refined, but the wicked will continue to be wicked. None of the wicked will understand, but those who are wise will understand. From the time that the daily sacrifice is abolished and the abomination that causes desolation is set up, there will be 1,290 days. Blessed is the one who waits for and reaches the end of the 1,335 days. As for you, go your way till the end. You will rest, and then at the end of the days you will rise to receive your allotted inheritance."'

What wonderful words the Lord Jesus leaves with Daniel. What wonderful words the Lord Jesus leaves with us as the book concludes.

Verse 9 is a repetition of verse 4, repeated again in verse 13 (although verse 13 adds a comment about Daniel's resurrection and inheritance). The exhortation to '[go] your way' is an encouragement to the ongoing, faithful witness that has characterized Daniel's life (his consistency is an important theme, for example, in Ch. 6). God expects His people to live distinctively in light of His rule. That is exactly what Daniel has done through his life and the Lord Jesus encourages him to continue.

Verse 10 is a repetition of verses 2 and 3. It speaks about the resurrection and division of humanity at the end, but also about how we should live now. In the world in which Daniel lived, and the world in which we live, there are two ways to live – the way of the righteous and the way of the wicked.

At first sight verses 11 and 12 might seem puzzling. The focus of chapter 12 is very much the time of the end. And yet the reference in verse 11 to the daily sacrifice being abolished and the abomination that causes desolation being set up suggests the Lord Jesus is talking about the specific events in the detailed visions in chapters 8 and 11. This is the language used of the persecution under Antiochus (e.g. 8:13). And yet the numerate references in 12:11-12 – '1,290 days' and '1,335 days' – are different from each other and from the '2,300 evenings and mornings' in 8:14. (In the earlier vision, the '2,300 evenings and mornings' was in response to a question about how long the persecution under Antiochus would last.) As we said in relation to verse 7 (above), in apocalyptic language these numbers simply mean a defined period of time ordained by God. Here in 12:11-12 we would suggest a meaning that focuses on the time of the end like verse 7 – whether the length of time to the end, or the time of great distress, the time of the Antichrist before the end. That's where we would lean in terms of interpretation, but of course such an interpretation is not exhaustive and embraces a specific interpretation to a time like Antiochus. Verses like this give us great confidence that God rules in history and over all history, but they are also intended as a challenge / encouragement to keep going and persevere. In Mark 13 Jesus speaks of 'the end...still to come' (v. 7) and of the need to stand firm and endure to the end (v. 13). Likewise, in the parables about the end times in Matthew's Gospel (Matt. 24 and 25), the importance of perseverance and watchfulness is emphasised; the wise servant continues his work although the master delays, while the wicked servant works against him (Matt. 24:47-51; 25:14-30).

Finally, verse 13. Again the encouragement from the Lord to Daniel: '[go] your way to the end'. At one level it is the repeated encouragement of verse 9 to live distinctively in light of God's rule until the end of his life. But the true 'end' in view is the time of the end when the Lord Jesus will return and Daniel will be raised to life and receive his allotted inheritance in the everlasting Kingdom of God, the New Creation.

God has revealed to Daniel all he needs to know. His revelation is sufficient. For Daniel that point had come. And in the Scriptures of the Old and New Testaments we have God's full and final revelation. The end of Revelation (the last words in the book of Revelation and the last words in the Bible as a whole) speak powerfully of the sufficiency of the Word of God. We are neither to add to them nor subtract from them, but to live in light of them as we wait for the Lord Jesus to return (Rev. 22:18-21). Daniel was astonishingly privileged in what was revealed to him. And yet we are far more privileged than Daniel in what has been revealed to us. Chapter 12 is an apt summary of the message of the book of Daniel – *God rules, is building an everlasting Kingdom, and calls people to live in light of that fact.*

From text to message

(1) Get the message clear

i) Big idea
God rules over the end of history and His everlasting Kingdom will come in its fullness.

ii) Key questions
Preaching or teaching on this passage should answer the following questions:

- What will happen at the end of history?

- What is the 'time of distress' before the end of history / time of the Antichrist?

- When the Lord Jesus returns, what will happen to all people?

- When the Lord Jesus returns, what will happen to God's people?

- When the Lord Jesus returns, what will happen to people who have rejected God's rule?

- How long will it be till Jesus returns?

- How are God's people to live now in light of God's rule over the end / His rule over all?

- Do we have God's full and sufficient revelation in Scripture?

(2) Engage the hearer

i) Point of contact
Both authors studied theology at New College, the University of Edinburgh (although in different millennia!) New College has a splendid theological library in a building that once was a church. Underneath the main library is a small

chapel where we used to sit and pray. On the wall of that chapel is a plaque commemorating a nineteenth-century minister with the words of Daniel 12:3 (in the King James Version): 'They that be wise shall shine as the brightness of the firmament; and they that turn many to righteousness as the stars for ever and ever.' A powerful verse for those studying to be ministers of the gospel. A powerful verse for all Christians. The eternal destiny of all believers is to shine like stars in the New Creation. On the way to glory (in this life) we are to turn many to righteousness.

ii) Dominant pictures / illustrations
A dominant picture here is the far horizon (from Daniel's perspective at least). In the visions Daniel has been given he has seen many mountain peaks. He has been led up a mountain and then shown a mountain range ahead of him. Here he sees the final summit of the final mountain on the farthest horizon.

The resurrection of all humanity at the end of history is a stark and sobering picture of division. Jesus uses various illustrations to describe that division in His parables (for example, the parable of the weeds and the parable of the net (Matt. 12-13)). Speaking about the final judgement in Matthew 25, Jesus describes the division / separation as like separating sheep from goats (Matt. 25:31-46). These are the best illustrations of the point.

The Lord Jesus speaks very personally and very movingly to Daniel. We have seen this already in the vision in the Lord's reassuring touch and words to Daniel. It's important we convey this personal, intimate relationship. The Lord's words to Daniel are truly spoken to every faithful believer: 'As for you, go your way till the end. You will rest, and then at the end of the days you will rise to receive your allotted inheritance' (12:13).

(3) *Work on application*

- Looking at this final vision as a whole, God rules through history (Ch. 11) and God rules over the end of history (Ch. 12). In applying the message of this final part of the vision, it is helpful to set it in the context of the vision as a whole.

- It is important when teaching this material to be clear as to where we stand in the timeline of biblical history. God's everlasting Kingdom has been inaugurated with the first coming of Christ. He reigns now as God's all-powerful, eternal King. We await His return at the end of history when the events prophesied in Daniel 12 will happen.

- In terms of the 'time of distress' / time of the Antichrist before the end of history, we need to be careful in making any definite applications to the times in which we live. God's people in a godless world suffer persecution all of the time. What will happen near the end is an intensifying of persecution and distress. Are we living in these times or the beginning of these times in the world? Perhaps a helpful answer is we don't know but we might be. The clear teaching in the New Testament is that we live in a state of readiness for the Lord's return (e.g. Mark 13).

- The question, 'how long?' was voiced in the earlier vision in 8:13-14. It is voiced again here in 12:6. The answers given are in apocalyptic numbers.

The point of these is that they are defined periods of time, set, determined and controlled by God. Whether it is the length of a period of stress / intense persecution, or the time between events, the time is determined by God. It will happen. That is what we need to know. That is all we need to know.

- You need to explain clearly the Bible's teaching on resurrection and division. It's all here in Daniel 12 in the Old Testament. All will be raised to face the Lord Jesus. There will be a division between God's people (those recorded in God's book) and those who have rejected God's rule. The eternal destiny for God's people will be to reign with Jesus in the New Creation. The eternal destiny for unbelievers will be hell, experiencing God's wrath. Both the New Creation and hell are physical places. Both have no end.

- The end of this final vision in the book (and the end of the book) is the last word of revelation Daniel receives. He wants to know more but God has revealed to him all he needs. We are in a far more privileged position than Daniel. Much of what was prophesied in the visions he received has been fulfilled. And we have the full and final revelation of God in Scripture. This is a very important point of application. We should not be looking for and do not need further revelation. The closing words of the book of Revelation make that clear.

- The final chapter aptly summarises the message of the book – *God rules, is building an everlasting*

Kingdom, and calls people to live in light of that fact.
In Daniel we see a great example of what it means
for a believer to live in light of God's rule. In a
concluding study to the book it would be helpful to
summarize Daniel's life and example drawing on
different episodes from the book.

• The encouragement to 'lead many to
  righteousness' is the responsibility of all believers
  in this life. It is not our responsibility to make
  them righteous (make them Christians). As we
  have seen in the book, God rules in salvation
  (Chs. 4 and 5). Our responsibility is to lead people
  to Jesus, in whom righteousness is to be found
  through faith.

• The last verses in the chapter (vv. 5-13), and the
  last verses in the book, mark a shift in perspective
  as the Lord Jesus is addressing Daniel personally.
  How has the book of Daniel spoken to us
  personally?

Outline for a sermon or talk

The first outline is on Daniel 12.

It is important to convey that chapter 12 is part of the
final vision that covers chapters 10–12. Setting chapter 12
in this context adds power and relevance to the talk.

We suggest an outline that follows the logic of the vision
systematically.

A second outline takes Daniel 11 and 12 together (this
might be appropriate for a shorter series on the book).

Outline 1

Title: God's rule in the end
Text: Daniel 12

Structure:

(1) The final vision (Chs. 10–12)

(2) God's rule of the end of history (vv. 1-4)

   i) *'At that time' (v. 1)*

   ii) *'time of distress' (v. 1)*

   iii) *Resurrection and judgement (vv. 1-3)*

   iv) *'seal the words' (v. 4)*

(3) Living in light of God's rule, then ruling with God for eternity (vv. 5-13)

   i) *Question (v. 6)*

   ii) *Answer (v. 7)*

   iii) *Question (v. 8)*

   iv) *Answer (vv. 9-13)*

Outline 2

Title: God's rule through history
Text: Daniel 11:2–12:13

Structure:

(1) God's rule in the details of history (Ch. 11)

(2) God's rule of the end of history (Ch. 12)

(3) Living in light of God's rule

Bible study on Daniel 12

Read chapter 12

(1) Introduce the issues

i) As we come to the end of the final vision and the end of the book, what do you think is the key message of this concluding chapter for God's people?

ii) From this chapter, and the book as a whole, what do we learn about God's rule (it might be helpful to summarize the message of the book)?

iii) From this chapter, and the book as a whole, what do we learn about living in light of God's rule (it might be helpful to summarize the message of the book)?

iv) From this chapter, and the book as a whole, what do we learn about the nature of God's revelation (it might be helpful to summarize the message of the book)?

(2) Study the passage

(i) Verses 1-4 focus on God's rule of the end of history. What is the meaning / significance of the following details? (Getting our heads around this will give us an important understanding of what will happen at the end of history.)

(a) 'At that time...' (v. 1)

(b) 'Michael...will arise' (v. 1)

(c) 'time of distress' (v. 1)

(d) 'But at that time your people – everyone whose name is found written in the book – will be delivered.' (v. 1)

(e) 'Multitudes who sleep in the dust of the earth will awake: some to everlasting life; others to shame and everlasting contempt.' (v. 2)

(f) 'Those who are wise will shine like the brightness of the heavens, and those who lead many to righteousness, like the stars for ever and ever.' (v. 3)

(g) 'But you, Daniel, roll up and seal the words of the scroll until the time of the end. Many will go here and there to increase knowledge.' (v. 4)

ii) In verses 5-13 the focus shifts from God's rule of the end of history (vv. 1-4) to living in light of God's rule. The text is structured in terms of questions and answers. The question and answer in verses 6-7 concern how long it will be for these things to be fulfilled. What 'things' are being referred to and what does the answer mean?

iii) What is the nature of the question in verse 8? How is the question answered in verses 9-12?

iv) Why is verse 13 a fitting conclusion to the message of the book?

(3) *Apply the passage*

i) What will happen at the end of history?

ii) What is the 'time of distress' before the end of history / time of the Antichrist?

iii) When the Lord Jesus returns, what will happen to all people?

iv) When the Lord Jesus returns, what will happen to God's people?

v) When the Lord Jesus returns, what will happen to people who have rejected God's rule?

vi) How long will it be till Jesus returns?

vii) How are God's people to live now in light of God's rule over the end / His rule over all?

viii) Do we have God's full and sufficient revelation in Scripture?

(4) Pray it through

Bible study on Daniel 11:2–12:13

Read chapter 11:2–12:13

(1) Introduce the issues

i) As we come to the end of the final vision (Chs. 10–12), and the end of the book, what do you think is the key message of chapters 11–12 for God's people?

ii) From these chapters, and the book as a whole, what do we learn about God's rule (it might be helpful to summarize the message of the book)?

iii) From these chapters, and the book as a whole, what do we learn about living in light of God's rule (it might be helpful to summarize the message of the book)?

iv) From these chapters, and the book as a whole, what do we learn about the nature of God's revelation (it might be helpful to summarize the message of the book)?

(2) *Study the passage*

    i) What is the meaning of the part of the vision in chapter 11? How does the perspective shift in the closing section (11:36-45)?

    ii) What is the meaning of the part of the vision in 12:1-4?

    iii) What is the meaning of the part of the vision in 12:5-13?

    iv) Why is verse 13 a fitting conclusion to the message of the book?

(3) *Apply the passage*

    i) What is human power like? Are the manifestations of human power we see here timeless in their application?

    ii) The vision in chapter 11 powerfully conveys God's rule through the details of history, whereas the vision in chapter 12 conveys God's rule over the end of history. In other words, God rules over the details and the big picture. Why are both important?

    iii) Both chapters 11 and 12 speak of persecution / distress for God's people. Why do God's people suffer? How does the material in chapters 11 and 12 encourage and inspire us to endure such times?

    iv) How will history end and what is the eternal future for God's people (those who have accepted God's rule)? What is the eternal future for unbelievers (those who have rejected God's rule)?

v) How are we to live now as we wait for that future glory (12:13)?

(4) *Pray it through*

FURTHER READING

There are a number of excellent commentaries on Daniel.

For a detailed exegetical study that nonetheless has an eye to the preacher or Bible teacher the stand out commentary is Dale Ralph Davis, *The Message of Daniel* (IVP, 2013) in the *Bible Speaks Today* series. Ralph Davis is a scholar and preacher and this commentary is a 'must have' on your shelf.

Other shorter applied commentaries, again with an eye to the preacher or Bible teacher are Bob Fyall's earlier commentary, *Daniel: A Tale of Two Cities* (Christian Focus, 2006) in the *Focus on the Bible* series and David Helm's, *Daniel for You* (Good Book Company, 2014).

In addition we want to warmly commend O. Palmer Robertson's, *The Christ of the Prophets* (P&R Publishing, 2004), a great introduction to the Old Testament Prophets. This book is a real help in unravelling the complexities of the prophetic material in Daniel.

Finally, John Lennox, *Against the Flow: The Inspiration of Daniel in an Age of Relativism* (Monarch Books, 2015).

This is not a commentary but a brilliant contemporary application of the message of Daniel to our time. John Lennox is one of the foremost evangelists and apologists of our time who sees Daniel as a book for our time.

If we had to settle for two alongside *Teaching Daniel*, we'd choose Ralph Davis and John Lennox.

PT Resources
RESOURCES FOR PREACHERS AND
BIBLE TEACHERS

PT Resources, a ministry of The Proclamation Trust, provides a range of multimedia resources for preachers and Bible teachers.

Teach the Bible Series (Christian Focus & PT Resources)
The Teaching the Bible Series, published jointly with Christian Focus Publications, is written by preachers, for preachers, and is specifically geared to the purpose of God's Word – its proclamation as living truth. Books in the series aim to help the reader move beyond simply understanding a text to communicating and applying it.

Current titles include: *Teaching Numbers, Teaching 1 Kings, Teaching Isaiah, Teaching Daniel, Teaching Amos, Teaching Matthew, Teaching Acts, Teaching Romans (in two volumes), Teaching Ephesians, Teaching 1 and 2 Thessalonians, Teaching 1 Timothy, Teaching 2 Timothy, Teaching 1 Peter, Teaching 1, 2, 3 John,* and *Teaching the Christian Hope.*

Practical Preacher series

PT Resources publish a number of books addressing practical issues for preachers. These include *The Priority of Preaching, Bible Delight, Hearing the Spirit* and *The Ministry Medical.*

Online resources

We publish a large number of audio resources online, all of which are free to download. These are searchable through our website by speaker, date, topic and Bible book. The resources include:

+ sermon series; examples of great preaching which not only demonstrate faithful principles but which will refresh and encourage the heart of the preacher

+ instructions; audio which helps the teacher or preacher understand, open up and teach individual books of the Bible by getting to grips with their central message and purpose

+ conference recordings; audio from all our conferences including the annual Evangelical Ministry Assembly. These talks discuss ministry and preaching issues.

An increasing number of resources are also available in video download form.

Online DVD

PT Resources have recently published online our collection of instructional videos by David Jackman. This material has been taught over the past 20 years on our PT Cornhill training course and around the world. It gives step by step instructions on handling each genre of biblical literature. There is also an online workbook. The videos are suitable for preachers and those teaching the Bible in a variety of different contexts. Access to all the videos is free of charge.

The Proclaimer

Visit the Proclaimer blog for regular updates on matters to do with preaching. This is a short, punchy blog refreshed daily which is written by preachers and for preachers. It can be accessed via the PT website or through www.theproclaimer.org.uk.

TEACHING
NUMBERS
From text to message
ADRIAN REYNOLDS

TEACHING
1 KINGS
From text to message
BOB FYALL

TEACHING
AMOS
From text to message
BOB FYALL

TEACHING
ACTS
Unlocking the book of Acts
for the Bible Teacher
DAVID COOK

TEACHING
EPHESIANS
From text to message
SIMON AUSTEN

TEACHING
1 & 2 THESSALONIANS
From text to message
ANGUS MACLEAY

TEACHING
1 TIMOTHY
From text to message
ANGUS MACLEAY

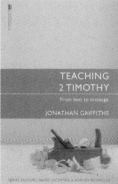

TEACHING
2 TIMOTHY
From text to message
JONATHAN GRIFFITHS

TEACHING
1 PETER
Unlocking the book of 1 Peter
for the Bible Teacher
ANGUS MACLEAY

Christian Focus Publications

Our mission statement –

STAYING FAITHFUL
In dependence upon God we seek to impact the world through literature faithful to His infallible Word, the Bible. Our aim is to ensure that the Lord Jesus Christ is presented as the only hope to obtain forgiveness of sin, live a useful life and look forward to heaven with Him.

Our books are published in four imprints:

CHRISTIAN FOCUS

Popular works including biographies, commentaries, basic doc-trine and Christian living.

CHRISTIAN HERITAGE

Books representing some of the best material from the rich heritage of the church.

MENTOR

Books written at a level suitable for Bible College and seminary students, pastors, and other serious readers. The imprint includes commentaries, doctrinal studies, examination of current issues and church history.

CF4·K

Children's books for quality Bible teaching and for all age groups: Sunday school curriculum, puzzle and activity books; personal and family devotional titles, biographies and inspirational stories – because you are never too young to know Jesus!

Christian Focus Publications Ltd,
Geanies House, Fearn, Ross-shire,
IV20 1TW, Scotland, United Kingdom.
www.christianfocus.com